THE BEST OF
EVERYDAY
COOKING

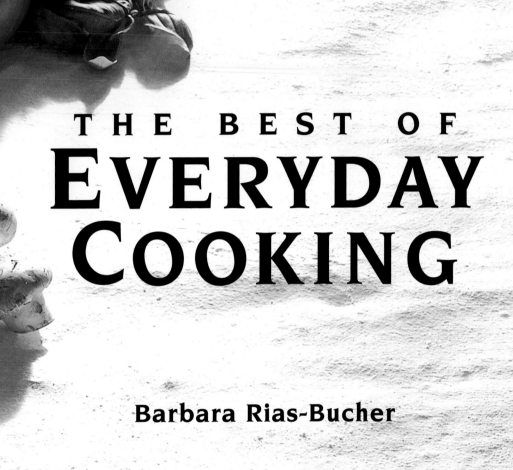

THE BEST OF
EVERYDAY
COOKING

Barbara Rias-Bucher

**Photography by
Susi and Pete A. Eising**

CHANCELLOR
PRESS

Contents

First published under the title
Naturlich Kochen - Kostlich wie noch nie

© Copyright Gräfe und Unzer GmbH, München

Previously published in English by
The Hamlyn Publishing Group
part of Reed International Books
under the title *The Best of Healthy Cooking*

This edition first published in 1992 by
Chancellor Press
Michelin House
81 Fulham Road
London SW3 6RB

Reprinted in 1992

© Copyright Reed International Books Limited 1987

ISBN 1 85152 121 6

Printed in Hong Kong

Useful Facts and Figures 6

Foreword 7

Introduction 8

Starters, Salads and Snacks 12

Dinner Party Starters 14

Satisfying Snacks 18

A Variety of Salads 20

Delicious Dips 28

For Breakfast or Brunch 30

Soups, Casseroles and Bakes 36

Soups for Starters 38

Hot, Substantial Soups 42

Unusual Soups 46

One-pot Suppers 50

Pastries and Bakes 56

Contents

Light Fish and Meat Dishes 62

Delectable Fish Dishes 64

Shellfish Specialities 72

Saucy Meat Dishes 74

Quick Meat Dishes 76

Ways with Larger Cuts 78

Full-flavoured Meat Dishes 82

Supper-party Specials 84

Chicken and Duck 86

Vegetarian Main Courses and Side Dishes 92

Light Main Dishes 94

Stuffed Vegetables 100

Vegetable Side Dishes 102

Versatile Potatoes 104

Pasta Specialities 110

Pancakes to Dumplings 113

Wholesome Ways with Grains 116

Tempting Tofu Ideas 123

Nuts and Pulses 125

Puddings Desserts and Drinks 128

Hearty Puddings 130

Dinner Party Desserts 134

Drinks, Sweet and Savoury 138

The Way to Healthy Eating 110

Wholefood Menu Suggestions 142

Useful Equipment 144

Glossary 145

Useful Food Values 154

Index 156

Useful Facts and Figures

Notes on metrication

In this book quantities are given in metric and Imperial measures. Exact conversion from Imperial to metric measures does not usually give very convenient working quantities and so the metric measures have been rounded off into units of 25 grams. The table below shows the recommended equivalents.

Ounces	Approx g to nearest whole figure	Recommended conversion to nearest unit of 25
1	28	25
2	57	50
3	85	75
4	113	100
5	142	150
6	170	175
7	198	200
8	227	225
9	255	250
10	283	275
11	312	300
12	340	350
13	368	375
14	396	400
15	425	425
16 (1 lb)	454	450
17	482	475
18	510	500
19	539	550
20 ($1\frac{1}{4}$ lb)	567	575

Note: When converting quantities over 20 oz first add the appropriate figures in the centre column, then adjust to the nearest unit of 25. As a general guide, 1 kg (1000 g) equals 2.2 lb or about 2 lb 3 oz. This method of conversion gives good results in nearly all cases, although in certain pastry and cake recipes a more accurate conversion is necessary to produce a balanced recipe.

Liquid measures The millilitre has been used in this book and the following table gives a few examples.

Imperial	Approx ml to nearest whole figure	Recommended ml
$\frac{1}{4}$ pint	142	150 ml
$\frac{1}{2}$ pint	283	300 ml
$\frac{3}{4}$ pint	425	450 ml
1 pint	567	600 ml
$1\frac{1}{2}$ pints	851	900 ml
$1\frac{3}{4}$ pints	992	1000 ml (1 litre)

Spoon measures All spoon measures given in this book are level unless otherwise stated.

Can sizes At present, cans are marked with the exact (usually to the nearest whole number) metric equivalent of the Imperial weight of the contents, so we have followed this practice when giving can sizes.

Oven temperatures

The table below gives recommended equivalents.

	°C	°F	Gas Mark
Very cool	110	225	$\frac{1}{4}$
	120	250	$\frac{1}{2}$
Cool	140	275	1
	150	300	2
Moderate	160	325	3
	180	350	4
Moderately hot	190	375	5
	200	400	6
Hot	220	425	7
	230	450	8
Very hot	240	475	9

Notes for American and Australian users

In America the 8 fl-oz measuring cup is used. In Australia metric measures are now used in conjunction with the standard 250-ml measuring cup. The Imperial pint, used in Britain and Australia, is 20 fl oz, while the American pint is 16 fl oz. It is important to remember that the Australian tablespoon differs from both the British and American tablespoons; the table below gives a comparison. The British standard tablespoon, which has been used throughout this book, holds 17.7 ml, the American 14.2 ml, and the Australian 20 ml. A teaspoon holds approximately 5 ml in all three countries.

British	American	Australian
1 teaspoon	1 teaspoon	1 teaspoon
1 tablespoon	1 tablespoon	1 tablespoon
2 tablespoons	3 tablespoons	2 tablespoons
$3\frac{1}{2}$ tablespoons	4 tablespoons	3 tablespoons
4 tablespoons	5 tablespoons	$3\frac{1}{2}$ tablespoons

An Imperial/American guide to solid and liquid measures

Solid measures

Imperial	America
1 lb butter or margarine	2 cups
1 lb flour	4 cups
1 lb granulated or caster sugar	2 cups
1 lb icing sugar	3 cups
8 oz rice	1 cup

Liquid measures

Imperial	American
$\frac{1}{4}$ pint liquid	$\frac{2}{3}$ cup liquid
$\frac{1}{2}$ pint	$1\frac{1}{4}$ cups
$\frac{3}{4}$ pint	2 cups
1 pint	$2\frac{1}{2}$ cups
$1\frac{1}{2}$ pints	$3\frac{3}{4}$ cups
2 pints	5 cups ($2\frac{1}{2}$ pints)

NOTE: When making any of the recipes in this book, only follow one set of measures as they are not interchangeable.

Foreword

What does cooking the natural way mean? It means cooking with fresh, naturally-grown produce so that food not only tastes delicious but is more wholesome and nourishing and better for you. Cooking the natural way is made easy with this new cookery book. I have included over 150 recipes for you to choose from, all made with natural produce and all with detailed instructions so that nothing can go wrong. The results should convert even those sceptics who have so far remained unconvinced by new ideas on diet.

Natural cooking and a healthy diet. That is what is wanted nowadays by all those 'informed' people who worry about the important matter of nutrition and its bearings upon our health. We are by no means powerless as regards scare stories about the harmful substances that go into food and our own poor eating habits. Despite the fact that it is impossible to buy foods free of additives, by choosing carefully what we buy and how we prepare it, we can go a long way towards cooking naturally.

To put it in more concrete terms – we can buy fresh, organically grown vegetables instead of canned or frozen ones; we can use natural fats such as butter or untreated vegetable oils rather than those produced by chemical processes. We can make our own Muesli instead of buying it ready packaged. Instead of white refined flour we can use wholemeal flour and use sugar only as a flavouring.

This book includes a comprehensive and easily understandable summary of all you need to known about what is described in general terms as wholefood cooking and makes the change to this somewhat different type of cooking extremely easy.

If you follow the instructions precisely the recipes will present no problems, even for those with no previous experience of cereals and pulses, nuts, seeds and sprouts. You will find all the products used in the recipes in health food or organic food shops, in your greengrocers or local market. Many are now available in good supermarkets – even the large chains are beginning to be influenced by the wishes of customers interested in healthy eating. The more frequently the customer expresses his preferences as a consumer, the quicker the shops will change the type of foods they stock.

Cooking naturally is a plus not only for the palate but also for our health. Famous chefs have been practising this new style of cookery for years, cooking with fresh vegetables, top quality meats and freshly caught fish. Think about it – you won't be served canned beans in a good restaurant, only vegetables with all their natural flavour. The great chefs have brought pulses back into favour and rescued such things as barley, buckwheat, wild herbs and elderblossom from obscurity. It is not only the health-conscious that will find this book useful, but it will appeal to the gourmet too, for it contains delicious dishes which have little in common with homely health food dishes. You will see this as you flick through the book, for each of the tempting recipes is illustrated in colour to give a foretaste of the pleasure the dish will give. You will also come across old favourites in this book – cannelloni and pizza, hamburgers and stocks – but they are old favourites with a difference. The cannelloni are made with tofu, the pizza with wholemeal flour and the stock entirely with vegetables.

You will find dishes which bring back pleasant memories of childhood – apple pancakes, curd cheese balls and semolina slices. I have hunted through old cookery books and modernised the old forgotten recipes such as millet pudding and barley soup, pot barley casserole and buckwheat dumplings. In addition the book provides a glimpse into international cuisine. You will find curries from India, fine dishes from Spain, Greece and Italy, light dishes from China – all made from natural ingredients of course.

The recipes are not restricted just to vegetarian dishes, for your own cooking and eating experiences will have determined whether you prefer to stick to a vegetarian diet. So there is a comprehensive chapter aimed at those among you who enjoy vegetables, salads, cereals and pulses but also like to treat yourselves to meat and fish. So let yourself be tempted by a juicy leg of lamb or a tender chicken, by herby fish fillets or grilled prawns. In the meat section I have stuck to lamb and poultry and omitted pork, veal and beef for these are rarely produced to the standard required. Lamb is not normally factory-farmed and fattened like pork or veal. And where poultry is concerned it is often possible to buy chickens and ducks reared naturally, by the free-range method. Bear in mind that a customer who does not put everything in his basket without thinking, but who occasionally asks questions or who refuses to buy class 1 products merely because they look nice, can make the shopkeeper reconsider. Our food can only improve if we return to the right values.

All the recipes in this book are easy to make even for the beginner. The method often explains why things are done in a certain way or mentions points to watch when preparing the dish. If you are unsure how to put together a complete menu or party buffet from natural dishes, turn to page 142 where you will find menus for every occasion with tips on preparation and timing. There is also a section on equipment where you can find out about the best pans to use, new utensils specially suitable for wholefood cooking and aids to make preparation and cooking easier. The short section on nutrition provides information on the composition of our foods and the nutrients our bodies need. You will learn the difference between animal and vegetable protein and discover something about organic value, fibre and vitamins. You will find everything you need to know about naturally produced, fresh produce in the glossary which starts on page 145. It gives information about all the ingredients, explains terms like kiln-dried and germinate, explains what is meant by 'organically grown' and suggests where you can buy free-range poultry and meat. This information on the various products will make you a discerning consumer concerned about production methods and quality.

But enough introduction – have a look through the book, choose a recipe and start cooking. May you and your family enjoy these delicious dishes secure in the knowledge that you are eating and living more healthily.

Enjoy your cooking and bon appetit!

Barbara Rias-Bucher

Introduction

For several years we have been told from all sides that we do not eat properly. According to a report published by the National Advisory Committee on Nutrition Education (NACNE), published in 1983, we eat too much fat, too much sugar and too much salt. We also give our bodies far more animal protein than they need. You may well ask what harm there can be in a thick, juicy steak when there are slimming diets consisting mainly of eggs and lean meat. Or why you should give up the cream cake with your coffee since it does no obvious harm and tastes delicious. We are also aware that the potato has been reassessed and is no longer considered to be fattening or a poor man's food, but to be a delicacy with great nutritional value. One thing that we are not so sure of is whether thin people or fat people live longer. Here expert opinion differs.

If you want to eat properly and still enjoy your food, you need information – information about the composition of foodstuffs, about the requirements of our bodies, about the things we need to eat to keep us healthy but which we can neither see, taste nor smell. Only then can we really judge if we are feeding ourselves properly. Then we can allow ourselves to kick over the traces occasionally because we will know how to make up for our minor sins.

The composition of our food

The human body is often compared to a machine which needs energy to function properly. But energy, as provided by fat, protein and carbohydrate, is not enough. The body also needs nutrients (vitamins, minerals and trace elements) for certain metabolic processes or – equally important – to allow it to break down the substances it needs such as protein or calcium for bones and teeth. When these nutrients are lacking we become ill or may even die. The same is true if we cut off the supply of energy. Prolonged hunger – starvation – eventually leads to death.

Every foodstuff contains these nutrients to varying degrees. But there is no one food which contains *all* the nutrients we need. So to eat correctly we need a varied diet. If we eat mostly meat we will have digestive problems for we will lack the fibre that takes food through the intestine. And if we eat too much fat – which is contained in many foods even though we can't see it – we put on weight for we are giving our bodies more energy than they need.

Protein

Protein is the basic building block of the human organism. It is responsible for building and maintaining tissue fabrics like muscles and organs for instance. Since the body continually uses up protein, we need to replenish it constantly by what we eat. This is not difficult since proteins are found in both animal and vegetable products. The protein we take in our food is broken down by digestion into its separate elements, the amino acids.

There are over twenty different amino acids, eight of which the body is incapable of producing itself. But these too are essential in the production of the body's own protein. Since these eight amino acids are essential to the functioning of the organism they are known as essential amino acids. Of course we need not worry about whether we are eating the essential amino acids; we do this automatically through our mixed diet. In the industrialised countries there is no deficiency due to shortage of protein, as there is in developing countries. Any deficiency arises from the lack of specific vitamins and minerals.

There are standard values covering protein requirements. Adults need around 0.8 g protein per kilogramme bodyweight every day. Children, pregnant mothers and old people require more. Of our total daily food intake 10 or 20 percent at the most should consist of protein. As a rule of thumb this protein should be made up of animal and vegetable proteins in equal proportions. Many dieticians recommend that we eat only one third animal and two thirds vegetable protein. On no account should one live entirely on meat or fish, milk products or eggs, but we should include cereal products and pulses. Even vegetables contain essential amino acids, albeit in small amounts. At first, when you are unfamiliar with the protein content of various products, you should find the nutritional values included in every recipe helpful. In time you will come to know which foods are rich in protein. But it is not only the protein content that we must consider, but the organic value of the protein as well.

Organic value of protein

The closer the composition of the protein in food to that of the protein in the human body, the better is its nutritional value. Protein that contains all eight essential amino acids in exactly the ratio the body requires to build up body protein is known as 'organically high-value protein'. Animal protein from meat, fish, milk products and eggs is extremely high in value for its composition is the same as body protein. Vegetable protein on the other hand is generally of lower value since it contains a lower proportion of essential amino acids and is often very unlike human protein. So our diets should not be restricted to one type of protein alone (pulses for instance) but should include a mixture of various proteins, from cereals, vegetables and milk for example. Essential amino acids may be low in some forms of protein but present in greater quantities in other proteins. If these are eaten together they complement each other, so by combining vegetable protein with other sources of protein you get high-value protein. An example will illustrate this. Milk is an organically high-value food and so is cereal, so by combining a milk product like cheese with wheat, as in the recipe for Tomatoes stuffed with wheat on page 100, you get an even higher organic value. The same is true of a breakfast muesli of yogurt and wheat flakes, a slice of wholemeal bread topped with cheese or even porridge made with rolled oats with milk or yogurt. Of course the idea is not simply to eat wheat and milk, but to turn these two ingredients into a meal. The important thing is to eat the two foods in the same meal.

Organic value of edible proteins

Egg (yolk and white)	100
Uncooked potatoes	86
Edam cheese	85
Cow's milk	85
Soya	84
Rye	83
Untreated rice	83
Maize	75
Beans	73
Sunflower seeds	70
Wheat	59

Vegetable proteins can be combined to make them as high or even higher in value than animal proteins.

Products whose proteins combine well together

- Potatoes with milk products
- Potatoes with egg
- Pulses with milk products
- Pulses with wheat or rye
- Rice, beans, soya, maize or wheat with egg
- Soya with sesame
- Beans with maize

You will find these combinations either in the recipes themselves or in the serving suggestions. The above list should, however, help you to think up your own combinations.

You will see from the table that meat or fish are not essential to healthy eating, although the body generally finds it easier to make body protein out of animal proteins. Animal protein is therefore of higher organic value than vegetable protein, but by properly combining various vegetable proteins your body will get all the essential amino acids it needs. There is one definite advantage of a low-meat diet and that is that vegetables rich in protein, such as pulses, cereal and potatoes, are much cheaper than meat. Secondly meat is rich in saturated fatty acids. One substance found chiefly in animal fat is cholesterol and a high cholesterol level in the blood gives rise to problems with the heart and arteries. Thirdly meat contains purine which the body changes into uric acid. Too much uric acid can cause gout and kidney stones in some people. Forthly meat provides the body with practically none of the roughage we need for a healthy digestion.

Fat

Fat provides the body with around twice as much energy as protein and carbohydrate. Like protein it consists of a number of basic substances, glycerine and fatty acids.

A little chemistry is needed at this point. Every chemical element, for example oxygen, carbon or iron, gold or copper can combine with another element under certain circumstances to produce a new substance. Our cooking salt for instance is a chemical mixture of sodium and chlorine. These chemical mixtures can also combine with elements and/or other mixtures to form new substances. Fatty acids are just such mixtures which in addition contain hydrogen. When they contain the maximum number of hydrogen atoms possible they are known as saturated fatty acids. If they contain only two hydrogen atoms less they are known as simple unsaturated fatty acids. With fewer hydrogen atoms still they are called polyunsaturated fatty acids. Whereas the body can produce its own saturated and simple unsaturated fatty acids, the polyunsaturates include one fatty acid which is essential, linoleic acid. The body has to take this in food. Products rich in polyunsaturated acids include vegetable oils from sunflower seeds, corn and maize as well as thistle oil, linseed oil, soya oil and walnut oil. Nuts and seeds in general also contain lots of polyunsaturated fatty acids. Saturated fatty acids are found mainly in animal products. As a comparison: corn oil contains about 50 percent polyunsaturated fatty acids, while butter has only 3 percent compared with 60 percent saturated fatty acids.

	Milk Milk prod.	Eggs	Bread Cereals	Maize	Potatoes	Pulses	Nuts Seeds
Milk Milk prod.			■		■	■	■
Eggs					■	■	
Bread Cereals	■					■	
Maize	■					■	
Potatoes	■	■					
Pulses	■	■	■	■			■
Nuts Seeds	■		■			■	

The coloured areas in the vertical and horizontal columns show suitable combinations to replace meat.

It has recently been discovered that even too much polyunsaturated fat may be bad for us. So it is best to combine animal and vegetable fats and, most important, to reduce total fat intake.

Fat should represent no more than 30 percent of our total daily energy intake, with around 1 g fat per kilogramme bodyweight. Of course we don't only take in fat in its pure form as oil or butter. Most foods contain hidden fats, often in large quantities. And it is here that the danger lies. If we eat too much fat we put on weight for the body does not get rid of excess fat but stores it in the form of fatty layers. So you should keep an eye on how much fat you eat each day and not merely cut down on the thickness of the butter you spread on your toast. Bear in mind that 1 g fat provides twice as much energy as the same amount of protein or carbohydrate. Fat is not only an important energy source, it is also responsible for our metabolism. In addition the body needs fat to be able to absorb fat-soluble vitamins such as vitamins A and E.

Carbohydrates

Carbohydrate is the main constituent of most vegetable food-stuffs. It can be divided into three groups: first the least soluble, starches, which are the most difficult to digest; secondly soluble sugar which passes quickly into the blood; and thirdly cellulose which is insoluble.

Starchy products such as cereal and potatoes are essential for a healthy diet. Starches are gradually broken down by the body into sugar and it is the slowness of the process which gives the welcome feeling of being full. Digestion begins with the saliva in the mouth. When we eat the easily soluble sugars we get an immediate full feeling, but one that does not last since the body has nothing more to do. In fact you will soon feel extremely hungry again for the blood-sugar level will fall just as quickly as it rose. In addition carbohydrates use up the body's vitamin B_1. Wholemeal bread, however, is rich in this vitamin so in this case digestion brings no vitamin loss. It is quite different with pure sugar. It is simply a

source of calories which supplies no vitamins but in fact robs the body of them. A shortage of vitamin B_1 also has the effect of making the body store any carbohydrate it does not use as fat. So a lot of sugar not only does you no good, it can do actual harm.

It would be best to look on sugar as we do salt, as a type of seasoning to be used sparingly, and to satisfy any urge for something sweet with fruit or an occasional slice of bread with honey or a bowl of muesli. Nor is brown sugar any more 'healthy'; it is merely unrefined, that is unpurified. If you experiment you will find that the use of sugar is no more than a habit. When baking, try using only two thirds of the amount of sugar given or replace sugar with honey or maple syrup (as they are more intensely sweet, less is needed). Try taking your tea or coffee without sugar. At first you will miss the sweetness, but in time you will get used to it. The main bonus is that you will rediscover your sense of taste, because dishes that previously tasted just sweet will now reveal their true flavours.

Introduction

Products made from white, highly refined flour should also be struck off your list. While they doubtless provide calories, (energy) they do not provide you with enough nutrients or fibre. If you want to eat healthy foods they must be processed as little as possible: bread, cakes and pastries made with coarse flour or better still wholemeal flour which contains all the natural goodness of the whole grain; natural brown rice from which the silvery skin and the vitamins it contains has not been removed. You will find more on individual products under separate headings in the glossary.

Carbohydrates should make up the lion's share of our food intake, providing about 55 percent of our daily energy requirements. At one time most people ate like this for the simple fact that carbohydrates such as potatoes or cereal were the cheapest foods available.

With improved living standards the amount of meat and fish we eat has increased for now we can afford a roast on weekdays as well as Sundays. Many of us are unaware that before it became commonplace to eat a lot of meat, to serve meat was considered a sign of wealth. Meat producers were quick to take advantage of and promote this feeling through factory-farming and fattening of animals.

The latest stage in this process is seen in the standardised frozen chicken, which has little more than its basic anatomy in common with the free-range farmyard chicken, and the lean EEC pigs which have to be fed on tranquillisers to prevent them meeting an early death from the stress they have to put up with in the course of their short lives.

Carbohydrates such as pulses and cereal also provide plenty of vegetable protein and so provide a good alternative to meat in both flavour and nutritional value.

Fibre

Fibre is the indigestible parts of vegetable products. It is formed by the cell walls of cereals, vegetables and fruit. Another less than flattering name for fibre – roughage – dates from a time when the best food was held to be that which was 100 percent digestible. Since for a long time fibre was thought to be valueless, it was also considered to be of no importance in diet. More recently it has been shown that it plays an important part in digestion in preventing chronic constipation. It is also believed to prevent stomach complaints and even cancer of the colon. Fibre has two functions: it absorbs a lot of liquid and thus increases the contents of the stomach so that it is transported and excreted more quickly. It also absorbs harmful and decaying substances which either form in the stomach or are ingested with food. Best of all for the functioning of the stomach is fibre such as cereal, wholemeal products and oat flakes. Some fibre, such as that from fruit and vegetables, can even lower the cholesterol level of the blood.

An extra bonus is the fact that fibre helps keep us slim for when it swells in the stomach it makes us feel pleasantly full.

Here once again the food industry has not been slow to latch on to the latest developments. Modern refined flours contain very little fibre, ie bran, and the bran that has been removed is sold back to us, attractively packaged, in health food shops at high prices. And we always have to pay more for coarse-ground or wholemeal flour than for the white superfine flour with its low nutritional value. There are different opinions on the standard value of fibre requirements. Many experts consider around 30 g per day to be sufficient, while others put the figure as high as 40 g. In either case you should eat an adequate amount of fibre. Of course it is impossible for the layman to calculate how much fibre a meal contains, but if you eat plenty of wholemeal products, brown rice, vegetables and fruit you will be eating a high-fibre diet.

Vital nutrients

By vital nutrients I mean those parts of our diet which supply no energy, but which are nevertheless essential to the human body – vitamins, minerals and trace elements, so called because the body needs only tiny amounts of them.

The body cannot make its own vitamins although it can store fat-soluble vitamins, A, D, E and K, so that we do not need to eat these every day.

The water-soluble vitamins, the various types of vitamin B and the familiar vitamin C, cannot be stored and if they are not taken in regularly in food signs of deficiency soon appear. Many vitamins, such as vitamin A, are contained in vegetable foodstuffs but only in rudimentary form. The body changes these rudimentary forms into pure vitamin A. It is not only insufficient vitamins that can be harmful but also too high a vitamin intake. Too much vitamin A, for example, changes the bone structure. A surplus of vitamins is impossible with a normal mixed diet, and vitamin deficiency is also quite rare if one eats a mixture of wholemeal and milk products and vegetables. With a good, mixed diet there will be no need for vitamin supplements. We get far too little of the B vitamins which are found in the outer layer of grain and the silver skin on rice. These are the parts which are removed to make refined flour and polished white rice, so it is important to eat grain and rice in their natural form fairly often. Foods which contain fat-soluble vitamins should always be eaten in conjunction with a little animal or vegetable fat so that the body can absorb the vitamins. So raw carrots, should be served with a few drops of oil or with yogurt.

Minerals and trace elements are basically one and the same thing, for the two terms refer to the amounts the body needs.

The daily requirement of minerals is measured in milligrammes (mg) or grammes while trace elements are measured in microgrammes and milligrammes. Minerals and trace elements are like vitamins in that the body cannot manufacture them but needs them for metabolism (magnesium, zinc), to build and maintain bones and teeth (calcium and phosphorus; fluoride prevents decay), for the blood (iron) or to control water retention (eg potash, sodium, chlorine). Our bodies usually get plenty of all these vital nutrients. The main exceptions are iron, fluoride and iodine where specific groups of people suffer deficiency. Women, for example, often suffer from iron deficiency through the blood loss in menstruation or childbirth. In areas where the drinking water contains too little fluoride caries is common. In certain areas of Europe many people suffer thyroid abnormalities (goitres) because they eat few foods that contain iodine (eg sea fish) and because air and water have a low iodine content.

Foods rich in iron
Duck, lamb, fennel, mâche or lamb's lettuce, dandelion, watercress, spinach.

Foods rich in fluoride
Milk, buttermilk, cod, chicken breast, soya beans, walnuts, spinach.

Foods rich in iodine
Milk, sole, trout, plaice, sardines, cod, sea-trout, haddock, radishes, watercress.

One fish meal per week will supply enough iodine, but you can also used iodised salt for seasoning.

Salt

Paracelsus, the great doctor and naturalist, formulated a basic rule which is especially applicable today in these times of excess: 'Everything is poison. It is the dose alone that makes a thing no longer a poison.'

This is more true of salt than any other seasoning. On the one hand it is essential for life, but on the other hand it is dangerous in too large quantities.

And we all eat too much salt. We need only 1 g per day and even unsalted food provide 3 g. On average we take in about 8–12 g per day. Although we have begun to eat less salt recently our intake is still too high. Cooking salt is a chemical mixture of the two elements sodium and chlorine which occur naturally in food. Both elements are minerals which serve to regulate the amount of water in the cells. Sodium retains water in the body, increasing the volume of the blood and raising blood pressure. High blood pressure eventually damages arteries and leads to heart disease and circulatory problems. We take in both sodium and chlorine in our food every day so that it is quite unnecessary to season with salt. As with sugar, we have got used to salt and believe it would be difficult to give it up. You should try nevertheless, even though you may be perfectly healthy.

Replace salt with fresh herbs which also contain a lot of minerals. Try a ripe uncooked tomato or a crunchy green pepper without salt occasionally. You will appreciate the flavour much more if you don't smother it in salt. The same is true of lamb and fish. Avoid at all costs processed foods such as canned foods, pre-cooked dishes, processed sauces and soups, smoked and cured products, bottled sauces and various mineral waters. These are the products responsible for such a drastic rise in salt consumption in the industrialised countries.

Enjoy your eating

Eating properly means eating better and this will increase your pleasure in eating as well as improving your health. Here are a few pointers for those of you who wish to change your eating habits or just to have a few guidelines to work on.

● Give your body time to get used to a high-carbohydrate, high-fibre diet. When you begin with organic foods don't immediately go for a grain and vegetable diet, but include some lighter, easily digestible foods and gradually increase the amount of vegetable products you eat.

● Vary your diet as much as possible for this will supply all your energy and nutrient requirements. At the same time you will reduce the risk of overloading your body with one kind of natural or chemical substance which may be harmful.

● In theory you can eat any type of food – the main question is how it has been produced. This is also true of meat. Look for a butcher who sells meat which is taken from animals reared naturally. Although it can be difficult to obtain beef and pork which has not been treated before marketing, lamb and poultry which has been reared naturally is available.

● Avoid processed foods such as canned items and products containing preservatives or artificial colourings and flavourings (the difference between foods and processed foodstuffs is given in the glossary which begins on page 145 under the appropriate headings).

Canned fruit, for instance, is not peeled by hand but by a chemical process. There are other substances which make the processing easier or improve the appearance of the product (like the bleaches used on canned fish, gelatine and walnut skins), separating agents which make it easier to get the cake out of the tin or acidity regulators which determine the acidity of wine. Since the end of 1983 it has been a legal requirement to list the additives in packaged foodstuffs, but you will usually find this to consist of columns of figures that you have to decipher. Several books about food additives, with detailed lists of E numbers (the EEC coding given to preservatives, colourings and flavourings), are available in bookshops.

● When preparing a meal always pay more attention to quality than quantity. This will be good for your palate as well as your figure.

● If you have problems with your weight keep telling yourself that eating is a pleasure you can enjoy every day. This will stop you eating as if there is no tomorrow.

● Eat something uncooked at the start of every meal. This helps digestion.

● Try to combine both cooked and uncooked foods in the same meal (eg fresh herbs or grated vegetables). This too helps digestion.

● Chew your food well for the digestion of carbohydrates begins in the mouth.

● Keep an eye on how much sugar and salt you eat per day and begin to gradually reduce the amounts.

● Gradually begin to replace all products made with white flour with wholemeal products. As far as foods made from dough or pastry are concerned, you can accustom yourself to the new regime with wheatgerm or soya pasta which do not have that 'healthy' taste and which, if you shut your eyes, are indistinguishable from ordinary pasta. There are different types of natural rice too and it is a good idea to try the various types until you find the one you prefer.

● Eat more foods containing vegetable protein. Pulses, cereals and potatoes will provide your body with all the carbohydrates and fibre it needs.

● Don't buy vegetables, fruit and salad stuffs for their looks alone. Such products are chemically treated. The classes under which they are sold refer only to appearance and not to quality.

● Don't buy hothouse foods, but stick to fresh seasonal fruit and vegetables. You cannot get home-grown strawberries in winter and imported ones may be full of harmful substances. Hothouse products are liable to pests and are chemically treated to prevent them.

● Include freshly grated vegetables in salads and don't stick just to leafy saladstuffs, which contain less vitamins and minerals and are less nutritious. You should avoid lettuce altogether in winter for they are more likely to be full of harmful substances from the fertiliser and insecticides.

● The skins of fruit and vegetables provide a natural form of packaging. If they are also encased in cling film it is better not to buy them. Firstly the extra packaging is not only unnecessary but also a burden on the environment and your purse (packing costs are added to the price of the food). Secondly prepackaging forces you to buy a certain quantity which may be more than you need. Thirdly it prevents you getting a good look at the products, for fruit and vegetables which look fine on top may often be damaged or going bad underneath. Pre-packaged foods serve the needs of industry rather than those of the consumer.

● Don't buy just because a product is labelled 'organic' but check whether it has really been produced in the right way. Look for information on the origins of the food. Check the list of ingredients used in preparing a product to make sure they are all acceptable.

● You should reduce the amount of meat and fish you eat, but don't give it up altogether. It is also important to eat animal protein in the form of milk products and cheese as well as animal fat. A strict vegetarian diet requires a thorough knowledge of the composition of our foods if you are to keep a balanced and healthy diet.

Crispy, flat, wholemeal breadcakes are delicious with both sweet and savoury spreads. Here they are served with a creamy cheese spread and a delicious avocado cream. In this chapter you will find a host of healthy treats which will appeal even to the most fastidious gourmet: a light salmon carpaccio, tomato quiche fresh from the oven or artichokes with a creamy tofu sauce.

Refreshing crudités are here, as well as light summer salads and delicious snacks to satisfy your hunger between meals. And the various breakfast ideas guarantee a good start to the day. Just try the porridge with fresh cream and dried fruit, muesli and wheatgerm or yogurt with fruit. You will learn how to make your own curd cheese, how to pickle trout fillets and how to combine unusual ingredients like tahini and couscous with more familiar ones to make delicious dishes.

Starters, Salads and Snacks

Pickled Fillets of Trout

3 cleaned fresh trout, about
*   350 g/12 oz each*
3 tablespoons lemon juice
3 tablespoons tarragon vinegar
375 ml/13 fl oz water
1 bay leaf
3 juniper berries
2 coriander seeds
1 teaspoon mustard seeds
1 teaspoon white peppercorns
100 g/4 oz fresh basil
2 tablespoons salt
1 tablespoon caster sugar

Rinse the trout inside and out in cold water and wipe thoroughly dry. Cut off the heads, fins and tails. Cut the fish open right along the stomach side, carefully open out and remove the backbone. It is best to use a knife with a thin, flexible blade. Start by loosening the large bones that lie flat in the fish. Then open up the fish as far as it will go and run the knife in short strokes along the left and right of the backbone. Once the bone is completely free of the flesh you can peel it back towards the tail. Remove all the small bones with tweezers, making sure you do not miss any. Separate the fish into fillets but do not skin.

Mix the lemon juice with the tarragon vinegar and water. Place the trout fillets in the liquid, cover the bowl and marinate for 8 hours in a cool place.

Remove the trout fillets from the marinade and wipe dry on absorbent kitchen paper.

Crumble the bay leaf between your fingers. In a mortar, coarsely crush the juniper berries, coriander, mustard seeds and peppercorns.

Rinse the basil in cold water, strip off the leaves, pat dry and finely chop.

Mix the seasonings in the mortar with the bay leaf, basil, salt and sugar.

Sprinkle the flesh side of half the fillets with this mixture and sandwich together in pairs with the skin to the outside. Press each pair of fillets together and wrap in foil. Place the packets between two trays or chopping boards and weight down.

Leave the trout fillets to press for 12 hours in a cool place.

Unwrap the fillets and scrape off the seasoning.

Next skin the fillets. To do this, place each fillet, skin side down, on the worktop and cut about 1 cm/½ in skin loose at the tail end. Hold this piece of skin and run the knife flat between the fillet and the skin.

Serve the pickled trout on individual plates, garnished to taste with lemon slices and fresh herbs.

Delicious with brown bread, horseradish cream and salad.

The quantities given will also make a light main course for 3.

Serves 6

Per Portion
about 115 calories
4 g carbohydrate
17 g protein · 2 g fat

Cook's Tip

Fresh salmon is also delicious pickled in this way. Marinate a tailpiece in the same way as the trout and skin after marinating. If you can't get fresh basil use dill. Eat both the trout and salmon as soon as possible after pickling for they lose their flavour if kept.

Salmon Carpaccio with Chervil

300 g/11 oz fresh salmon (tail piece)
handful of fresh chervil
5 white peppercorns
1 tablespoon white wine vinegar
2 tablespoons lemon juice
3 tablespoons dry white wine
salt
pinch of caster sugar
1 tablespoon capers
4 tablespoons cold-pressed olive oil

To cut the salmon into really thin slices you will need a special salmon knife with a long, flexible, very sharp blade. The best idea is to ask your fishmonger to fillet, skin and slice the salmon. If you prefer to fillet and skin the fish yourself, proceed as in the trout fillets recipe on the opposite page. Any slices that are too thick can be placed between pieces of cling film and gently flattened with the ball of your hand. Arrange the salmon slices on four plates.

Pick over and wash the chervil, pat thoroughly dry and chop very finely.

Place the peppercorns on a board and crush with the blade of a strong knife.

Stir the white wine vinegar with the lemon juice, white wine, salt to taste and sugar until the salt has completely dissolved. Coarsely chop the capers and add them. Beat in the olive oil a tablespoon at a time.

Mix the chervil and peppercorns into the vinaigrette.

Spoon the chervil vinaigrette over the salmon and serve the carpaccio immediately, with wheatgerm rolls or wholemeal bread and butter.

Serves 4

Per Portion
about 300 calories
3 g carbohydrate
15 g protein · 25 g fat

Cook's Tip
For a slightly stronger flavour you can replace the chervil with snipped fresh chives.

Artichokes with Tofu Sauce

salt
1 lemon
4 globe artichokes
100 g/4 oz tofu
150 ml/¼ pint natural yogurt
1 tablespoon crème fraîche or soured cream
1 clove garlic
freshly ground white pepper
1 teaspoon vegetable oil
5 tablespoons chopped mixed fresh herbs (chives, parsley, dill, borage, lemon balm, tarragon and basil)

Bring plenty of salted water to the boil in a pan which is large enough to take all the artichokes at once.

Meanwhile, halve the lemon. Squeeze one half and keep the juice to one side. Wash the artichokes well in cold water. Cut off the artichoke stalks close to the base. Using kitchen scissors snip off the top half of each leaf. Rub all the cut edges with the second lemon half to prevent discolouring. Then squeeze the lemon half into the fast-boiling water.

Add the artichokes. Return to the boil and cook for 20 to 30 minutes over a low to moderate heat. They are cooked when the leaves come away easily.

Meanwhile, make the sauce by blending the tofu with the yogurt and crème fraîche in a liquidiser or food processor to give a smooth, creamy consistency. Peel the garlic and squeeze through a garlic press into the tofu paste. Season to taste. Stir in the reserved lemon juice, oil and herbs.

Serve the drained artichokes with the tofu sauce.

Serves 4

Per Portion
about 135 calories
16 g carbohydrate
6 g protein · 5 g fat

Fried Mozzarella

about 250 g/9 oz mozzarella cheese
1 egg
1 tablespoon wholemeal flour
3–4 tablespoons stale rye breadcrumbs
1–2 tablespoons olive oil

Drain the mozzarella, pat dry and cut into 4 slices.

Beat the egg in a dish with a fork until the white and yolk are completely mixed. Put the wholemeal flour and rye crumbs into dishes.

Coat the mozzarella slices first in wholemeal flour, then in egg and finally in breadcrumbs.

Heat the olive oil in a frying pan. Fry the mozzarella slices over a moderate heat for about 2 minutes on each side until the cheese is soft and the crumbs golden brown.

Serve immediately on individual warmed plates, garnished with sliced tomato, and sprinkled with fresh herbs and a little olive oil.

Serves 4

Per Portion
about 200 calories
8 g carbohydrate
11 g protein · 13 g fat

Cook's Tip
Mozzarella is a soft Italian cheese made from cow's or buffalo's milk. When it is fresh it is soft and slightly sticky at the centre. Slices of tomato and mozzarella arranged alternately on a plate and sprinkled with chopped fresh basil and cold-pressed olive oil make a delicious light starter for summer.

Dinner Party Starters

Celery Gratin

1 head celery (about 400 g/
*   14 oz)*
100 g/4 oz soya bean sprouts
75 g/3 oz cheese (preferably Bel
*   Paese, Gruyère or fairly stale*
*   Gouda)*
small bunch of fresh parsley
125 ml/4 fl oz freshly made vege-
*   table stock (recipe*
*   page 38)*
salt
freshly ground black pepper

Cut off the base of the celery,
separate the stalks, trim and
wash. Cut off the leaves and
keep to one side. Peel off any
tough threads with a small
pointed knife. Wipe the sticks
of celery dry and cut into 1 cm/
½ in lengths. Dry the leaves.

Tip the bean sprouts into a
sieve, wash thoroughly under
cold running water and drain.

Coarsely grate the cheese.
Wash the parsley, strip the
leaves from the stalks, wipe dry
and finely chop with the celery
leaves.

Bring the vegetable stock to
the boil. Add the celery and
bean sprouts and simmer over a
moderate heat for about 3
minutes.

Drain the vegetables and
spoon into 4 gratin or other
shallow ovenproof dishes.
Season to taste with salt and
black pepper and sprinkle with
the chopped parsley and celery
leaves. Scatter with the cheese.

Put the dishes into a moderately hot oven (200 C, 400 F, gas
6), on the second shelf from the
bottom, and bake for 20 to 25
minutes until the cheese is
melted and golden brown.

Serves 4

Per Portion
about 100 calories
6 g carbohydrate
7 g protein · 5 fat

Mushroom Gratin

½ lemon
250 g/9 oz button mushrooms
1 shallot
1 clove garlic
1 bunch of fresh parsley
150 g/5 oz mozzarella cheese
1 tablespoon olive oil
salt
freshly ground white pepper
1 tablespoon sesame seeds

Squeeze the juice from the
lemon. Wash the mushrooms, if
necessary, and then trim the
stalks and slice. Sprinkle with
the lemon juice to prevent
discolouring.

Peel and finely chop the
shallot and garlic. Wash the
parsley, shake dry and chop the
leaves. Dry the mozzarella and
finely dice.

Heat the olive oil in a frying
pan and fry the shallot and
garlic until transparent. Add
the mushrooms and fry over a
high heat until the liquid produced has evaporated and the
mushrooms are dry.

Season to taste with salt and
white pepper and divide between four gratin or other shallow ovenproof dishes. Scatter
with the parsley and then with
the mozzarella and sesame
seeds.

Place the dishes in a moderately hot oven (200 C, 400 F, gas
6), on the second shelf from the
bottom, and bake for about
15 minutes until the cheese is
melted and golden brown.

Serves 4

Per Portion
about 160 calories
5 g carbohydrate
8 g protein · 11 g fat

17

Tomato Quiche

*300 g/11 oz wholemeal or
    wheatmeal flour*
6 eggs
1 tablespoon vegetable oil
salt
*3–4 tablespoons water (if
    necessary)*
1 kg/2¼ lb ripe tomatoes
*bunch each of fresh chives and
    basil*
6 sprigs of fresh thyme
125 ml/4 fl oz milk
*250 ml/8 fl oz crème fraîche or
    soured cream*
*75 g/3 oz Parmesan cheese,
    freshly grated*
freshly ground white pepper
pinch of cayenne pepper
freshly grated nutmeg
butter for the baking sheet
flour for rolling

Mix the flour with 2 eggs, the
oil, salt to taste and a little
water to make a smooth pasta
dough. After kneading the
dough should not be sticky or it
will be difficult to roll later. If it
is too dry work in more water a
few drops at a time.

Shape the dough into a ball,
wrap in greaseproof paper and
leave to rest for 30 minutes to
allow the flour to swell.

Meanwhile, blanch the tomatoes in boiling water for 30
seconds, rinse in cold water and
peel. Using a sharp knife cut
out the cores and slice the tomatoes crossways. Carefully
scrape out all the seeds for they
contain a lot of moisture and
would make the quiche too
soft.

Wash the herbs and shake
dry. Snip the chives into short
lengths. (You should never
chop chives: the delicate stems
need a clean cut if they are to
give their full flavour.) Strip off
the basil leaves and cut into
thin strips. Strip the thyme
leaves from the stalks and leave
whole.

Whisk the remaining eggs
with the milk, crème fraîche or
soured cream and Parmesan.
Stir in the herbs and season to
taste with salt, pepper, cayenne
and nutmeg.

Grease a 23 × 33-cm/9 × 13-
in, deep Swiss roll tin or a
roasting tin with butter.

Divide the dough into 4 to 6
pieces. On a lightly floured
worktop, roll out the dough as
thinly as possible. Line the baking tin with dough, overlapping
the pieces by about 0.5 cm/¼ in
and making a rim 1–2 cm/½ to
¾ in high around the edge.

Arrange the tomato slices on
the dough base. Pour over the
egg and milk mixture.

Place the baking sheet in a
moderately hot oven (200 C,
400 F, gas 6), on the second
shelf from the bottom, and
bake for 30 to 40 minutes until
the egg mixture has set and the
top is golden brown.

Delicious as a starter or, with
a colourful mixed salad, as a
light lunch.

Serves 6

Per Portion
about 470 calories
43 g carbohydrate
19 g protein · 22 g fat

Cook's Tip

The thinner the dough
the better the quiche will
taste. You can make
really thin sheets of
dough in a hand-operat-
ed pasta machine. To use
this, you do not need to
knead the dough for so
long. Instead allow the
dough to rest, then divide
it into pieces and pass
them through the ma-
chine several times until
really smooth. Then roll
the sheets of dough on
the thinnest setting. If
you have any dough over
you can make noodles,
spaghetti or vermicelli. If
you are not intending to
use the pasta immedi-
ately, spread out on tea
towels until completely
dry.

Satisfying Snacks

Flat Bread Cakes

500 g/18 oz wholemeal flour
salt
½ teaspoon freshly ground
*   caraway*
1 teaspoon freshly crushed
*   coriander*
150 ml/¼ pint natural yogurt
250 ml/8 fl oz lukewarm water

In a bowl, mix the wholemeal
flour with a generous pinch of
salt, the caraway and coriander.

Beat the yogurt with the
water and pour on to the flour.
Work the ingredients together,
then knead the dough vigorously until smooth. Shape into
a ball, wrap in greaseproof paper and leave to rest for at least
8 hours.

Divide the dough into about
15 equal portions. Knead each
piece vigorously once more,
and then roll out on a lightly
floured worktop into thin
rounds.

Heat a heavy griddle or cast
iron frying pan over a low to
moderate heat without allowing

it to get too hot. Add the bread
cakes, one at a time, and cook
on both sides until lightly
browned and slightly bubbly.

Serve the bread cakes with
either avocado cream and/or
olive cheese or simply with
melted butter, flavoured with a
little garlic if liked.

Makes 15

Per Portion
about 130 calories
24 g carbohydrate
5 g protein · 1 g fat

Avocado Cream

50 g/2 oz Roquefort or Gorgon-
*   zola cheese*
1 tablespoon blanched almonds
1 ripe avocado
juice of ½ lemon
freshly ground white pepper

Cream the cheese with a fork
until as smooth as possible.

Tip the almonds on to a
board and finely chop using a
strong knife or grind in a nut
mill or coffee grinder.

Halve the avocado and re-
move the stone. Peel the avocado halves using a small, sharp
knife and sprinkle immediately
with lemon juice to prevent
discolouring. Mash the avocado with a fork.

Add the cheese and almonds
and mix to a smooth paste.
Season to taste with pepper.

Serves 6

Per Portion
about 245 calories
3 g carbohydrate
2 g protein · 23 g fat

Olive Cheese

100 g/4 oz black olives
1 clove garlic
small bunch of fresh basil
1 tablespoon natural yogurt
125 g/4½ oz cream cheese
1 tablespoon gomasio
freshly ground white pepper

Drain the olives well, remove
the stones and chop very finely.
Peel and chop the garlic. Wash
the basil in cold water, shake
dry and chop the leaves.

Stir the yogurt into the cream
cheese until smooth. Stir in the
olives, garlic and basil. Season
to taste with gomasio and
pepper.

Serves 6

Per Portion
about 195 calories
3 g carbohydrate
5 g protein · 18 g fat

Romanian-style Marinated Vegetables

500 g/18 oz fennel
250 g/9 oz carrots
3 tomatoes
3 cloves garlic
juice of ½ lemon
250 ml/8 fl oz dry white wine
125 ml/4 fl oz freshly made vege-
    table stock (recipe page 38)
3 black peppercorns
1 bay leaf
6 sprigs of fresh thyme
6 sprigs of fresh parsley
salt
6 tablespoons cold-pressed olive
    oil

Trim the feathery leaves from
the fennel and set aside. Halve
the fennel bulbs lengthways.
Wash the halves, drain and cut
lengthways twice more.

Peel the carrots and cut into
sticks about 5 cm/2 in long and
1 cm/½ in thick.

Blanch the tomatoes in boiling water for 30 seconds, rinse
in cold water and peel. Quarter
the tomatoes lengthways and
remove the core and the seeds.
Peel the garlic.

Put the lemon juice, wine,
vegetable stock, peppercorns
and bay leaf in a saucepan and
bring to the boil. Wash the
thyme and parsley and add to
the pan.

Add the fennel, carrots and
garlic. Return to the boil, cover
and cook gently for about 8
minutes until half cooked.

Add the tomatoes and cook
for a further 2 minutes. Remove all the vegetables from
the stock with a slotted spoon
and transfer to a serving dish.
Season lightly with salt.

Strain the stock and then boil
to reduce by half, stirring continuously. Add the olive oil and
reheat. Pour over the
vegetables.

Finely chop the reserved fennel leaves and sprinkle over the
vegetables. Leave to cool, then
cover and marinate at room
temperature.

Serves 4

Per Portion
about 230 calories
16 g carbohydrate
4 g protein · 16 g fat

A Variety of Salads

Mooli Salad with Cheese Dressing

2 mooli or daikon (white
*   radishes)*
herb salt
bunch of fresh chives
20 g/¾ oz Gorgonzola or
*   Roquefort cheese*
125 ml/4 fl oz single cream,
*   crème fraîche or soured cream*
2 tablespoons lemon juice
freshly ground white pepper
pinch of caster sugar
1 tablespoon sunflower oil
handful of watercress or 1 box
*   mustard and cress*

Trim, peel and coarsely grate
the mooli. Place in a bowl,
sprinkle with herb salt and
leave to stand for about 5 minutes. This draws some of the
moisture out of the mooli so
that the salad is not watery.

Meanwhile, rinse the chives
in cold water, pat dry and cut
up. Crush the Gorgonzola or
Roquefort with a fork and
work in the cream to make a
smooth paste. Stir in the lemon
juice and season the cheese
dressing with pepper to taste
and the sugar. Add the chives
and oil and mix gently.

Pour off any liquid that has
formed in the mooli bowl.
Squeeze dry the mooli by hand
and transfer to a clean bowl.
Pour the cheese dressing over
the mooli and fold in (or serve
the dressing separately).

Pick over the watercress,
wash well and pat dry. Chop
thick stems and scatter over the
salad with the leaves. If using
mustard and cress, snip off with
scissors and scatter over the
salad.

Serves 4

Per Portion
about 175 calories
7 g carbohydrate
4 g protein · 14 g fat

Uncooked Vegetable Salad

1 green and 1 red pepper
1 carrot
½ cucumber
1 large beef tomato
bunch of spring onions
bunch of radishes
bunch each of fresh chives and
*   dill or 3 tablespoons chopped*
*   mixed fresh herbs*
1 clove garlic
salt
3 tablespoons red wine vinegar
1 tablespoon dry red wine
pinch of caster sugar
freshly ground black pepper
5 tablespoons cold-pressed olive
*   oil*

Remove the stalks from the
peppers, cut lengthways into
quarters and cut out the white
pith with the seeds. Wash in
cold water, wipe dry and cut
into strips or squares.

Peel the carrot and cucumber
and then slice or dice. Wash,
dry and dice the tomato, removing the core and seeds.

Wash, dry and trim the
spring onions and radishes. Cut
the onions with about one third
of the green leaves into rings
and thinly slice the radishes.
Mix the salad ingredients
together in a bowl.

Wash the chives and dill and
shake dry. Cut up the chives
and chop the dill. Peel and chop
the garlic and crush with a little
salt.

Beat the red wine vinegar
and red wine with the sugar,
and salt and pepper to taste.
Gradually beat in the oil. Add
the herbs and garlic.

Pour the dressing over the
salad, stir in gently and serve
immediately.

Serves 4

Per Portion
about 155 calories
7 g carbohydrate
1 g protein · 13 g fat

A Variety of Salads

Fennel Salad with Sesame Dressing

50 g/2 oz tofu
2 tablespoons lemon juice
125 ml/4 fl oz water
herb salt
2 tablespoons tahini (sesame paste)
500 g/18 oz fennel
2 tablespoons chopped fresh mixed herbs (eg parsley, dill, chives, lemon balm, chervil)
freshly ground white pepper
2 tablespoons shelled walnuts

Drain the tofu and blend with the lemon juice and water in a liquidiser. Stir in a little herb salt and the tahini.

Halve the fennel bulbs lengthways, wash and drain. Cut out the wedge-shaped stalk. Cut off the feathery leaves and keep to one side to garnish the salad. Cut the fennel across the grain into strips.

Arrange the fennel strips on four plates and sprinkle with the chopped herbs. Pour the sesame dressing over the fennel and season to taste with pepper.

Using a sharp knife, coarsely chop the walnuts. Finely chop the reserved fennel leaves. Scatter the fennel salad with the walnuts and leaves and serve.

Serves 4

Per Portion
about 160 calories
14 g carbohydrate
6 g protein · 8 g fat

Cook's Tip
Dressings with tahini need quite a lot of liquid because if the sesame paste comes into contact with undiluted acids, such as vinegar or lemon juice, it forms lumps that you can't get rid of. So always mix all the other dressing ingredients before adding the tahini.

Spinach Salad with Pine Nuts

100 g/4 oz fresh young spinach
handful of young nettle leaves
2 tablespoons raspberry vinegar
pinch of sugar
herb salt
freshly ground white pepper
1 teaspoon Dijon mustard
4 tablespoons cold-pressed olive oil
2 tablespoons pine nuts

Pick over the spinach and nettles. The nettles must be really young and tender or they are not suitable for salad. (Older nettles can be blanched and served like spinach as a hot vegetable.) Wash the spinach several times in plenty of water. Then wash the nettles and shake both dry.

Stir the raspberry vinegar with the sugar and herb salt and pepper to taste until the salt has dissolved. Add the mustard and beat in the olive oil a tablespoon at a time.

Add the spinach, nettles and pine nuts to the dressing, mix gently and serve immediately while the leaves are still nice and crisp.

Serve with garlic bread or crispbread and butter.

Serves 4

Per Portion
about 165 calories
4 g carbohydrate
2 g protein · 15 g fat

Cook's Tip
In late spring when the first fresh herbs reappear, leave out the spinach and make up the salad only with wild and garden herbs. You can use parsley, chervil, burnet and dandelion as well as the nettles.

Couscous Salad

75 g/3 oz couscous
2 small courgettes, about 100 g/
    4 oz each
5 tablespoons sunflower oil
500 g/18 oz ripe tomatoes
1 onion
1 clove garlic
1 small red pepper
3 tablespoons herb vinegar
4 tablespoons chopped fresh
    mixed herbs (eg parsley, dill,
    chives, lemon balm, chervil,
    borage and mint)
salt

Soak the couscous in hot water
for 1 hour, then drain
thoroughly.

Wash and dry the courgettes.
Trim off the ends. Cut lengthways into 1 cm/½ in slices and
then into sticks 1 cm/½ in wide.

Heat 2 tablespoons sunflower
oil in a frying pan. Fry the
courgette pieces over a moderate heat until lightly browned
and beginning to soften. Drain
on absorbent kitchen paper and
leave to cool slightly.

Meanwhile, wash, dry and
dice the tomatoes, removing the
core and seeds. Peel and finely
dice the onion and garlic.

Remove the stalk from the
red pepper, cut in half and
scrape out the white pith and
seeds. Wash the peppers in cold
water and cut into fine strips.

Mix the courgettes, tom-
atoes, onion, garlic and red
pepper with the couscous. Add
the vinegar, herbs, remaining
oil and salt to taste. Cover the
bowl and leave to marinate at
room temperature for 45
minutes.

Stir through with a fork before serving.

Serves 4

Per Portion
about 230 calories
24 g carbohydrate
4 g protein · 13 g fat

Bean Salad with Tomato Vinaigrette

300 g/11 oz green beans
bunch of fresh savory
1 red onion
1 tablespoon mild herb vinegar
1 tablespoon balsam vinegar
salt
freshly ground black pepper
1 teaspoon whole grain mustard
3 tablespoons cold-pressed olive
    oil
1 large beef tomato

Wash and drain the beans. Top
and tail the beans and pull off
any strings.

Wash the savory and keep
two sprigs to one side for the
vinaigrette.

In a saucepan, bring about
two fingers depth of water to
the boil. Add the beans and savory, cover the pan and cook
over a low to moderate heat for
about 5 to 8 minutes until the
beans are tender but still firm.

Meanwhile, peel and finely
chop the onion. Stir the two
vinegars with salt and pepper to
taste. Add the mustard and
beat in the olive oil a tablespoon at a time. Add the
chopped onion.

Wash, dry and dice the tomato, removing the core and
seeds. Finely chop the reserved
savory.

Drain the beans, rinse in cold
water and drain well.

Mix the diced tomato and
chopped savory into the vinaigrette. Arrange the warm beans
on a flat dish and pour on the
vinaigrette. Serve with garlic
bread.

Serves 4

Per Portion
about 100 calories
6 g carbohydrate
2 g protein · 8 g fat

Rice Salad with Chicken and Bean Sprouts

1 (1.3 kg/2½ lb) chicken
150 g/5 oz celeriac
1 carrot
1 leek
1 onion
1 clove garlic
2 cloves
sprig of fresh thyme
4 black peppercorns
1 bay leaf
salt
2 litres/3½ pints water
1 teaspoon instant vegetable
   stock granules
500 g/18 oz long-grain brown
   rice
2 bunches of spring onions
1–2 cucumbers (about 700 g/
   1½ lb)
bunch of fresh parsley
1 lemon
300 g/11 oz mung bean sprouts
herb salt
2 tablespoons cold-pressed olive
   oil

Place the chicken in a large saucepan. Add sufficient cold water just to cover and bring slowly to simmering point over a moderate heat.

As soon as small bubbles begin to form, reduce the heat. The chicken should cook at just below boiling point if the meat is to be tender and moist. Half cover the pan and keep checking that it is not boiling. If necessary add more hot water to keep the chicken just covered throughout. Cook in this way for 30 minutes.

Meanwhile, peel the celeriac and carrot and cut into fairly large pieces. Trim the leek, wash well and halve lengthways. Peel the onion and garlic. Halve the onion and stick the cloves into it.

Add all the vegetables, the garlic, thyme, peppercorns and bay leaf to the chicken. Increase the heat until the stock begins to simmer again. Season to taste with salt. Cook the chicken for another hour, until cooked.

Meanwhile, bring the water

to the boil with the instant vegetable stock. Add the rice, cover the pan and cook over the lowest possible heat for 25 to 30 minutes or until the rice is tender and has absorbed all the liquid. Transfer the rice to a large bowl and leave to cool.

Lift the chicken out of the stock. Remove the meat from the carcass, discarding all skin and bones, and cut the meat into bite-sized pieces. Remove fat and gristle as you go.

Strain the stock through a sieve lined with muslin. Squeeze the liquid out of the vegetables and flavourings before discarding them. Measure off 375 ml/ 13 fl oz stock and set aside.

Cut the spring onions into thin rings. Peel the cucumber. Cut in half across and then lengthways and scrape out the seeds using a teaspoon. Cut into small cubes.

Wash the parsley, pluck off the leaves, pat dry and finely chop. Squeeze the juice from the lemon.

Wash the bean sprouts well in cold water. Bring the re-

served stock to the boil and cook the bean sprouts for 3 minutes.

Add the chicken meat and the bean sprouts with their stock to the cooled rice. Add the spring onion rings, diced cucumber and parsley.

Stir the lemon juice with herb salt to taste until the salt has dissolved, then beat in the olive oil. Pour the dressing over the salad and stir in.

Serves 10

Per Portion
about 360 calories
42 g carbohydrate
24 g protein · 9 g fat

Carrots with Nut Vinaigrette

500 g/18 oz young carrots
75 g/3 oz shelled hazelnuts or
*   walnuts*
juice of 1 lemon
2 tablespoons mild herb vinegar
1 pinch of sugar
salt
freshly ground white pepper
2 tablespoons cold-pressed olive
*   oil*
2 tablespoons chopped fresh
*   parsley*

Trim and scrape the carrots. Rinse under cold running water, dry and finely grate.

On a board coarsely chop the nuts using a strong knife.

Mix the lemon juice with the herb vinegar. Add the sugar and salt and pepper to taste and stir until the salt and sugar have dissolved. Beat in the oil a tablespoon at a time. Stir the nuts and 1 tablespoon parsley into the vinaigrette.

Pour over the carrots and stir in. Serve immediately, sprinkled with the remaining parsley. Makes a delicious starter or, with wholemeal bread and butter, a light supper.

Serves 4

Per Portion
about 220 calories
14 g carbohydrate
4 g protein · 17 g fat

Variation
Beetroot with Apple
Peel and grate 300 g/11 oz beetroot. Core 1 large (125 g/ 4½ oz) fairly tart apple, then peel and grate. Stir 3 tablespoons mild raspberry vinegar with a pinch of sugar and salt and freshly ground white pepper to taste until the salt and sugar have dissolved. Beat in ½ tablespoon cold-pressed olive oil. Mix the grated beetroot and apple with the vinaigrette. Fold in 250 ml/8 fl oz natural yogurt or soured cream and serve.

Sprouted Salad

2 tablespoons each dried mung
   beans, lentils, chickpeas and
   wholewheat grain (wheat
   berries)
125 ml/4 fl oz freshly made vegetable stock (recipe page 38)
bunch of spring onions
3 ripe tomatoes
1 clove garlic
3 tablespoons mild herb vinegar
1 teaspoon chive mustard
salt
freshly ground white pepper
4 tablespoons sunflower oil
1 box of mustard and cress
2 tablespoons sunflower seeds

Tip the mung beans, lentils,
chickpeas and wheat into separate germinating trays and
spread out in a single layer. The
mung beans will germinate best
in the bottom tray as they don't
need much light. Fill the trays
with water according to the
instructions and either renew or
top up the water every day. (If
you don't have a seed sprouter,
you can use glass jars covered
with muslin secured with a rubber band.)

Rinse the sprouted seeds and
shake dry. Bring the vegetable
stock to the boil and blanch the
mung bean sprouts for 1
minute. Drain.

Cut the spring onions into
thin rings. Dice the tomatoes,
removing the core and the
seeds. Peel and finely chop the
garlic.

Beat the vinegar with the
mustard, and salt and pepper to
taste. Beat in the sunflower oil
a tablespoon at a time. Snip off
the cress with kitchen scissors.
Add all the sprouted seeds and
the cress to the dressing and
mix well. Sprinkle with the sunflower seeds and serve.

Serves 4

Per Portion
about 240 calories
21 g carbohydrate
8 g protein · 14 g fat

Onion and Mushroom Salad with Smoked Salmon

2 bunches of spring onions
125 ml/4 fl oz freshly made vegetable stock (recipe page 38)
   or chicken stock
1 tablespoon dry white wine
200 g/7 oz mushrooms
1 tablespoon lemon juice
4 slices smoked salmon
salt
freshly ground black pepper
2 tablespoons cold-pressed olive
   oil
1 box of mustard and cress

Trim the spring onions, wash
well under cold running water,
wipe dry and, with about two
thirds of the green leaves, cut
into 3 cm/1¼ in lengths.

Bring the vegetable or
chicken stock to the boil with
the white wine. Add the spring
onions, return to the boil, cover
the pan and cook over a low
heat for 3 to 5 minutes until the
onions are tender but still firm
to bite. When ready, drain well.

Meanwhile, trim the mush-
rooms, wash if necessary, cut
into thin slices and sprinkle immediately with lemon juice to
prevent discolouring.

Cut the salmon into fairly
wide strips.

Arrange the spring onions,
mushrooms and salmon on
four plates and season to taste
with salt (preferably from a
mill) and pepper. Sprinkle the
vegetables with the olive oil.

Snip off the cress with
kitchen scissors and use to garnish the salad. Serve with rye
bread and butter.

Serves 4

Per Portion
about 170 calories
4 g carbohydrate
12 g protein · 10 g fat

A Variety of Salads

Bean Sprout Salad with Prawns

200 g / 7 oz cooked fresh or frozen prawns, peeled
1 lemon
1 small red pepper
2 spring onions
400 g / 14 oz mung bean sprouts
3 tablespoons sunflower oil
125 ml / 4 fl oz freshly made vegetable stock (recipe page 38)
2 tablespoons soy sauce
1 tablespoon dry sherry
pinch of sugar
salt

If using frozen prawns, allow to thaw first and drain well. Squeeze the lemon and sprinkle half the juice over the prawns.

Remove the stalk from the red pepper, cut in half and scrape out the white pith and seeds. Rinse in cold water to get rid of the remaining seeds, then wipe dry and cut across into very thin strips.

Trim, wash and dry the spring onions and then cut into thin rings with about two thirds of the green leaves.

Tip the bean sprouts into a sieve, rinse well in cold water and shake dry. Heat 1 tablespoon oil in a frying pan and add the bean sprouts. Cook for 30 seconds, stirring continuously. Add the stock and soy sauce and cook for 1 minute.

Tip the bean sprouts and the cooking liquid into a bowl and mix in the prawns, red pepper and spring onions.

Beat the remaining lemon juice with the sherry, sugar, remaining oil and salt to taste. Stir gently with the salad.

Marinate for 30 minutes at room temperature before serving.

Serves 4

Per Portion
about 160 calories
8 g carbohydrate
12 g protein · 9 g fat

Leek Salad with Chicken and Almonds

4 boneless chicken breasts (450 g / 1 lb total weight)
2 tablespoons chopped fresh parsley
2 tablespoons dry sherry
2 tablespoons cold-pressed olive oil
400 g / 14 oz leeks
2 teaspoons chopped fresh thyme
125 ml / 4 fl oz freshly made vegetable stock (recipe page 38)
salt
freshly ground white pepper
2 tablespoons wine vinegar
2 tablespoons lemon juice
1 teaspoon walnut oil
1 teaspoon butter
3 tablespoons chopped almonds

Skin the chicken breasts. Mix the parsley with the sherry and 1 tablespoon olive oil. Brush on to the chicken and leave to marinate.

Trim and wash the leeks and cut into 1-cm/½-in lengths.

Cook the leeks and thyme in the stock for 2 to 3 minutes until the leeks are tender but still firm. Drain, reserving 3 tablespoons stock. Season the reserved stock to taste. Stir in the wine vinegar, lemon juice, the remaining olive oil and the walnut oil. Arrange the leeks on four warmed plates and spoon on the dressing.

Heat the butter and fry the almonds until golden. Remove from the pan and set aside.

Pat the chicken breasts dry. Fry the breasts over a high heat for about 2 minutes on each side or until cooked. Season the chicken, cut into thin slices and arrange over the leeks. Sprinkle with the almonds and serve.

Serves 4

Per Portion
about 245 calories
16.5 g carbohydrate
16.5 g protein · 12 g fat

Delicious Dips

Dips with Vegetables

200 g / 7 oz tofu
125 ml / 4 fl oz single cream
½ tablespoon lemon juice
1 tablespoon salted shelled
  pistachios
bunch of fresh basil
freshly ground white pepper
2 tablespoons sesame seeds
1 box of mustard and cress
250 g / 9 oz cream cheese
125 ml / 4 fl oz soured cream
salt
250 g / 9 oz ripe tomatoes
1 onion
1 clove garlic
freshly ground black pepper
pinch of caster sugar
Tabasco sauce

To make the tofu dip, finely dice the drained tofu and blend with the cream and lemon juice in a liquidiser or food processor. Finely chop the pistachios. Wash the basil, shake dry and finely chop. Mix the pistachios and basil into the dip and season to taste with white pepper.

To make the cream cheese dip, first toast the sesame seeds in a dry frying pan, stirring continuously. Snip off the cress. Stir the cream cheese with the soured cream until smooth and mix in the sesame seeds and cress. Season to taste with salt and white pepper.

To make the tomato dip, first blanch the tomatoes in boiling water for 30 seconds, and then rinse in cold water. Peel the tomatoes, remove the core and seeds and blend in a liquidiser or food processor. Peel and very finely chop the onion and garlic and mix into the tomato purée. Season to taste with salt, black pepper, sugar and Tabasco sauce.

Serve the dips with fresh vegetables cut into sticks. Try kohlrabi, carrot, cucumber, celery, mushrooms and strips of green pepper. Also serve wholemeal or wheatgerm bread or rolls.

Serves 8

Per Portion
about 465 calories
11 g carbohydrate
16 g protein · 39 g fat

Home-made Curd Cheese with Herbs and Pumpkin Seeds

3.5 litres/6 pints milk
150 ml/¼ pint lemon juice
100 g/4 oz cottage cheese
1 tablespoon single cream or
  crème fraîche
pinch of caster sugar
freshly ground white pepper
1 onion
1 box of mustard and cress
½ bunch each of fresh parsley,
  dill and chives
handful of fresh chervil
few young leaves of dandelion,
  nettle, sorrel and lemon balm
1–2 tablespoons pumpkin seeds
1 teaspoon sunflower oil

There are two methods of making curd cheese. The first uses untreated milk which is left to sour naturally over a period of several days. Untreated milk is difficult to obtain, and this method calls for careful cleaning of all utensils.

The second method, which is used in this recipe, uses pasteurised milk and a souring agent – lemon juice – to produce the curds.

Heat the milk slowly to 48.5C/120F. Add the lemon juice and stir well, then leave for about 15 minutes or until the milk has separated. Line a colander with clean muslin and drain the curds through it. Tie the corners of the cloth together and hang the cheese over a bowl to drain completely; this should take about 1 hour.

Mix the resulting curds with the cottage cheese and cream or crème fraîche and season with the sugar and pepper to taste.

Peel and finely chop the onion. Snip off the cress with scissors. Pick over the herbs and leaves, remove any tough stalks and wash well under cold running water. Shake until dry and finely chop.

Tip the pumpkin seeds on to a wooden board and chop using a large heavy knife.

Mix the onion, cress, herbs, leaves, pumpkin seeds and sunflower oil into the curds.

Serve with radishes, cucumber and tomatoes and fresh wholemeal bread.

Serves 6

Per Portion
about 235 calories
7 g carbohydrate
21 g protein · 12 g fat

Variations
The following ideas can all be used to make simple curd cheese spreads or dips.

Tomato and Basil
Peel and chop some tomatoes, then mix them into the curd cheese. Add some chopped fresh basil and freshly ground white pepper.

Minted Garlic Dip
Crush one or two cloves of garlic and mix into curd cheese. Add some chopped fresh mint and a little olive oil. Season with a little salt and freshly ground white pepper. Serve well chilled.

Walnut Spread
Finely chop some walnuts and mix them into curd cheese. Add some chopped fresh parsley and freshly ground white pepper. Stir in a little celery salt and press the mixture into a dish. Chill well before serving.

Cucumber Dip
Grate a large piece of cucumber and leave it to drain in a sieve or colander for 30 minutes. Squeeze all the liquid out of the cucumber. Stir the grated cucumber into the curd cheese and add some chopped fresh mint. Season lightly with freshly ground white pepper and a little garlic salt. Chill for 10 minutes before serving but do not leave for too long or the dip will become very runny.

29

Porridge with Dried Fruit

*100 g/4 oz mixed dried ready-to-
eat apricots and prunes*
750 ml/1¼ pints water
pinch of salt
100 g/4 oz porridge oats
½ tablespoon sugar
6 tablespoons single cream

It is best to buy unsul-
phurised dried fruit in a
healthfood store. To be on the
safe side you should always
wash dried fruit thoroughly
under hot running water; this
will remove most of the sulphur, if there is any.

Tip the dried fruit into a
bowl and cover with 250 ml/
8 fl oz of the water. Cover the
bowl and leave the fruit to soak
for 5 hours.

Drain the soaked fruit and
cut up.

To make the porridge, bring
the remaining water to the boil
with the salt. Add the oats and
simmer over a low heat for 10
minutes, stirring frequently to
prevent the porridge sticking.

Pour the porridge into two
dishes, top with the dried fruit
and sprinkle with the sugar.
Pour the cream over the porridge and serve.

Serves 2

Per Portion
about 485 calories
79 g carbohydrate
10 g protein · 13 g fat

Cook's Tip
Soaking does not make
dried fruit easier to di-
gest. It simply softens it
and improves its flavour.
So for a quick breakfast,
serve the porridge with
dried fruit that has been
cut up without soaking.

Banana and Sesame Purée

2 tablespoons sesame seeds
1 lemon
2 ripe bananas
*2 tablespoons unsalted tahini
(sesame paste)*
1 firm banana

Heat a dry frying pan and toast
the sesame seeds over a low to
moderate heat, stirring continuously, until you begin to smell
their aroma. Toasting brings
out the flavour of sesame seeds
and gives them a nice nutty
taste. Set aside.

Wash the lemon well in hot
water and wipe dry. Cut off a
2 cm/¾ in piece of rind very
thinly so that you get no white
pith with it for this has a bitter
taste. Chop this piece of rind
very finely and squeeze the juice
from the lemon.

Peel the ripe bananas and
mash well using a fork or blend
in a liquidiser or food processor. Mix the lemon rind and
juice immediately into the banana (keeping 1 tablespoon
juice in reserve). Stir the tahini
into the banana. Spoon the
purée into four bowls.

Peel the firm banana and cut
on a slant into slices. Arrange
on top of the purée and sprinkle with the reserved lemon
juice. Sprinkle on the toasted
sesame seeds.

Serve with wheatgerm rolls
or crispbread. You can spread
the bread with tahini rather
than butter.

Serves 4

Per Portion
about 135 calories
19 g carbohydrate
3 g protein · 5 g fat

For Breakfast or Brunch

Vanilla Quark with Grapes

100 g/4 oz mixed green and
  black grapes
3 tablespoons Quark or other
  soft cheese (20 percent fat)
1 teaspoon crème fraîche or
  soured cream
1 teaspoon lemon juice
1 tablespoon butter
1 tablespoon porridge oats
2 teaspoons vanilla sugar

Wash the grapes, dry well and
pull off the stalks. Cut in half
and remove the pips.
  Stir the Quark with the crème
fraîche and lemon juice until
smooth. Stir the grapes into the
mixture.
  Heat the butter in a small
pan without allowing it to
brown. Tip the oats into the
butter, sprinkle with the vanilla
sugar and cook over a moderate heat, stirring continuously,
until golden brown. Sprinkle
over the grape mixture.

Serves 1

Per Portion
about 400 calories
52 g carbohydrate
11 g protein · 15 g fat

Cook's Tip
To make vanilla sugar,
slit open a vanilla pod
using a very sharp knife.
Scrape out the inside and
mix with sugar in a
screw-topped jar. Add
the vanilla pod. It will
keep for months.

Cherry Quark

1 slice stale wholemeal bread
125 g/4½ oz fresh cherries
50 g/2 oz Quark or other soft
  cheese (20 percent fat)
2 tablespoons each crème fraîche
  and natural yogurt
maple syrup or honey
1 tablespoon freshly ground
  hazelnuts

Grate the wholemeal bread to
make fine crumbs. Wash and
drain the cherries and remove
stalks and stones. Stir the
Quark with the crème fraîche
and yogurt until smooth and
sweeten to taste with maple
syrup or honey.
  In a bowl, arrange layers of
cherries, breadcrumbs and the
Quark mixture. Sprinkle with
the hazelnuts before serving.

Serves 1

Per Portion
about 435 calories
56 g carbohydrate
14 g protein · 17 g fat

Strawberry Quark

1 tablespoon chopped almonds
125 g/4½ oz fresh strawberries
125 g/4½ oz Quark or other soft
  cheese (20 percent fat)
2 tablespoons single cream
1 teaspoon lemon juice
1 tablespoon cranberry jelly

Dry-fry the almonds over a low
heat, stirring continuously, until golden. Set aside.
  Crush the strawberries
coarsely with a fork. Stir in the
Quark with the cream and
lemon juice. Mix in the strawberries and cranberry jelly.
Serve sprinkled with the
almonds.

Serves 1

Per Portion
about 335 calories
19 g carbohydrate
20 g protein · 19 g fat

Muesli with Flakes and Fruit

400 g/14 oz fresh fruit (eg apricots, peaches, plums, strawberries, blackberries)
1–2 tablespoons oat flakes
1–2 tablespoons wheat flakes
1–2 tablespoons millet flakes
1 tablespoon sunflower seeds
750 ml/1¼ pints milk
maple syrup or honey
4 tablespoons corn flakes

Blanch the apricots and peaches in boiling water for a few minutes, then rinse in cold water and peel. Halve, stone and slice the fruit.

Wash the plums, strawberries and blackberries and drain well. Halve, stone and slice the plums. Hull the strawberries and halve or slice larger ones.

Arrange the fruit in 4 bowls. Mix the cereal flakes with the sunflower seeds and scatter over the fruit. Pour the milk over the muesli and sweeten to taste with maple syrup or honey. Sprinkle with the corn flakes and serve immediately.

Serves 4

Per Portion
about 260 calories
34 g carbohydrate
19 g protein · 13 g fat

Muesli with Wheatgerm

4 tablespoons wholewheat grain (wheat berries)
2 small bananas
2 oranges
2 apples
200 g/7 oz fresh pineapple
2 tablespoons sunflower seeds

Moisten the wheat grain with water and leave to germinate. This is easiest in a special germinating tray available from health food and organic food shops. Alternatively you can use a preserving jar or shallow dish. The grain should be watered every day but should not lie in water or they will go mouldy. Wheatgerm always forms a delicate white down which does not mean it is going mouldy. Stand the germinating tray in a warm place and cover it, for wheat germinates best in a warm damp environment. Leave to sprout for about 3 days, when they are at their most nutritious.

Tip the germinated wheat into a sieve, wash thoroughly under cold running water and drain well.

Peel the bananas and mash using a fork. Halve and squeeze the oranges. Pour the juice over the bananas.

Wash the apples thoroughly under hot running water for you are not going to peel them. Dry, quarter, core and dice the apples and mix immediately with the banana and orange juice. The acids in the juice will prevent the apples going brown.

Peel and dice the pineapple and add to the fruit.

Scatter the wheatgerm and sunflower seeds over the fruit and serve.

Serves 4

Per Portion
about 250 calories
49 g carbohydrate
6 g protein · 4 g fat

Cook's Tip
If you prefer a sweeter muesli, stir in a little honey, malt extract or maple syrup rather than sugar.

For Breakfast or Brunch

Three-grain Muesli with Fruit

4 tablespoons each rolled oats,
*   wholewheat grain (wheat ber-*
*   ries) and buckwheat grain*
about 250 ml/8 fl oz cold water
4 small oranges
2 apples
2 bananas
4 tablespoons shelled walnuts
1 teaspoon honey or maple syrup
2 tablespoons currants
4 tablespoons single cream

Crush the oats, wheat and
buckwheat. Do this in a pestle
and mortar or food processor.
Alternatively, you can buy
cracked wheat in healthfood
shops and crush the buckwheat
yourself.

Mix the crushed grain with
enough of the cold water to
make a thick paste. The quantity of water will vary according
to the type of grain. Cover and
leave to soak overnight in a
cool place. In summer you will
need to put it in the fridge for

at room temperature there is a
risk of mould forming.
Uncooked cereal should always
be soaked well in water before
eating or it is indigestible.

When the grain has soaked,
squeeze two of the oranges and
keep the juice to one side. Peel
the remaining oranges, removing all the pith, separate into
segments and cut these up,
catching the juice in a bowl and
removing pips. Add the orange
to the juice in the bowl.

Wash the apples thoroughly
and wipe dry. Quarter and core
the apples, then cut into small
pieces. Mix immediately with
the orange pieces. The juice
from the orange will prevent
the apple going brown.

Peel the bananas and mash
using a fork. Mix the banana
with the rest of the fruit.

Coarsley chop the walnuts.

Stir the soaked grain with the
reserved orange juice and
honey or maple syrup. Mix the
fruit, walnuts and currants into
the muesli. Divide between four
bowls and pour on the cream.

Serves 4

Per Portion
about 395 calories
66 g carbohydrate
8 g protein · 11 g fat

Variation
Crushed Muesli
Crush 4 tablespoons mixed
muesli grains (obtainable from
healthfood shops) and mix with
about 8 tablespoons cold water
to make a thick paste. Cover
and leave to soak overnight in a
cool place. The following day
wash 4 dried apricots and
stoned prunes, drain and chop.
Prepare 100 g/4 oz fresh fruit,
eg apples, plums or soft fruit,
and cut up where necessary.
Coarsely chop 4 tablespoons
shelled hazelnuts. Mix the
soaked cereal with about 4
teaspoons honey or maple syrup and the dried and fresh fruit.
Transfer the muesli to four
bowls. Sprinkle each portion
with 1 tablespoon barley flakes
and pour on 1 tablespoon milk.
Serve sprinkled with the
hazelnuts.

Roasted Malted Muesli
The grains used in muesli can
be roasted in a dry, heavy-
based frying pan until lightly
browned. Stir the grains often
to prevent them from
overcooking. Stir a little malt
extract with the hot grains so
that it coats them evenly and
thinly.

Mix with dried fruits and
nuts, or with fresh fruit and
serve with yogurt or apple juice.
The roasted grains can be
cooled, mixed with dried fruits
and nuts, then cooled and
stored in an airtight jar for several weeks.

For a change, try mixing a
small amount of roasted sesame
seeds with the muesli grains.
Honey can be used to sweeten
the muesli and to add an inter-
esting flavour to the cereal.

Apple Yogurt

4 dried apricots
300 ml/½ pint natural yogurt
1 large apple
½ orange
1 tablespoon maple syrup
½ teaspoon ground cinnamon
1 tablespoon shelled hazelnuts
2 tablespoons porridge oats

Wash the apricots well in hot water, drain and chop. Whisk the yogurt vigorously. Peel, core and grate the apple.

Squeeze the orange and stir the juice into the yogurt with the apple and apricot. Sweeten with maple syrup and season with cinnamon.

On a board coarsely chop the hazelnuts using a strong knife. Serve the apple yogurt immediately, sprinkled with the chopped nuts and porridge oats.

Serves 2

Per Portion
about 390 calories
56 g carbohydrate
12 g protein · 12 g fat

Variation
Yogurt with Nuts
Whisk 300 ml/½ pint natural yogurt until creamy. Chop 100 g/4 oz mixed shelled walnuts, hazelnuts and blanched almonds using a strong knife. Stir the nuts into the yogurt with 1 tablespoon raisins. Sweeten to taste with honey and sprinkle with bran or cereal flakes.

Variation
Yogurt with Oranges
Whisk 300 ml/½ pint natural yogurt until creamy. Fry 1–2 tablespoons pine nuts in a little hot oil until golden. Peel 2 oranges, remove pith and cut into small pieces, catching the juice and removing any pips. Stir the orange pieces and juice with the pine nuts into the yogurt and sweeten to taste.

For Breakfast or Brunch

Oat Flake Waffles with Soft Fruit

200 g/7 oz rolled oats or oat
*   flakes*
2 tablespoons crunchy toasted
*   oat flakes*
500 ml/17 fl oz buttermilk
½ lemon
salt
½ tablespoon vanilla sugar
½ teaspoon ground cinnamon
2 eggs
300 g/11 oz mixed soft fruit (eg
*   strawberries, redcurrants,*
*   raspberries, blackberries)*
3 tablespoons honey
1 tablespoon orange marmalade
oil for the waffle iron

Stir the oats into the buttermilk and leave to soak for about 3 hours in a covered bowl.

Wash the lemon thoroughly under hot running water, dry well and finely grate the rind.

Mix the soaked oat flakes with the lemon rind, salt to taste, vanilla sugar, cinnamon and eggs and beat well. Cover the batter and set aside.

Wash the soft fruit well, drain and remove stalks. Place the honey and marmalade in a saucepan and stir continuously over a very low heat until liquid. Pour over the soft fruit. Set aside.

Preheat the waffle iron according to the manufacturer's instructions and brush with a little oil. Spoon about 4 tablespoons batter into the iron for each waffle, close and cook for about 6 minutes until golden brown on both sides.

Keep the cooked waffles warm in the oven until all eight are cooked. Brush the iron with oil before cooking each waffle.

Serve the waffles topped with the fruit or serve the fruit separately.

Serves 4

Per Portion
about 390 calories
52 g carbohydrate
16 g protein · 12 g fat

Wholemeal Waffles

120 g/4½ oz butter
½ tablespoon caster sugar
4 eggs
grated rind of 1 lemon
salt
250 ml/8 fl oz soured cream
150 g/5 oz wholemeal flour
oil for the waffle iron
maple syrup

Cream the butter with the sugar until the sugar is completely worked in. The more air you incorporate into the mixture the creamier it becomes.

Separate the eggs. Refrigerate the whites so that they will whisk up well later. Beat the egg yolks one at a time into the creamed butter. Stir in the grated lemon rind, a pinch of salt and the soured cream.

Whisk the egg whites with a pinch of salt until stiff. Spoon the whites on to the waffle batter and sprinkle with the wholemeal flour. Gently fold in with a wooden spatula to give a uniform mixture. Do not beat or the egg whites will lose the air beaten into them and the waffles will be heavy.

Preheat the waffle iron according to the manufacturer's instructions and brush with a little oil. Use the batter to make eight waffles. Sprinkle with maple syrup and serve hot.

Serves 4

Per Portion
about 515 calories
26 g carbohydrate
13 g protein · 38 g fat

Soups, Casseroles and Bakes

Tasty stocks made entirely with vegetables are the basis for delicious, nutritious soups. With the addition of fresh broccoli, tender kohlrabi and golden pancakes, as in the photo, they are equal to the finest creations of Nouvelle cuisine, a feast both for the eyes and the palate. But with special-occasion soups such as potato soup with cream and fresh spring herbs, you will also find filling everyday dishes: Barley casserole and Cheese and semolina bake, Vegetable strudel and Millet pudding. With pizza and cannelloni, chilli and chickpea balls you can try your hand at inter-national specialities, with ingredients that you can buy anywhere. Or you can treat yourself to dishes our grandmothers used to make. The recipe for Pumpkin soup, for example, is one which has been taken from an old cookery book. The Tofu ragout Provençal-style, full of aromatic herbs, Gratin with spinach beet and a delicious Fish soup with sorrel will be welcomed by all those who like to try colourful and unusual dishes.

Cold Cucumber Soup

2 (300 g/11 oz) cucumbers
1 onion
3 cloves garlic
2 bunches of fresh dill
300 ml/½ pint natural yogurt
125 ml/4 fl oz single cream
salt
freshly ground white pepper
2 tablespoons snipped chives

Peel the cucumbers and cut them in half lengthways. Use a teaspoon to scrape out the seeds. Cut into pieces.

Peel the onion and garlic. Rinse the dill in cold water, pat dry and finely chop.

Blend the cucumber with the onion and garlic in a liquidiser or food processor.

Beat the yogurt with the cream until light and fluffy, then fold into the cucumber mixture. Stir in the dill and season to taste with salt and pepper. Sprinkle with the chives and serve.

Serves 4

Per Portion
about 160 calories
8 g carbohydrate
5 g protein · 11 g fat

Vegetable Stock

250 g/9 oz leeks
350 g/12 oz carrots
1 (250 g/9 oz) fennel bulb
450 g/1 lb celery
1 onion
1 clove garlic
bunch of fresh parsley
few sprigs of fresh thyme
1 bay leaf
4 white peppercorns
2 juniper berries
2 cloves
1.5 litres/2¾ pints water
salt

The ingredients should be cut up as finely as possible to allow the flavour to be fully absorbed by the stock.

Cut the roots and any limp leaves off the leeks. Cut a cross in the remaining leaves down as far as the white. This allows the leaves to separate so that all the dirt that has collected between them can be washed away under cold running water. Cut the leeks into rings.

Peel, wash and dice the carrots. Halve the fennel bulbs and cut out the wedge-shaped stalk with a sharp knife. Rinse in cold water and cut across into 1 cm/½ in strips.

Cut the bottom off the celery, separate the sticks and wash. Cut off the leaves and pull off any tough threads. Chop the celery. Peel and halve the onion and garlic. Rinse the parsley and thyme.

Place all these ingredients in a large saucepan with the bay leaf, peppercorns, juniper berries and cloves. Add the water and bring to the boil. Cover the pan and simmer the stock over a low heat for about 30 minutes.

Line a sieve with muslin, place it over a pan and pour the stock through the muslin. Press the vegetables and flavourings with a wooden spatula and then discard them.

Season the vegetable stock to taste with salt and reheat. Pour into warmed dishes and add a few freshly-cooked vegetables and chopped fresh herbs, or use as a basis for other soups.

Makes scant 1.5 litres/2¾ pints

This stock contains so few calories that it is not worth giving the figures.

Soups for Starters

Chilled Tomato Soup with Herbs

1 kg/2¼ lb ripe tomatoes
1 large onion
3 cloves garlic
bunch of fresh parsley
bunch of fresh basil
sprig of fresh savory
sprig of fresh thyme
salt
freshly ground black pepper
5 tablespoons cold-pressed olive
*   oil*
2–3 slices wholemeal bread

Wash the tomatoes, wipe dry and cut into quarters, removing the core and the seeds. Peel the onion and garlic. Cut the onion into quarters

Wash the parsley, basil, savory and thyme and shake dry. Strip the savory and thyme leaves from the stalks.

Blend the tomatoes with the onion, 1 clove garlic, the parsley and basil in a liquidiser or food processor. Stir the savory and thyme leaves into the tomato mixture. Season to taste with salt and pepper and stir in 2 tablespoons olive oil. Chill the soup.

Finely chop the remaining garlic. Dice the bread.

Heat the remaining olive oil in a frying pan and fry the bread over a moderate to high heat, stirring continuously, until beginning to brown. Stir in the chopped garlic, fry for a few minutes longer, stirring, and drain on absorbent kitchen paper. Use these fried croûtons to garnish the soup.

Serves 4

Per Portion
about 240 calories
22 g carbohydrate
5 g protein · 13 g fat

Vegetable Soup with Cornmeal Pancakes

bunch of fresh parsley
75 g/3 oz cornmeal (polenta)
25 g/1 oz wholemeal flour
3 tablespoons milk
2 eggs
salt
250 g/9 oz broccoli
1 (200 g/7 oz) young kohlrabi
3 tablespoons vegetable oil
bunch of fresh chives
1.5 litres/2¾ pints freshly made vegetable stock (recipe page 38)

Wash the parsley, strip the leaves off the stalks, pat dry and finely chop.

Whisk the cornmeal with the wholemeal flour, parsley, milk, eggs and a pinch of salt to make a thin pancake batter. Cover and leave to rest for 15 minutes to allow the flour to swell. If the batter has become too thick after standing stir in a little more milk.

While the batter is standing, wash the broccoli and remove large leaves and the tough ends of the stalks. Cut off the florets for they cook faster than the stalks.

Peel the kohlrabi. Cut off the feathery green leaves and keep to sprinkle on the soup. Wash and quarter the kohlrabi. Cut into slices and then into sticks.

To cook the pancakes, heat 1 tablespoon oil in a frying pan. Spoon enough batter into the pan to make a thin layer, tilting the pan to spread out the batter evenly. Cook until set and golden on both sides. Slide from the pan and keep hot while you make the remaining pancakes, oiling the pan as necessary.

Rinse the chives and kohlrabi leaves in cold water and pat dry. Snip the chives with scissors and coarsely chop the leaves.

Bring the stock to the boil in a saucepan and cook the broccoli stalks and kohlrabi for about 3 minutes. Add the

broccoli florets and cook for a further 2 to 3 minutes until all the vegetables are tender but still firm to bite.

Cut the pancakes into thin strips.

Pour the vegetable soup into warmed bowls. Add the strips of pancake and serve immediately, sprinkled with chives and kohlrabi leaves.

Serves 5

Per Portion
about 205 calories
21 g carbohydrate
8 g protein · 9 g fat

Variation
Vegetable Soup with Tofu
Cut 250 g/9 oz tofu into 1 cm/½ in cubes. Mix with 1 tablespoon soy sauce, cover and marinate for 30 minutes, turning occasionally. Wash 4 sticks celery, cut off the leaves and keep to one side. Pull off any tough threads and cut into 0.5 cm/¼ in pieces. Scrape and wash 250 g/9 oz young carrots and cut into sticks. Heat 1–2

tablespoons vegetable oil in a frying pan and fry the tofu cubes for about 5 minutes, stirring continuously. Meanwhile bring 1 litre/1¾ pints freshly made vegetable stock to the boil. Add the vegetables and cook for about 4 minutes until tender but still firm to bite. Flavour the soup with 1 tablespoon each dry sherry and soy sauce and pour into four warmed bowls. Add the tofu to the soup. Serve immediately, sprinkled with chopped celery leaves, parsley or watercress.

Soups for Starters

Leek and Chicory Soup

250 g/9 oz leeks
250 g/9 oz chicory
2 (40 g/1½ oz) slices rye bread
3 cloves garlic
30 g/1¼ oz butter
375 ml/13 fl oz milk
250 ml/8 fl oz freshly made vege-
  table stock (recipe page 38)
½ teaspoon caraway seeds
salt
freshly ground white pepper
freshly grated nutmeg

Trim the leeks and chicory, wash well and drain. Cut the leek with about two thirds of the pale green part into thin rings. Cut out the bitter, wedge-shaped stalk of the chicory using a sharp pointed knife and cut the chicory crossways into 0.5 cm/¼ in strips.
Dice the rye bread. Peel and finely chop the garlic.
Heat about one-quarter of the butter in a saucepan without allowing it to brown. Add the leek and chicory and stir until transparent. Add the milk, stock and caraway seeds. Season the soup to taste with salt, pepper and nutmeg. Bring to the boil, cover the pan and simmer gently over a low heat for 5 minutes.
Meanwhile, heat the remaining butter in a frying pan until frothy but not brown. Add the bread cubes and fry over a moderate heat, stirring continuously, until crisp and golden brown. Add the garlic and fry for a few minutes more, reducing the temperature if necessary (garlic burns easily).
Serve the soup garnished with the garlic croûtons.

Serves 4

Per Portion
about 220 calories
20 g carbohydrate
3 g protein · 10 g fat

Carrot and Courgette Soup

250 g/9 oz carrots
250 g/9 oz courgettes
1 onion
1 clove garlic
1 tablespoon butter
250 ml/8 fl oz milk
500 ml/17 fl oz freshly made
  vegetable stock (recipe
  page 38)
salt
freshly ground white pepper
freshly grated nutmeg
bunch of fresh parsley
1 tablespoon pumpkin seeds

Peel the carrots (tender young ones only need light scraping or scrubbing), wash under cold running water and wipe dry. Slice lengthways and then cut into thin sticks. Wash and dry the courgettes. Top and tail them and without peeling cut into fairly thick slices as they cook faster than carrots. Peel and very finely chop the onion and garlic.
Heat the butter in a saucepan without allowing it to brown. Fry the onion and garlic until transparent. Add the carrots and courgettes and cook until they are coated in a thin film of fat, stirring continuously. Add the milk and stock.
Season the soup to taste with salt, pepper and nutmeg and bring to the boil. Reduce the heat, cover the pan and simmer gently over a low heat for about 5 minutes until the vegetables are tender but still firm to bite.
Meanwhile, wash the parsley, strip the leaves off the stalks, pat dry and finely chop.
Pour the soup into heated bowls and sprinkle with parsley and pumpkin seeds.

Serves 4

Per Portion
about 130 calories
13 g carbohydrate
5 g protein · 7 g fat

41

Vegetable Soup with Pasta

500 g/18 oz mixed fresh vegetables (select from carrots, broccoli, cauliflower, peas, beans and leeks, for example)
1.5 litres/2¾ pints freshly made vegetable stock (recipe page 38)
100 g/4 oz wholewheat pasta shapes
freshly grated Parmesan cheese to serve

Peel or trim the vegetables according to type, then wash and dry. Slice the carrots, separate the broccoli and cauliflower into florets, shell the peas, break the beans in half and slice the leeks.

Bring the vegetable stock to the boil in a saucepan. Add the pasta and simmer for 10 minutes. Add the prepared vegetables and cook over a low to moderate heat for a further 5 to 10 minutes until the vegetables are tender but still firm to bite and the pasta is tender but not too soft.

Pour the vegetable soup into bowls and serve sprinkled with Parmesan cheese.

Serves 4

Per Portion
about 345 calories
34 g carbohydrate
11 g protein · 16 g fat

Hot, Substantial Soups

Millet Soup with Vegetables

100 g/4 oz millet
1 onion
1 clove garlic
1 tablespoon butter
1 tablespoon sunflower oil
1 litre/1¾ pints freshly made
*   vegetable stock (recipe*
*   page 38)*
1 (100 g/4 oz) leek
250 g/9 oz white cabbage
½ bunch of fresh parsley or a
*   handful of fresh chervil*
herb salt
freshly ground white pepper
freshly ground caraway

Tip the millet on to a tray or large, flat dish to pick over. Using tweezers, discard any black seeds or other impurities. Then tip the millet into a sieve, wash under lukewarm water and drain thoroughly. Peel and finely chop the onion and garlic.

Heat the butter and oil in a saucepan. Fry the onion and garlic until transparent, stirring continuously. Add the millet and stir until the seeds are completely coated in fat.

Add the stock and bring to the boil. Reduce the heat, cover the pan and cook over a low heat for about 15 minutes.

Meanwhile, cut the roots and limp outer leaves off the leek. Cut a cross through the remaining leaves down as far as the white. Wash the leek thoroughly under cold running water, opening the cut leaves so that you can wash away any dirt between them. Cut the leek into 1 cm/½ in lengths with about half the green part.

Cut the stalk out of the cabbage together with any thick ribs. Wash the cabbage and cut into strips.

Add the leek and cabbage to the pan and cook for about 5 minutes more until the vegetables are tender but still firm to bite.

Rinse the parsley or chervil in cold water and shake dry. Strip parsley leaves from the stalks and finely chop. Chop the chervil with the stalks.

Season the soup to taste with herb salt, pepper and a generous pinch of caraway and serve sprinkled with parsley and chervil.

Serves 4

Per Portion
about 175 calories
23 g carbohydrate
4 g protein · 7 g fat

Cook's Tip
Although millet is the hardest of all the cereals – and the one with the smallest grains – it cooks quickly and does not need to be soaked. Most people look on it merely as birdseed nowadays. Yet millet is easy to digest and rich in vitamins and minerals. It contains trace elements which are good for the hair and skin. You can buy millet whole or flaked in healthfood or wholefood shops. The grain is excellent in soups or in sweet and savoury puddings (see recipe for Millet pudding, page 54). Flakes are used like oat flakes. Cooked like rice or risotto as a side dish, millet is delicious (see recipe for Millet casserole with herbs, page 53).

Barley Soup with Herbs

100 g/4 oz pot barley
1.5 litres/2¾ pints freshly made
  vegetable stock (recipe
  page 38)
400 g/14 oz young carrots
bunch of fresh parsley or chervil
bunch of fresh chives
herb salt
freshly ground white pepper

Pick over the barley, tip into a sieve and wash well under cold running water. Drain thoroughly.

Bring the vegetable stock to the boil in a saucepan. Add the barley and return to the boil. Reduce the heat and gently simmer the barley for about 45 minutes.

Meanwhile, trim, scrape, wash and halve the carrots. Cut lengthways into thin slices and then into matchsticks.

Rinse the parsley or chervil and chives under cold running water and pat thoroughly dry.

Strip the parsley leaves from the stalks and finely chop. Chop chervil with the stalks. Snip the chives.

Add the carrots to the barley soup, return to the boil and simmer over a low heat for about 3 minutes.

Season to taste with herb salt and pepper. Stir in the herbs and serve immediately in warmed bowls.

Serves 6

Per Portion
about 90 calories
18 g carbohydrate
3 g protein · 0.5 g fat

Bulgur Soup

1 tablespoon butter
2 tablespoons wholemeal flour
60 g/2½ oz bulgur
750 ml/1¼ pints freshly made
  vegetable stock (recipe
  page 38)
2–3 spring onions
yeast extract or salt

Heat the butter in a saucepan until frothy but not brown. Add the flour and bulgur and stir until it gives off a light spicy smell. Add the stock and continue stirring until it comes to the boil.

Reduce the heat, cover the pan and simmer gently for about 10 minutes, stirring from time to time to prevent the bulgur sticking to the pan. The cooked soup should have a creamy appearance and the bulgur should be broken down.

While the soup is cooking, cut the roots and any limp leaves off the spring onions. Wash well and cut into very thin rings using about half the

pale green leaves.

Season the soup to taste with yeast extract or salt and pour into warmed bowls. Sprinkle with the spring onion rings and serve immediately.

Serves 4

Per Portion
about 100 calories
15 g carbohydrate
3 g protein · 4 g fat

Cook's Tip

The same method can be used to make Semolina soup (from wholemeal semolina) or Buckwheat soup (from coarsely crushed grain). Suitable herbs include chervil or thyme.

Hot, Substantial Soups

Pumpkin Soup

400 g/14 oz pumpkin
1 large onion
1 tablespoon butter
1–2 teaspoons wholemeal flour
1 litre/1¾ pints freshly made
 vegetable stock (see page 38)
½ bunch of fresh parsley
salt
freshly ground white pepper
freshly grated nutmeg
125 ml/4 fl oz single cream or
 3 tablespoons crème fraîche

Peel the pumpkin, remove the seeds and cut the flesh into small cubes. Peel and finely chop the onion.

Melt the butter in a saucepan without allowing it to brown. Cook the onion in the butter until transparent. Add the pumpkin and stir well.

Sprinkle on the flour and cook until it gives off a light aroma. Gradually stir in the vegetable stock and bring to the boil. Reduce the heat, cover and simmer for 10 minutes.

Meanwhile, wash the parsley, strip the leaves off the stalks, pat dry and finely chop.

Give the soup a good stir to distribute the soft pumpkin evenly and to make the soup creamy. Season to taste with salt, pepper and nutmeg. Stir in the cream. Serve sprinkled with parsley.

Serves 4

Per Portion
about 190 calories
13 g carbohydrate
3 g protein · 14 g fat

Cook's Tip
You can make this creamy soup with courgettes, broccoli or cauliflower instead of pumpkin. Sprinkle courgette soup with chives and lemon balm, and broccoli or cauliflower soup with chervil.

Potato Soup with Herbs

500 g/18 oz floury potatoes
1 onion
1 tablespoon butter
250 ml/8 fl oz double cream
1 lemon
about 500 ml/17 fl oz hot freshly
 made vegetable stock (recipe
 page 38)
1 tablespoon fresh thyme leaves
salt
freshly ground white pepper

Peel, wash and finely dice the potatoes. Peel and finely chop the onion.

Heat the butter in a saucepan without allowing it to brown and cook the onion until transparent. Add the diced potato and stir until completely coated in butter.

Pour on the cream and bring to the boil, then cover the pan and cook over a low heat for 12 to 15 minutes until the potatoes are soft, stirring frequently to prevent sticking.

Meanwhile, cut a 2 cm/¾ in piece of lemon rind. Cut it thin enough to avoid including any white pith for this has a bitter taste. Finely chop the rind. Squeeze the lemon and keep the juice to one side.

Stir the stock into the potato mixture with the lemon rind and thyme leaves. Season to taste with the lemon juice, salt and pepper and serve immediately.

Serves 4

Per Portion
about 340 calories
25 g carbohydrate
5 g protein · 24 g fat

Unusual Soups

Herb Soup

*500 g/18 oz mixed young wild
    herbs (eg nettles, salad burnet
    and dandelion leaves)*
bunch of fresh parsley
1 onion
1 clove garlic
1 tablespoon butter
*750 ml/1¼ pints freshly made
    vegetable stock (recipe
    page 38)*
*250 ml/8 fl oz double cream or
    crème fraîche*
2 tablespoons whipped cream
salt
freshly ground white pepper
freshly grated nutmeg

Pick over the herbs, removing
any tough stalks. Strip the parsley leaves from the stalks.
Wash the wild herbs and parsley several times and pat dry.
Chop very finely with a knife.
Never try to chop herbs in a
blender or grinder as the blades
tear the delicate leaves releasing
bitter substances and tannins.
    Peel and finely chop the
onion and garlic.

Melt the butter in a saucepan
without allowing it to brown.
Fry the onion and garlic until
transparent, stirring frequently.
Add the stock and cream or
crème fraîche and bring to the
boil. Reduce the heat and simmer for 3 minutes.
    Keep about 2 tablespoons
herbs in reserve to garnish and
add the remaining herbs and
whipped cream to the pan.
Season to taste with salt, pepper and nutmeg. Sprinkle with
the reserved herbs and serve in
heated bowls.

Serves 4

Per Portion
about 310 calories
14 g carbohydrate
5 g protein · 25 g fat

Clear Vegetable
Soup with Plaice

2 (75 g/3 oz) plaice fillets
½ lemon
bunch of fresh chives
1 fennel bulb (about 200 g/7 oz)
100 g/4 oz young carrots
3 spring onions
*scant 1 litre/1¾ pints freshly
    made vegetable stock (recipe
    page 38)*
salt

Rinse and thoroughly dry the
plaice fillets. Cut across the
grain into strips 1 cm/½ in wide
and arrange in four bowls.
    Using a potato peeler, cut 2
very thin pieces of lemon rind
and cut these into thin strips.
Squeeze the juice from the
lemon. Wash, dry and cut up
the chives.
    Mix the lemon rind with the
chives and scatter over the fish.
Sprinkle the fish with the lemon
juice and leave to marinate
while you make the soup.
    Trim the fennel and set aside

the feathery leaves for the garnish. Cut the fennel bulb in
half. Using a pointed knife cut
out the wedge-shaped stalk.
Wash the fennel and pat dry.
Cut lengthways into quarters
and then across into thin strips.
    Scrape and wash the carrots
and cut into thin sticks. Trim
and wash the spring onions and
cut into thin rings including
about two thirds of the green
leaves.
    Bring the stock to the boil in
a saucepan. Add the vegetables
and cook for about 2 minutes
until just tender. Season to taste
with a little salt.
    Pour the boiling soup over
the plaice. The fish will cook in
the hot soup. Serve
immediately.

Serves 4

Per Portion
about 80 calories
9 g carbohydrate
13 g protein · 0.5 g fat

Fish Soup with Vegetables and Cress

1.5 kg/3 lb mixed fish (eg cod, halibut, turbot, salmon trout or salmon)
750 g/1½ lb fish trimmings (bones and heads of salmon, turbot and sole)
1 onion
1 leek
1 stick celery
400 g/14 oz carrots
bunch of fresh parsley
sprig of fresh thyme
few celery leaves
4 white peppercorns
2 juniper berries
1 bay leaf
1 piece lemon rind
500 ml/17 fl oz dry white wine
750 ml/1¼ pints water
2 shallots
1–2 cloves garlic
1 fennel bulb (about 250 g/9 oz)
250 g/9 oz ripe tomatoes
3 tablespoons olive oil
100 g/4 oz sorrel or spinach

3 tablespoons dry vermouth
250 ml/8 fl oz single cream
salt
freshly ground white pepper
2 boxes of mustard and cress

You will probably need to order the fish and trimmings in advance. Have the fishmonger skin and fillet the fish but ask him to give you the heads and bones for the stock.

Cut the gills off the heads because these will give the stock an oily taste. Make sure you get rid of the gills themselves as well as the outer gill covering. Place all the trimmings in a saucepan.

Peel and quarter the onion. Trim the leek and celery. Peel 2 carrots. Wash these vegetables and cut into fairly large pieces. Wash the parsley, thyme and celery leaves and shake dry. Add the vegetables, parsley, thyme, celery leaves, peppercorns, juniper berries, bay leaf and lemon rind to the fish pan. Pour on the wine and water, bring to the boil and then simmer for 25 minutes.

While the stock is cooking, rinse the fish fillets in cold water, pat dry and cut into bite-sized pieces. Peel and finely chop the shallots and garlic. Halve the fennel bulb and cut out the stalk. Wash and dry the halves and cut across into strips. Peel and wash the remaining carrots and cut into sticks. Blanch the tomatoes in boiling water for 30 seconds and then rinse in cold water. Peel and dice the tomatoes, removing the core and the seeds.

Strain the fish stock (without pressing the fish trimmings and vegetables as this would make the stock cloudy) and discard all the solid ingredients.

Heat the olive oil in a clean saucepan. Fry the shallots and garlic until transparent. Add the fennel, carrot and tomato and fry for a few minutes. Add the fish stock and bring to the boil, then cover the pan and simmer over a low heat for 8 to 10 minutes until the vegetables are tender but still firm to bite.

Meanwhile, wash and dry the sorrel or spinach and coarsely

chop. Add to the soup. Stir in the vermouth and cream. Add the pieces of fish, cover the pan and cook over a very low heat for about 3 minutes. Season to taste.

Snip off the cress with scissors and sprinkle over the soup before serving.

Serves 6

Per Portion
about 490 calories
20 g carbohydrate
40 g protein · 20 g fat

47

Chickpea Soup with Lamb

400 g/14 oz dried chickpeas
1 litre/1¾ pints water
1 litre/1¾ pints freshly made
  unsalted vegetable stock
  (recipe page 38)
500 g/18 oz lean boneless lamb,
  for example trimmed shoulder
  or leg
1 carrot (about 100 g/4 oz)
1 large leek (about 150 g/5 oz)
100 g/4 oz celeriac
1 onion
1 clove garlic
few sprigs of fresh thyme
¼ bunch of fresh parsley
1 tablespoon vegetable oil
1 bay leaf
salt
freshly ground white pepper
cayenne pepper

Tip the chickpeas into a sieve and wash well under cold running water. Cover the chickpeas with the measured water and stock and soak in a covered bowl for 7 to 8 hours.

When ready, bring the chickpeas to the boil in the soaking liquid, cover the pan and simmer very gently for about 2 hours.

Meanwhile, cut the fat off the piece of lamb. Remove any skin or gristle and cut into equal bite-sized pieces.

Peel the carrot. Cut the roots and coarse leaves off the leek. Peel the celeriac. Wash all the vegetables under cold running water and then dry and chop. Peel and finely chop the onion and garlic.

Wash the thyme and parsley and shake dry. Strip the parsley leaves off the stalks and keep to one side. The stalks are used in the soup.

Heat the oil in a large saucepan. Fry the meat in batches over a moderate to high heat, transferring them from the pan to a sieve when they are sealed. Place the sieve over a basin to collect the juice. (The sealed meat should not be left to sit in its juices or it continues to cook and becomes leathery.)

When you have sealed all the meat, cook the onion and garlic in the same fat until transparent. Add the chopped vegetables and cook for a few minutes, stirring frequently. Return the lamb to the pan and add the chickpeas with the cooking liquid. Add the thyme, the parsley stalks and bay leaf. Bring to the boil, then reduce the heat, cover the pan and simmer for 30 minutes.

Finely chop the parsley leaves. Remove the herbs from the soup. Season well with salt, pepper and cayenne and serve sprinkled with the chopped parsley.

Serves 6

Per Portion
about 470 calories
43 g carbohydrate
25 g protein · 21 g fat

Cook's Tip

Opinions differ on whether pulses should be cooked in the soaking water or in fresh water. The soaking water can contain harmful substances as well as vitamins. Since pulses are rich in vitamin B which is soluble in water I tend not to throw the soaking water away. You can reduce the danger of harmful substances by buying organically grown pulses. Pulses should always be cooked in unsalted water or stock otherwise they will not become soft.

Potato Soup with Lamb Meatballs

350 g/12 oz lamb bones
1.5 litres/2¾ pints freshly made
  vegetable stock (recipe
  page 38)
100 g/4 oz celeriac
1 carrot
1 leek (about 100 g/4 oz)
1 onion
3 cloves garlic
bunch of fresh parsley
2 white peppercorns
1 bay leaf
1 slice rye toast
125 ml/4 fl oz lukewarm water
1 shallot
sprig of fresh thyme
250 g/9 oz minced lamb
1 egg yolk
salt
freshly ground white pepper
300 g/11 oz floury potatoes
1–2 bunches of fresh chives
125 ml/4 fl oz buttermilk or
  soured cream

Rinse the lamb bones in cold
water and place in a saucepan.

Add the cold vegetable stock
and bring slowly to the boil.
Reduce the heat and cook gently at just below simmering
point for about 1 hour. There
should be only tiny bubbles rising to the surface. You do not
need to remove the grey scum
which forms, for it contains
protein which clarifies the stock
and collects on the bottom of
the pan.

Meanwhile, peel and wash
the celeriac and carrot then cut
into fairly large pieces. Cut the
roots and dark green leaves off
the leek and cut a cross down
through the remaining leaves as
far as the white. Open the
leaves and wash out any dirt
under cold running water. Cut
the leek into fairly large pieces.

Peel and halve the onion and
1 clove garlic. Wash the parsley
and shake dry. Strip the leaves
off the stalks. Finely chop the
leaves and keep to one side to
go in the lamb balls.

Add the vegetables, parsley
stalks, peppercorns and bay
leaf to the stock and simmer
gently for 1 hour.

Soak the rye toast in the
lukewarm water and squeeze
out well. Peel and finely chop
the shallot and the remaining
garlic. Rinse the thyme, pat dry
and strip the leaves off the
stalks. Mix the soaked toast,
shallot, garlic, thyme and
chopped parsley with the
minced lamb and egg yolk.
Season to taste and shape into
walnut-sized balls.

Strain the lamb stock and
discard the bones, vegetables
and herbs. Bring the stock back
to the boil.

Drop the lamb balls into the
boiling stock, reduce the heat
and cook the balls over a low to
moderate heat for 10 minutes.

Peel and wash the potatoes,
and grate straight into the
soup. Cook for about 5 minutes
until the potato is soft and
thickens the soup.

Wash, dry and cut up the
chives. Stir the buttermilk or
soured cream into the hot soup.
Reheat the soup to just below
simmering point, but do not let
it boil, and pour into a heated
soup terrine.

Sprinkle with the cut chives
and serve very hot with
wheatgerm rolls and butter.

Serves 6

Per Portion
about 220 calories
16 g carbohydrate
11 g protein · 12 g fat

Chilli with Lamb

100 g/4 oz dried pinto beans
100 g/4 oz each dried red kidney
  beans, black beans and white
  haricot beans
300 ml/½ pint unsalted freshly
  made vegetable stock (recipe
  page 38)
250 ml/8 fl oz dry red wine
1 kg/2¼ lb ripe tomatoes
1 large onion
1 clove garlic
2 tablespoons vegetable oil
750 g/1½ lb minced lamb
1 tablespoon dried oregano
hot chilli powder
salt
2 tablespoons chopped parsley

Rinse the beans in cold water.
Cover with the vegetable stock
and soak for 12 hours.

The following day add the
red wine, bring to the boil and
boil hard for 5 minutes. Reduce
the heat and cook the beans
gently for about 30 minutes.

Meanwhile, blanch the tomatoes in boiling water for 30
seconds, rinse in cold water and
peel. Dice the tomatoes, removing the seeds.

Peel and finely chop the
onion and garlic. Heat the oil in
a saucepan. Cook the minced
lamb over a moderate to high
heat, stirring continuously, until it is grey in colour and of
crumbly texture. Add the onion
and garlic and fry until transparent. Add the tomatoes and
cook until they form a juice.

Add the beans and their
cooking liquid and stir in well.
Season with the oregano and a
generous pinch of chilli powder.
Bring to the boil, then cover the
pan and cook over a low heat
for about 1½ hours until the
beans are tender but not
mushy. Stir frequently as it
cooks, adding a little more
stock from time to time if
necessary.

Season to taste with salt and
chilli powder and serve
sprinkled with parsley.

Serves 6

Per Portion
about 570 calories
46 g carbohydrate
47 g protein · 20 g fat

Vegetable Stew with Chickpea Balls

500 g / 18 oz dried chickpeas
1 onion
4 cloves garlic
bunch each of fresh chives and
*   parsley*
½ teaspoon turmeric
1 teaspoon ground anise or
*   cumin*
½ tablespoon ground coriander
pinch of hot chilli powder
salt
freshly ground black pepper
2 tablespoons wholemeal flour
600 g / 1¼ lb mixed seasonal vege-
*   tables (eg carrots, fennel,*
*   white cabbage, leeks, broccoli,*
*   aubergines, courgettes, green*
*   peppers and tomatoes)*
1 Spanish onion
few leaves fresh sage and 1 leaf
*   fresh lovage (optional)*
250 ml / 8 fl oz sunflower oil
125 ml / 4 fl oz freshly made vege-
*   table stock (recipe page 38)*
1 teaspoon dried thyme

Wash the chickpeas, cover with water and soak for 12 hours.

The following day, peel the onion and 2 cloves garlic. Quarter the onion. Rinse the chives and parsley in cold water and shake dry. Cut up the chives. Strip the parsley leaves off the stalks and finely chop.

Drain the chickpeas and blend in a liquidiser or food processor with the onion quarters and peeled garlic. Add the chives, parsley, turmeric, aniseed or cumin, coriander, chilli powder and salt and pepper to taste. Work in the flour to give a firm malleable dough. If the dough is sticky work in a little more flour; if it is too firm work in a few drops of water. Cover the dough and set aside.

Trim all the vegetables, wash and dry. Peel carrots and cut into sticks. Halve fennel, cut out the stalk and cut across into strips. Cut the stalk and thick ribs out of white cabbage and then shred. Cut leeks with about two thirds of the pale green leaves into 2 cm/¾ in lengths. Separate broccoli into

florets. Slice aubergines and courgettes. Halve peppers, remove seeds and white pith, rinse and cut into strips. Blanch the tomatoes in boiling water for 30 seconds, rinse in cold water and then peel and dice, removing the core and the seeds.

Peel the Spanish onion and cut into rings. Wash the sage and lovage in cold water and shake dry. Peel the remaining garlic.

Using wet hands, shape the chickpea mixture into walnut-sized balls.

Keep 1 tablespoon sunflower oil to one side and heat the rest in a frying pan. Fry the chickpea balls, in batches, for about 4 minutes, turning to brown evenly. Drain the fried balls on absorbent kitchen paper and keep hot in the oven.

While the balls are being fried, place the vegetables in a saucepan with the whole garlic, herbs, vegetable stock and remaining sunflower oil and bring to the boil. Cover the pan and cook over a low heat for 5

to 10 minutes until the vegetables are tender but still firm to bite. Remove the herbs and season the vegetables to taste.

Serve the vegetables and chickpea balls separately.

Serves 6

Per Portion
about 550 calories
63 g carbohydrate
18 g protein · 24 g fat

Baked Courgettes and Tomatoes

1 kg/2¼ lb ripe tomatoes
1 kg/2¼ lb small young
  courgettes
1 Spanish onion
2 cloves garlic
bunch of fresh parsley
6 sprigs of fresh thyme
2 sprigs of fresh rosemary
125 ml/4 fl oz olive oil
salt
freshly ground black pepper

Blanch the tomatoes in boiling water for 30 seconds and then rinse in cold water. Peel and quarter the tomatoes and remove the core and the seeds. Wash and top and tail the courgettes. Dry them and cut lengthways into 0.5 cm/¼ in slices.

  Peel the onion and garlic. Cut the onion into thin rings and finely chop the garlic. Wash and dry the herbs. Finely chop the parsley leaves. Strip the thyme and rosemary leaves

from the stalks. Heat about half the olive oil in a frying pan and fry the courgette slices, in batches, until golden brown on both sides. Remove them from the pan when they are cooked and drain on absorbent kitchen paper. When you have fried all the courgettes, fry the onion and garlic in the pan until transparent.

  Arrange the courgettes and tomato slices in layers in an ovenproof dish, seasoning each layer and scattering with onion, garlic and herbs. Sprinkle with the remaining olive oil. Place in a hot oven (220c, 425f, gas 7) and bake for 30 minutes until tender but still firm to bite.

Serves 6

Per Portion
about 285 calories
16 g carbohydrate
5 g protein · 22 g fat

Provençal-style Tofu Ragoût

300 g/11 oz tofu
3 cloves garlic
½ tablespoon fresh rosemary
  leaves
3 tablespoons lemon juice
125 ml/4 fl oz olive oil
400 g/14 oz aubergines
salt
400 g/14 oz ripe tomatoes
250 g/9 oz courgettes
8 black olives
125 ml/4 fl oz freshly made vege-
  table stock (recipe page 38)
1 teaspoon dried Provençal herbs
freshly ground black pepper

Dice the tofu. Peel and chop the garlic. Coarsely chop the rosemary. Mix the lemon juice with the garlic, rosemary and 2 tablespoons olive oil. Pour over the tofu, cover and leave for 2 hours.

  Wash the aubergines, trim and slice lengthways. Sprinkle with salt and set aside.

  Meanwhile, blanch the tom-

atoes in boiling water for 30 seconds. Rinse in cold water, then peel and dice the tomatoes, removing the seeds. Wash, dry and trim the courgettes. Cut into sticks.

  Pat the aubergine slices dry. Heat the remaining oil in a frying pan and fry the aubergines until golden brown on both sides, then remove them from the pan. Fry the courgettes until golden and remove from the pan.

  Lay the aubergine slices in the pan. Top with the courgettes, tomatoes, olives and tofu. Add the stock, Provençal herbs and salt and pepper to taste. Cover and cook over a moderate heat for about 5 minutes.

Serves 4

Per Portion
about 410 calories
12 g carbohydrate
8 g protein · 34 g fat

Country-style Casseroles

Millet Casserole with Herbs

1 large onion
2 cloves garlic
200 g/7 oz millet
1 tablespoon sunflower oil
350–400 ml/12–14 fl oz freshly made vegetable stock (recipe page 38)
salt
freshly ground white pepper
2 handfuls of mixed fresh cultivated herbs and wild herbs (eg parsley, chervil, dandelion leaves, nettles, chickweed)
1 tablespoon butter
4 tablespoons crème fraîche or soured cream

Peel and finely chop the onion and garlic. Pick over the millet, tip into a sieve, rinse in cold water and drain.

Heat the oil in a saucepan. Fry the onion and garlic over a moderate heat until transparent, stirring continuously. Add the millet and stir until completely coated in fat. Add the vegetable stock and bring to the boil. Season to taste, cover the pan tightly and simmer gently over a low heat for about 35 minutes.

Remove the pan from the heat but leave covered and allow the millet to swell for 10 minutes.

Meanwhile, pick over herbs, wash, shake dry and finely chop.

Using a fork, fold the herbs, butter and crème fraîche into the millet and reheat without boiling. Serve the millet in a heated serving dish, with Uncooked vegetable salad (recipe page 21).

Serves 4

Per Portion
about 290 calories
41 g carbohydrate
7 g protein · 11 g fat

Barley Casserole

1 (100 g/4 oz) carrot
1 large onion
2 cloves garlic
300 g/11 oz pot barley
3 tablespoons oil
about 600 ml/1 pint freshly made vegetable stock (recipe page 38)
250 g/9 oz mushrooms
1 tablespoon lemon juice
bunch of fresh parsley
2–3 tablespoons crème fraîche or soured cream
salt
freshly ground white pepper

Peel, wash and dice the carrot. Peel and finely chop the onion and garlic.

Rinse the barley until the water runs clear. This removes the starch and stops the barley sticking together as it cooks.

Heat 2 tablespoons oil in a saucepan. Fry the onion and garlic until transparent. Add the carrot and fry for 2 minutes. Add the barley and stir until coated in fat.

Add the vegetable stock, cover the pan and cook over a low heat for 45 minutes.

Meanwhile, trim the mushrooms and wash if necessary. Thinly slice and sprinkle immediately with lemon juice to prevent them going brown.

Wash, dry and finely chop the parsley. Heat the remaining oil in a frying pan. Add the mushrooms and fry, stirring continuously, until the juice that forms has evaporated. Stir in the parsley and crème fraîche.

Stir the mushrooms into the cooked barley and season to taste.

Serves 4

Per Portion
about 400 calories
63 g carbohydrate
10 g protein · 11 g fat

Cheese and Semolina Bake

250 ml/8 fl oz freshly made vege-
*   table stock (recipe page 38)*
250 ml/8 fl oz milk
salt
freshly ground white pepper
freshly grated nutmeg
100 g/4 oz wholemeal semolina
2 eggs
150 g/5 oz Emmental cheese,
*   freshly grated*
25 g/1 oz butter
2 tablespoons chopped fresh
*   mixed herbs*

Bring the vegetable stock to the
boil with the milk and a little
salt, pepper and nutmeg. Remove the pan from the heat and
gradually stir in the semolina.
Cover the pan and leave to
stand for about 10 minutes.

Beat the eggs with a fork until frothy. Stir into the semolina
mixture with half the
Emmental.

Grease a baking dish with a
little of the butter. Fill with the
semolina mixture and smooth
the top. Place in a moderately
hot oven (200 C, 400 F, gas 6),
on the second shelf from the
bottom, and bake for 10
minutes.

Turn the oven temperature
up to very hot (240 C, 475 F, gas
9) and bake for a further 10
minutes.

Mix the remaining Emmental
with the herbs and spread over
the dish. Dot with the remaining butter and bake for a further 10 minutes until the top is
nice and brown. Serve with
Bean salad with tomato vinaigrette (recipe page 23) or
Sprouted salad (recipe page 26).

Serves 4

Per Portion
about 335 calories
21 g carbohydrate
18 g protein · 19 g fat

Millet Pudding

1 onion
1 clove garlic
200 g/7 oz millet
1 tablespoon vegetable oil
500 ml/17 fl oz freshly made
*   vegetable stock (recipe*
*   page 38)*
500 g/18 oz fresh green cabbage
4 eggs
100 g/4 oz Emmental cheese,
*   grated*
salt
freshly ground white pepper
freshly grated nutmeg
1 tablespoon butter

Peel and finely chop the onion
and garlic. Tip the millet into a
sieve, rinse under cold water,
drain and pick over.

Heat the oil in a saucepan
and fry the onion and garlic
over a moderate heat until
transparent, stirring continuously. Add the millet and stir
until completely coated in oil.

Add the stock, bring to the
boil, cover the pan and simmer
for 20 minutes.

Meanwhile, blanch the
washed cabbage leaves in
plenty of boiling water for 2
minutes. Drain, rinse in cold
water and finely chop.

Cool the millet until lukewarm. Separate the eggs. Stir
the yolks into the millet with
the cabbage and cheese. Season
to taste with salt, pepper and
nutmeg. Whisk the egg whites
until stiff and fold into the millet mixture.

Grease a baking dish with a
little butter. Fill with the millet
mixture and dot with the remaining butter.

Bake in a moderately hot
oven (200 C, 400 F, gas 6) for
about 40 minutes or until
browned on top. Serve immediately with a salad of tomatoes
and onions.

Serves 4

Per Portion
about 460 calories
42 g carbohydrate
22 g protein · 21 g fat

Polenta Bake

scant 750 ml/1¼ pints water
150 g/5 oz cornmeal
salt
2 tablespoons chopped fresh
  parsley
500 g/18 oz courgettes
500 g/18 oz tomatoes
2 onions
2 cloves garlic
2 sprigs of fresh thyme
sprig of fresh rosemary
3–4 tablespoons sunflower oil
500 g/18 oz minced lamb
freshly ground black pepper
100 g/4 oz Emmental cheese,
  grated
30 g/1¼ oz butter

Bring the water to the boil in a saucepan. Add the cornmeal and salt to taste and stir. Cover the pan and allow the mixture to cook over a low heat until it comes away from the sides of the pan, stirring frequently.

Stir in the parsley, spread on a baking sheet and leave for about 30 minutes until solid enough to cut.

Meanwhile, wash, dry and trim the courgettes. Cut lengthways into slices 0.5 cm/¼ in thick. Blanch the tomatoes in boiling water for 30 seconds, rinse in cold water and peel. Dice the tomatoes, removing the core and the seeds. Peel and finely chop the onions and garlic. Wash the herbs and strip off the leaves.

Heat about 3 tablespoons oil in a frying pan. Fry the courgettes until brown on both sides, and arrange in a baking dish.

Heat the remaining oil and fry the lamb. Add the onion and garlic and fry until transparent. Add the tomatoes and cook until the liquid evaporates. Stir in the herbs, season, and spread over the courgettes.

Cut the polenta into pieces about 5 × 10 cm/2 × 4 in. Arrange on the lamb and top with Emmental. Dot with the butter.

Bake in a very hot oven (240 C, 475 F, gas 9) for 10 to 15 minutes until browned.

Serves 4

Per Portion
about 590 calories
35 g carbohydrate
27 g protein · 35 g fat

Bean Sprout Pie

FOR THE WHEATMEAL PASTRY
350 g/12 oz wheatmeal flour
175 g/6 oz margarine
about 4 tablespoons water
beaten egg to glaze
FOR THE FILLING
400 g/14 oz mushrooms
1 onion
300 g/11 oz mixed sprouted
*   mung beans and chickpeas*
25 g/1 oz butter
3 tablespoons chopped fresh
*   parsley*
salt
freshly ground black pepper

To make the pastry, put the flour in a bowl and add the margarine, cut into pieces. Rub the fat into the flour until the mixture resembles fine breadcrumbs. Work in just enough water to bind the dough.

Roll out two-thirds of the pastry and use to line a 23-cm/9-in ovenproof pie dish.

Trim and wash the mushrooms if necessary and cut into thin slices. Peel and finely chop

the onion. Wash the sprouted beans in cold water and drain.

Heat the butter in a frying pan and fry the onion until transparent. Add the mushrooms and cook over a high heat, stirring continuously, until the liquid that forms has evaporated again. Stir in the sprouts and parsley and season.

Turn the filling into the lined pie dish and brush the edges of the pastry with a little water. Roll out the remaining pastry to cover the pie. Lift it over the filling, press the edges together well and trim off excess pastry. Make a hole in the middle of the pie and decorate with re-rolled pastry trimmings.

Brush the top of the pie with a little beaten egg and bake in a moderate oven (180 C, 350 F, gas 4) for about 45 minutes or until the pastry is golden.

Serves 5

Per Portion
about 590 calories
15 g carbohydrate
7 g protein · 35 g fat

Variations
For a change why not flavour the pastry used to make the pie? You can use a variety of herbs or other ingredients.

Herb Pastry
Add 2 tablespoons chopped fresh herbs to the pastry when the fat has been rubbed in.

Cheese Pastry
Add 50 g/2 oz grated matured cheese to the pastry when the fat has been rubbed in.

Sesame Crust
When you have made the pie, brush it with the glaze and sprinkle with some unroasted sesame seeds.

Walnut Pastry
Grind 50 g/2 oz walnuts to a powder and mix them into the pastry once the fat has been rubbed in.

Sunflower Pastry
Add 50 g/2 oz finely chopped sunflower seeds to the pastry once the fat has been rubbed in.

Cook's Tip

To line a pie dish with pastry, roll out the pastry, then carefully fold it over the rolling pin and lift it over the dish. Gently ease the pastry down into the dish using your fingers, at the same time lifting the edge of the dough over the rim of the dish to prevent it from cracking.

When adding the decoration to the pie, you may find it easier to cut leaves and strips from the pastry trimmings if you use a pair of kitchen scissors. Once you have completed the pie, leave it in the refrigerator to chill the pastry for at least 30 minutes, or longer if you have the time.

Pastries and Bakes

Vegetable Pasties

double quantity wheatmeal pastry (recipe page 56)
beaten egg to glaze
FOR THE ONION FILLING
175 g/6 oz onions
1 tablespoon vegetable oil
4 tablespoons soured cream
1 egg
½ teaspoon caraway seeds
½ teaspoon dried thyme
freshly ground white pepper
FOR THE QUARK FILLING
2 cloves garlic
250 g/9 oz Quark or other soft
  cheese (20 percent fat)
2 tablespoons chopped mixed
  fresh herbs
1 tablespoon single cream
freshly ground black pepper
FOR THE COURGETTE FILLING
175 g/6 oz courgettes
4 sprigs of fresh thyme
2 cloves garlic
2 tablespoons sesame seeds
2 tablespoons olive oil
FOR THE TOMATO FILLING
250 g/9 oz ripe tomatoes
100 g/4 oz feta cheese
1 clove garlic

2 tablespoons chopped fresh
  parsley
2 tablespoons fresh wholemeal
  breadcrumbs
FOR THE MUSHROOM FILLING
2 bunches of fresh basil
1 clove garlic
2 tablespoons pine nuts
2 tablespoons freshly grated
  pecorino or Parmesan cheese
5 tablespoons vegetable oil
175 g/6 oz mushrooms
FOR THE KOHLRABI FILLING
200 g/7 oz kohlrabi
2 tablespoons soured cream
1 egg
1 tablespoon freshly grated
  Emmental cheese
freshly grated nutmeg

Make the pastry according to
the recipe instructions.
    To make the onion filling,
peel and thinly slice the onions.
Heat the oil and fry the onions
until transparent. Leave to
cool. Stir in the remaining
ingredients.
    To make the Quark filling,
peel and finely chop the garlic.
Mix the Quark with the garlic,
herbs, cream and pepper.

    For the courgette filling,
wash, dry and top and tail
the courgettes. Cut into
matchsticks. Wash and dry the
thyme and pull the leaves off
the stems. Peel and finely chop
the garlic. Mix all these ingredients with the sesame seeds and
oil and season to taste.
    For the tomato filling,
blanch the tomatoes in boiling
water for 30 seconds, rinse in
cold water and peel. Dice the
tomatoes, removing the core
and the seeds. Mash the cheese.
Peel and finely chop the garlic.
Mix the tomatoes with the
cheese, garlic, parsley and
breadcrumbs.
    For the mushroom filling,
wash and dry the basil and
chop the leaves. Peel and finely
chop the garlic. In a mortar
work the basil, garlic, pine nuts,
cheese and 4 tablespoons oil to
a paste. Trim and chop the
mushrooms and fry in the remaining oil over a high heat.
Season to taste and stir into the
basil paste.
    For the kohlrabi filling, peel
and grate the kohlrabi and mix

with the soured cream, egg and
cheese. Season to taste with
salt, pepper and nutmeg.
    Cut the pastry into 12 pieces.
Roll out each piece into a
15-cm/6-in circle. Divide the
fillings between the pastry cir-
cles and dampen the edges.
Fold the pieces of pastry in half
and press the edges with a fork
to seal in the filling. Brush with
beaten egg and bake in a moderately hot oven (200 C, 400 F,
gas 6) for 25 to 30 minutes.

Makes 12

Per Portion
about 755 calories
73 g carbohydrate
23 g protein · 39 g fat

Cannelloni with Tofu and Spinach

150 g/5 oz wheatmeal flour
salt
1 egg
1–3 egg yolks
1 tablespoon vegetable oil
1 kg/2¼ lb spinach
1 onion
1 clove garlic
500 g/18 oz tofu
freshly ground white pepper
freshly grated nutmeg
250 ml/8 fl oz single cream
100 g/4 oz Parmesan cheese,
 freshly grated
oil for the dish
20 g/¾ oz butter

Work the flour with a pinch of salt, the egg, 1 egg yolk and the oil to make a smooth pasta dough. The dough should not be sticky, but if it is too solid or even crumbly, work in 1 or 2 further egg yolks. Wrap in foil and leave to rest for 30 minutes.

Meanwhile, make the filling. Pick over the spinach, cutting out tough stems, and wash well several times in cold water. Drain the spinach.

Bring plenty of water to the boil with a little salt. Blanch the spinach in batches in the boiling water for about 1 minute. Lift each batch out on a slotted spoon, drain well and then press with a wooden spoon to remove as much liquid as possible. Finely chop the spinach.

Peel and finely chop the onion and garlic.

Drain the tofu. Crush about three quarters of it with a fork or blend in a liquidiser or food processor. Mix the puréed tofu with the spinach, onion and garlic and season to taste with salt, pepper and nutmeg.

Blend the remaining tofu with the cream in a liquidiser or food processor and stir in the grated cheese.

Divide the pasta dough into portions and roll out on a lightly floured worktop. It is much quicker and easier to roll the pasta in a hand-operated pasta machine. This also makes it unnecessary to knead the dough by hand. Set the rollers at the widest setting and roll one piece of dough. Fold one end to the centre and the other end over it, turn the dough through 90 degrees and reroll. Continue in this way until all the dough is smooth. Then reset the rollers at the required thickness and roll out each portion thinly.

Cut the pasta into 10 × 15 cm/4 × 6 in pieces. Spread each with the tofu and spinach mixture and roll up.

Brush a shallow baking dish with the oil and place the cannelloni side by side in the dish. Pour on the tofu cream and dot with the butter. Bake in a hot oven (220 C, 425 F, gas 7), on the second shelf from the bottom, for about 45 minutes until the top is nice and brown.

Serves 6

Per Portion
about 490 calories
28 g carbohydrate
21 g protein · 32 g fat

Cook's Tip

If you can't get fresh spinach, use 2 packets frozen spinach (about 900 g/2 lb). After thawing, squeeze it out very well and finely chop.

The cannelloni are just as good made with spring greens, prepared in the same way as the spinach. Or mix the tofu with peeled, seeded puréed tomatoes. Season this filling with fresh basil or, in winter, dried oregano.

Pastries and Bakes

Courgette Gratin

1 kg/2¼ lb small courgettes
2 large ripe tomatoes
bunch of spring onions
10 black olives
about 250 g/9 oz mozzarella
cheese
bunch of fresh parsley
herb salt
freshly ground black pepper
125 ml/4 fl oz double cream

Wash the courgettes in cold
running water and wipe dry.
Top and tail them and cut in
half lengthways.

Blanch the tomatoes in boiling water for 30 seconds, rinse
in cold water and peel. Dice the
tomatoes, discarding the core
and seeds.

Trim the spring onions, wash
well and cut into thin rings with
about one third of the green
leaves.

Halve, stone and finely chop
the olives. Drain and dice the
mozzarella. Wash the parsley,
strip the leaves off the stalks,
pat dry and finely chop.

Mix the tomato with the
onion rings, olives, mozzarella
and parsley and season to taste
with herb salt and pepper.

Place the courgette halves in
a baking dish, sprinkle with a
little salt and cover with the
tomato mixture. Pour the
cream around the sides of the
dish.

Bake in a moderately hot
oven (200 c, 400 f, gas 6), on the
second shelf from the bottom of
the oven, for about 30 minutes
until the cheese has melted and
is nice and brown.

Serve with potatoes boiled in
their jackets and a salad.

Serves 4

Per Portion
about 360 calories
22 g carbohydrate
15 g protein · 23 g fat

Stuffed Cucumber

2 (500 g/18 oz) cucumbers
1 shallot
350 g/12 oz tomatoes
½ avocado
1½ bunches each of fresh dill and
parsley
100 g/4 oz minced lamb
salt
freshly ground white pepper
cayenne pepper
1 tablespoon vegetable oil
100 g/4 oz Edam cheese
1 tablespoon pine nuts
250 ml/8 fl oz crème fraîche or
soured cream
4 tablespoons single cream
30 g/1¼ oz butter

Peel the cucumbers and cut in
half across then lengthways.

Peel and coarsely chop the
shallot. Wash and dry the
tomatoes and cut out the core.
Stone the avocado and scoop
the flesh out of the skin. Purée
the tomatoes with the avocado
in a liquidiser or food
processor.

Wash and dry the herbs;
chop finely. Mix about half the
herbs into the purée with the
shallot and lamb. Season with
salt, pepper and cayenne.

Brush a baking dish with the
oil. Place the cucumber in the
dish and fill with the lamb
mixture.

Blend the Edam with the pine
nuts in a liquidiser or food processor. Add the crème fraîche
and cream and blend again to a
smooth paste. Stir in the remaining herbs and season to
taste. Pour the mixture over the
cucumbers and dot with the
butter. Bake in a hot oven
(220 c, 425 f, gas 7), for about
40 minutes.

Serves 4

Per Portion
about 405 calories
34 g carbohydrate
12 g protein · 8 g fat

Wholemeal Pizza with Tomato and Mushrooms

300 g/11 oz wholemeal or
wheatmeal flour
30 g/1¼ oz fresh yeast
125 ml/4 fl oz lukewarm water
1 tablespoon vegetable oil
1 egg yolk
1 tablespoon low-fat Quark or
other soft cheese
salt
750 g/1½ lb ripe tomatoes
about 400 g/14 oz mozzarella
cheese
250 g/9 oz mushrooms
bunch of fresh basil
sprig of fresh thyme
3 tablespoons olive oil
flour for rolling
2 tablespoons freshly grated
Parmesan
2 teaspoons dried oregano
freshly ground black pepper

To make the yeast dough, tip the flour into a bowl, make a well in the centre and crumble in the yeast. Sprinkle about 2 tablespoons lukewarm water over the yeast. Mix a little of the flour into the yeast, cover the bowl and leave to rise in a warm place for 15 minutes.

Work in the remaining lukewarm water, the oil, egg yolk, Quark and a pinch of salt. Knead the dough until elastic and then beat it to work in air. Cover the bowl with a tea towel and leave the dough to rise in a warm place for a further 30 minutes.

Meanwhile, blanch the tomatoes in boiling water for 30 seconds, rinse in cold water, peel and core. Finely chop half the tomatoes and slice the rest from the stalk end downwards. Remove the seeds.

Drain and slice the mozzarella. Trim the mushrooms, rinse if necessary and thinly slice. Rinse the mushrooms under cold running water only if absolutely necessary (if you can't remove dirt with a damp cloth) for they easily absorb water and lose their flavour. For this reason mushrooms should never be left to soak in water.

Rinse the basil and thyme in cold water and shake dry. Chop the basil finely and strip the thyme leaves from the stems. Grease a baking sheet with a little olive oil.

Cut the yeast dough into two portions and roll out each portion on a lightly floured worktop into a thin round. Place the rounds side by side on the baking sheet, cover with a tea towel and leave to rise for a further 10 minutes.

Prick the dough rounds several times with a fork so that they cook evenly without forming bubbles. Cover the dough with the chopped tomatoes, then the sliced tomatoes and mushrooms. Scatter with the Parmesan, basil, thyme, oregano, and salt and pepper to taste. Top with the mozzarella slices and sprinkle with the remaining olive oil.

Bake the pizza in a moderately hot oven (200 C, 400 F, gas 6), on the second shelf from the bottom, for 15 to 20 minutes until crisp around the edges and the mozzarella is soft and slightly browned. Serve with a colourful mixed salad.

Serves 4

Per Portion
about 760 calories
67 g carbohydrate
30 g protein · 39 g fat

Cook's Tip

Try making pizza with sliced aubergine and courgette fried in oil, diced green pepper and spring onion rings. Any pizza should automatically include tomato and mozzarella.

Crispy Gratins with Potatoes and Vegetables

Potato and Tomato Gratin

500 g / 18 oz floury potatoes
400 g / 14 oz ripe tomatoes
salt
freshly ground black pepper
250 ml / 8 fl oz double cream
100 g / 4 oz cheese (Bel Paese, Emmental, Gruyère or mature Gouda), grated
about 30 g / 1¼ oz butter

Peel the potatoes, wash and wipe dry. Using a mandolin, cut into 1 mm/$\frac{1}{16}$ in slices. Wipe the slices dry on absorbent kitchen paper, for the less moisture they contain, the crispier the gratin.

Wash and dry the tomatoes and cut out the cores. Cut downwards into 0.5 cm/¼ in slices. Arrange the potato and tomato slices in layers in a gratin dish and season each layer.

Pour the cream around the edge of the dish. Sprinkle with the grated cheese and dot with the butter.

Bake in a hot oven (220 c, 425 f, gas 7), on the second shelf from the bottom, for 20 to 25 minutes until the cheese is nice and brown, the potatoes tender and the liquid absorbed. If necessary add a little more cream to the edge of the dish. It is impossible to give an exact quantity of liquid for this depends on the variety of potato and the amount of moisture in the tomatoes.

Serve the gratin at once for if left to stand the cheese will become tough.

Serves 4

Per Portion
about 460 calories
25 g carbohydrate
11 g protein · 34 g fat

Spinach Beet Gratin with Garlic Bread

500 g / 18 oz spinach beet
salt
125 g / 4½ oz tofu
125 ml / 4 fl oz freshly made vegetable stock (recipe page 38)
1 tablespoon lemon juice
2 tablespoons rye breadcrumbs
2 tablespoons sesame seeds
6 tablespoons olive oil
4 cloves garlic
bunch of fresh parsley or box of mustard and cress
freshly ground black pepper
4 slices rye bread (40 g / 1½ oz each)

Wash the spinach beet, shake dry and coarsely chop. Place in a gratin dish and season to taste with salt.

Blend the drained tofu with the vegetable stock and lemon juice in a liquidiser or food processor and pour over the spinach beet. Scatter with the breadcrumbs and sesame seeds and sprinkle with 1 tablespoon olive oil.

Bake in a hot oven (220 c,

425 f, gas 7) for 35 to 40 minutes until browned.

Peel the garlic and squeeze through a garlic press or chop very finely. Wash the parsley, strip the leaves from the stalks, pat dry and chop very finely (snip cress with scissors). Mix the garlic with the parsley or cress, pepper to taste and the remaining olive oil.

Toast the rye bread, spread with garlic paste and serve hot with the gratin.

Serves 4

Per Portion
about 370 calories
26 g carbohydrate
10 g protein · 22 g fat

61

Healthy cooking does not in any way mean going without meat and fish. In modern, nutrition-conscious cooking fish has made an established name for itself. It is amazingly versatile. Compare plaice fillets or trout in a creamy herb sauce with steamed cod served on a bed of vegetables with a tasty dill butter sauce or tench or mackerel on a bed of juicy tomatoes. If we take a look at foreign cooking we find a succulent Chinese-style fish dish or a Spanish paella.

A juicy leg of lamb seasoned with plenty of garlic and thyme is a treat you can allow yourself without worrying. The tender meat of young lamb blends wonderfully with fresh herbs and young vegetables or even with fruit and yogurt. See for yourself how delicious lamb tastes with tarragon, spinach beet or quinces. If you prefer poultry, try duck with spring onions, juicy chicken rissoles or a tender braised chicken cooked with wine and dried apricots.

Light Fish and Meat Dishes

Plaice Fillets in Herb Sauce

2 plaice (600 g/1¼ lb each)
300 g/11 oz fish heads and bones
2 shallots
bunch of fresh parsley
1 carrot
1 small leek
1 stick celery
4 white peppercorns
1 bay leaf
250 ml/8 fl oz water
250 ml/8 fl oz dry white wine
½ bunch of fresh dill
2 handfuls of fresh chervil
5 leaves fresh sorrel
handful of wild herbs (eg dandelion leaves, nettle and salad burnet)
2 tablespoons lemon juice
salt
freshly ground white pepper

Have your fishmonger skin and fillet the plaice, but take the heads and bones with you to add to the other fish trimmings for the stock. Cut the gills off all the fish heads (the fishmonger will do this if you ask him) for they give the stock an oily taste. Make sure you remove the whole gill and not just the gill covering.

Peel and halve the shallots. Wash the parsley and shake dry. Strip the leaves off the stalks and keep to one side for the sauce. The stalks are used in the stock.

Peel and wash the carrot and halve it lengthways. Cut the roots and limp leaves off the leek. Cut a cross through the leaves down as far as the white, open the leaves and wash well. Cut the leek into two pieces. Wash the celery and cut in half.

Tie the parsley stalks, carrot, leek and celery into a bundle with cooking string.

Put the fish heads and bones, the bundle of vegetables, the peppercorns, bay leaf, water and half the wine in a saucepan and bring to the boil. Cover the pan and simmer over a low heat for 25 minutes. Do not overcook the stock or it will have a bitter taste.

Strain the stock into another pan, wide enough to take the plaice fillets side by side, through a sieve lined with absorbent kitchen paper. Do not squeeze out the fish trimmings or seasonings as this would make the stock cloudy.

Pick over the herbs and remove any tough stalks. Rinse, shake dry and chop fairly coarsely with the parsley leaves.

Add the remaining wine and the lemon juice to the fish stock and bring to the boil. Reduce by about half over a high heat, stirring frequently.

Season the plaice fillets. Add the herbs to the stock, then add the fillets and cook over a low heat for about 2 minutes.

Lift the fish gently out of the pan on to warmed plates and spoon on the herb sauce. Serve with potatoes or wholemeal French bread and salad.

Serves 4

Per Portion
about 225 calories
8 g carbohydrate
30 g protein · 2 g fat

Cook's Tip

The sauce will be richer, but higher in calories, if you whisk in a little butter. Arrange the cooked plaice fillets on warmed plates. Cut about 50 g/2 oz chilled butter into small pieces and whisk into the herb sauce.

Delectable Fish Dishes

Trout with Cream and Herbs

*4 cleaned fresh trout, about
 300 g/11 oz each
salt
freshly ground white pepper
1 box of mustard and cress
large bunch of fresh parsley
few leaves fresh lemon balm
350 ml/12 fl oz double cream
1 bay leaf*

Rinse the trout inside and out in cold water and wipe thoroughly dry. On a plate mix a little salt with plenty of pepper and rub into the inside and outside of the trout. Place the trout side by side in a baking dish.

Snip off the cress with scissors. Wash the parsley, strip the leaves off the stalks, pat dry and finely chop. Wash and dry the lemon balm and cut into strips. Stir the herbs into the cream, pour over the trout and add the bay leaf.

Bake the trout in a moderately hot oven (200 C, 400 F, gas 6) for 20 to 25 minutes, basting repeatedly with the herb cream.

Transfer the cooked trout to a warmed plate. Pour the herb cream into a saucepan. Remove the bay leaf. Boil to reduce the cream over a high heat until thickened.

Serve the trout and sauce separately, with jacket-boiled potatoes and salad.

Serves 4

Per Portion
about 450 calories
5 g carbohydrate
27 g protein · 33 g fat

Cook's Tip
Instead of lemon balm you can use a piece of thinly cut lemon rind. Cut this into fine strips and stir into the cream with the cress and parsley.

Delectable Fish Dishes

Fish in Foil

2 sea trout (600 g/1¼ lb each),
    cleaned
1 lemon
2 shallots
2 bunches of fresh parsley
salt
freshly ground white pepper

Rinse the sea trout inside and out with cold water and wipe dry, making sure you dry the stomach cavity too.

Wash the lemon in hot water, wipe dry and thinly slice, removing the pips. Peel and finely slice the shallots. Wash the parsley and shake dry. Strip the leaves from one bunch and finely chop. Separate the other bunch into sprigs but do not chop. These will be used to stuff the trout.

Season the trout inside and out. Arrange half the lemon and shallot slices with the parsley sprigs in the stomach cavity.

Place each trout on a large sheet of double-strength foil. Place the remaining lemon and shallot slices on the trout and sprinkle with the chopped parsley. Wrap the trout loosely in the foil but seal the edges well so that the juice that forms during baking cannot escape.

Place the wrapped trout directly on the second shelf from the bottom in a hot oven (220 C, 425 F, gas 7) and bake for about 20 minutes

Open the foil carefully to avoid spilling the juice. Serve the trout with the juice, accompanied by potatoes and salad.

Serves 4

Per Portion
about 190 calories
3 g carbohydrate
31 g protein · 3 g fat

Herby Fish in Lemon Butter

1 lemon
bunch of fresh parsley or 2 hand-
    fuls of fresh chervil
4 white fish fillets (125 g/4½ oz
    each)
40 g/1½ oz butter
salt
freshly ground white pepper

Squeeze the juice from the lemon. Wash the parsley. Strip the leaves from the stalks, pat dry and finely chop. If you use chervil this should be picked over, washed and shaken dry before chopping both leaves and stems. Rinse the fish fillets in cold water and wipe dry.

Select a frying pan or fish pan large enough to take all the fillets side by side. Melt the butter in the pan over a low to moderate heat until it bubbles gently but does not brown.

Add the lemon juice to the butter and heat through.

Place the fish fillets in the lemon butter and cook the first side for 4 minutes over a low to moderate heat.

Add the parsley to the butter. (Chervil is added only for the last minute of cooking as the longer it cooks the more flavour it loses.) Turn the fish and cook the second side for a further 4 minutes without allowing it to brown.

Transfer the fish to warmed plates, spoon on some of the lemon herb butter and season to taste.

Serve with jacket-boiled potatoes and Sprouted salad (recipe page 26) or mixed salad.

Serves 4

Per Portion
about 265 calories
1 g carbohydrate
28 g protein · 22 g fat

Delectable Fish Dishes

Steamed Cod on Vegetables

1 lemon
bunch of fresh dill
250 g/9 oz young carrots
250 g/9 oz kohlrabi
bunch of spring onions
250 ml/8 fl oz water
1 bay leaf
3 white peppercorns
1 juniper berry
4 cod cutlets, about 4 cm/1½ in thick
herb salt
freshly ground white pepper
1 egg yolk
100 g/4 oz chilled butter

Wash the lemon under hot running water, dry and cut in half. Cut a thin slice off one half for the stock. Then squeeze the two halves and keep the juice in reserve for the sauce.

Rinse the dill in cold water and shake dry. Break off the ends of the stalks for the stock. Keep the leaves for the sauce but do not chop yet.

Trim, scrape and wash the carrots. Peel the kohlrabi, cut out any tough parts and then wash. Cut the roots and limp leaves off the spring onions. Wash well and shake dry. Cut the carrots and kohlrabi first into 0.5 cm/¼ in slices and then into thin sticks. Cut the spring onions, including about half the length of the green leaves, into 1 cm/½ in pieces.

Bring the water to the boil with the lemon slice, the dill stalks, bay leaf, peppercorns and juniper berry in a fish kettle or steamer.

Rinse the cod cutlets in cold water, wipe dry and season both sides with herb salt and pepper. Arrange the vegetables on the rack in the steamer and top with the cutlets. Cover and steam the fish and vegetables for about 20 minutes.

Arrange the fish and vegetables on heated plates and keep hot in the oven.

Finely chop the dill leaves.

To make the sauce fill a frying pan with hot water and place on the hob. Keep the

water hot over a low heat. Stand a deep container, preferably stainless steel, in the water. Into this container pour 3 tablespoons of the steaming liquid, the lemon juice and egg yolk and beat with a hand or electric whisk to a thick, frothy mixture. The water should be hot throughout but not boiling or the egg yolk will separate.

Cut the butter into small pieces and gradually whisk into the sauce. Stir in the chopped dill and season to taste with pepper.

Pour the sauce over the fish cutlets and vegetables and serve at once with jacket-boiled potatoes.

Serves 4

Per Portion
about 415 calories
9 g carbohydrate
37 g protein · 23 g fat

Cook's Tip
The cooking times given for fish may be shorter than you are used to. But try this modern, time-saving and delicious way of cooking fish. When fish fillets or cutlets are properly cooked the flesh should still look transparent at the thickest point, usually the centre. With whole fish the backbone should be pinkish in colour with the flesh still attached to it. Fish is overcooked if the backbone pulls away easily or if the flesh falls apart as you serve it. Remember that fish will continue to cook when kept hot.

67

Whole Fish with Tomatoes

2 oily fish such as tench or
mackerel (about 600 g/1¼ lb
each), cleaned
½ lemon
750 g/1½ lb ripe tomatoes
1 (300 g/11 oz) Spanish onion
2 cloves garlic
salt
sprig of fresh rosemary
5 black peppercorns
2 fresh bay leaves
scant 125 ml/4 fl oz dry white
wine
4 tablespoons cold-pressed olive
oil
½ bunch of fresh parsley

Rinse the fish inside and out
under cold running water and
wipe dry. Using a sharp knife
make a few slanting slits in the
skin on the top of the fish so
that it can absorb the flavour of
the seasonings.

Squeeze the lemon juice over
the fish and leave to stand for
about 20 minutes.

Meanwhile, blanch the tomatoes in boiling water for 30
seconds, rinse in cold water and
peel. Cut out the core, remove
the seeds and chop the flesh.

Peel the onion and garlic.
Chop the onion. Halve the garlic cloves and crush with a little
salt.

For the seasoning, rinse the
rosemary, shake dry and strip
the leaves from the stalk. Crush
the peppercorns on a board
with the blade of a strong knife.
Add the rosemary and bay
leaves to the peppercorns and
coarsely chop.

Cover the bottom of a baking dish with half the tomato,
onion and garlic. Place the fish
in the dish and season inside
and out with salt and the seasoning mixture. Scatter the remaining tomato, onion and
garlic over the fish. Pour the
white wine around the edge of
the dish and sprinkle all over
with the olive oil.

Bake in a moderately hot
oven (200 c, 400 f, gas 6) for
about 40 minutes.

Wash the parsley and shake

dry. Strip the leaves from the
stalks and finely chop.

Serve the fish straight from
the dish, sprinkled with parsley.
Serve with jacket-boiled potatoes, wheatgerm rolls or
wholemeal French bread with
Uncooked vegetable salad
(recipe page 21).

Serves 4

Per Portion
about 380 calories
14 g carbohydrate
30 g protein · 29 g fat

Cook's Tip
This recipe is also excellent made with cod or sea
trout fillets. These should
be seasoned with the juice
of 1 lemon, salt and
freshly ground black pep-
per before arranging in
layers in a baking dish
with the other ingredients
given in the recipe. For a
more delicate flavour re-
place the wine with
250 ml/8 fl oz double
cream or crème fraîche
and omit the olive oil. In
this case the parsley
should be chopped and
half of it mixed with the
cream to be poured over
the fish. The remaining
parsley is sprinkled over
the fish just before serving. The fish will bake in
a preheated oven in 15
minutes.

Delectable Fish Dishes

Steamed Fish with Ginger

2 cleaned trout
salt
4 spring onions
piece of fresh root ginger, about
  6 cm/2½ in long
1–2 cloves garlic
4 tablespoons dry sherry
2 tablespoons soy sauce
½ teaspoon caster sugar
1 tablespoon sunflower oil

Rinse the fish and wipe thoroughly dry. Place the fish flat on the worktop and season sparingly with salt, inside and out.

Cut the roots and limp leaves off the spring onions, wash well and cut into strips. Finely shred about a quarter of the spring onions and shred both ends of two pieces to set aside for the garnish. Peel the root ginger like a potato, wash, dry and cut into very thin slices. Peel and finely chop the garlic.

Beat the sherry with the soy sauce, sugar and sunflower oil. Stir in the ginger and garlic.

Cover the bottom of a fish kettle or steamer with water. Place the spring onions and fish on the rack, sprinkling the fine shreds of onion on top of the fish. Pour on the marinade.

Steam the fish for 15 to 20 minutes. Bone the steamed fish and serve on heated plates, garnished with the reserved spring onions. Brown rice or wholemeal French bread and a salad can be served with the fish.

Serves 4

Per Portion
about 230 calories
7 g carbohydrate
27 g protein · 8 g fat

Cook's Tip
Instead of spring onions you can use thin strips of leek.

Fish with Vegetables

750 g/1½ lb skinned firm-fleshed
*   white fish fillets*
1 tablespoon cornflour
1 tablespoon dry sherry
2 tablespoons soy sauce
1 clove garlic
bunch of spring onions
2 sticks celery
handful of mung bean sprouts
5 tablespoons vegetable oil
125 ml/4 fl oz freshly made vege-
*   table stock (recipe page 38)*
salt
cayenne pepper

Remove any bones in the fish
fillet with tweezers. Rinse the
fish under cold running water
and wipe thoroughly dry. Using
a sharp knife cut the fish into
3 cm/1¼ in cubes. Try to get
them all the same size so that
they cook evenly.

Beat the cornflour with the
sherry and soy sauce, pour over
the fish and stir to mix in.
Cover and leave to stand while

you prepare the vegetables.

Peel and very finely chop the
garlic. Cut the roots and limp
leaves off the spring onions.
Wash the onions well, shake
dry and cut into 0.5 cm/¼ in
rings, including about one third
of the green leaves. Using a
small sharp knife peel off any
tough threads from the celery.
Wash and dry, then cut off the
leaves (reserve for the garnish)
and cut the celery sticks into
0.5 cm/¼ in pieces. Tip the bean
sprouts into a sieve, wash under
cold water and drain.

Heat 1 tablespoon oil in a
frying pan. Cook the garlic over
a low to moderate heat, stirring, until transparent. Do not
allow it to brown or it will be
bitter.

Add all the vegetables and
turn up the heat. Stirring continuously, fry the vegetables
over a moderate to high heat
for 2 to 3 minutes.

Add the vegetable stock and
season to taste with salt and
cayenne. Cover the pan and
cook over a moderate heat for 1
minute until the vegetables are

tender but still firm to bite.

Transfer the vegetables to a
shallow warmed dish and keep
hot while you cook the fish.

Heat 2 tablespoons oil in the
frying pan and fry the fish in
batches for 3 to 4 minutes,
turning them continually and
keeping them hot with the vegetables until they are all cooked.
You will need to heat more oil
for each batch. When all the
fish is cooked stir it gently into
the vegetables and serve at
once, scattered with the celery
leaves.

Serve with rice, wholemeal
bread or wholemeal French
bread.

Serves 4

Per Portion
about 260 calories
9 g carbohydrate
18 g protein · 16 g fat

Cook's Tip
You must use a firm-
fleshed fish for this dish,
such as cod, huss, had-
dock or halibut. Even
with firm fish the cubes
tend to fall apart to some
extent during cooking.
You can avoid this by
deep-frying the fish but
this adds extra calories
and makes the fish
harder to digest. Instead
of fish you could use
fresh or frozen cooked
shelled prawns. You will
find how to prepare
prawns in the recipe for
Prawns in herb sauce
(page 72).

Herring Fillets with Potatoes and Quark Sauce

1 kg/2¼ lb small new potatoes
1 tart eating apple
1 red onion
bunch of fresh dill
bunch of fresh chives
250 g/9 oz Quark or other soft cheese (20 percent fat)
125 ml/4 fl oz single cream
1–2 tablespoons freshly grated horseradish
salt
freshly ground white pepper
8 matjes herring fillets

Scrub the potatoes well under cold running water so that they can be eaten in their skins. Bring a little water to the boil in a saucepan, add the potatoes, cover and cook over a low heat for 20 to 30 minutes, until tender.

Meanwhile, peel, core and dice the apple. Peel and chop the onion. Wash the dill and chives and pat dry. Chop the dill and cut up the chives.

Stir the Quark with the cream until smooth. Mix in the apple, onion, herbs and horseradish. Season to taste with salt and pepper.

Cover the bottom of a shallow dish with ice cubes. Wash the herring fillets under cold running water to remove some of the salt. Wipe dry and arrange on the ice. Drain the cooked potatoes and allow the steam to evaporate. Serve with the Quark sauce and herring fillets. Accompany with green beans tossed in a little butter.

Serves 4

Per Portion
about 690 calories
57 g carbohydrate
31 g protein · 36 g fat

Fish and Cucumber Stew

100 g/4 oz shallots or very small onions
1 (400 g/14 oz) cucumber
1 tablespoon butter
1 tablespoon lemon juice
125 ml/4 fl oz freshly made vegetable stock (recipe page 38)
salt
freshly ground white pepper
600 g/1¼ lb white fish fillet
1 teaspoon made English mustard
bunch of fresh dill

Peel the shallots and cut into wedges. Wash the cucumber. Cut it in half across and then into quarters lengthways. Scrape out the seeds with a teaspoon. Cut the cucumber into 1 cm/½ in pieces.

Heat the butter in a large saucepan without allowing it to brown. Cook the shallots and cucumber in the butter, stirring, until transparent. Add the lemon juice and stock. Season to taste and bring to the boil, then cover the pan and simmer over a low heat for 8 to 10 minutes.

Meanwhile, rinse the fish fillet, wipe thoroughly dry and cut into 2 cm/¾ in cubes.

Stir the mustard into the vegetables. Tip the fish on to the vegetables, season to taste, cover the pan again and cook over the lowest possible heat for about 8 minutes.

Meanwhile, wash, dry and finely chop the dill, discarding any tough stalks.

Transfer the fish stew to a heated dish and serve at once, sprinkled with dill. Accompany with jacket-boiled potatoes or rice, and tomato salad generously seasoned with fresh herbs.

Serves 4

Per Portion
about 230 calories
9 g carbohydrate
28 g protein · 9 g fat

71

Prawns in Herb Sauce

12 uncooked Mediterranean or
  Dublin Bay prawns
1 onion
1 leek
2 carrots
½ celeriac
½ bunch of fresh parsley
1 tablespoon butter
125 ml/4 fl oz dry white wine
2 white peppercorns
1 bay leaf
½ bunch of fresh dill
125 ml/4 fl oz double cream
1 teaspoon lemon juice
salt
freshly ground white pepper

Rinse and peel the prawns, then
remove the black thread-like
intestine.

Peel and quarter the onion.
Trim and thoroughly wash the
leek. Peel and wash the carrots
and celeriac. Coarsely chop the
leek, carrots and celeriac. Wash
the parsley, strip off the leaves.
Keep 3 stalks for the stock.

Melt the butter in a saucepan
and fry the prawn shells and
vegetables until the shells are
red in colour. Add the wine and
stir well to mix. Add the parsley
stalks, peppercorns and bay
leaf.

Simmer for 30 minutes, then
strain. Bring the stock back to
the boil in a clean pan. Add the
prawns and simmer for about 8
minutes.

Wash the dill and finely chop
with the parsley leaves.

Lift the prawns out of the
stock and keep hot on four
warmed plates.

Boil to reduce the stock by
half. Gradually add the cream
and continue boiling until
creamy and saucelike, stirring
continuously. Stir in the herbs
and lemon juice and season to
taste with salt and pepper. Pour
over the prawns.

Serves 4

Per Portion
about 270 calories
2 g carbohydrate
22 g protein · 16 g fat

Grilled Prawns

12 uncooked Mediterranean or
  Dublin Bay prawns in the shell
½ lemon
3 cloves garlic
bunch of fresh parsley
3–4 tablespoons olive oil
salt
freshly ground black pepper

Preheat the grill or barbecue.
Cutting on the in-curving side,
cut the prawns in half lengthways without cutting right the
way through. Open up the
prawns so that the shells crack
and the prawns lie as flat as
possible on the worktop.

Squeeze the juice from the
lemon. Peel the garlic and
squeeze in a garlic press, or
chop to a pulp. Wash the parsley. Strip the leaves off the
stalks, pat dry and finely chop.

Beat the lemon juice with the
garlic, parsley and olive oil to
form a paste. Spread the paste
on to the flesh side of the
prawns. Place under a
preheated grill, or on the hot

grid of the barbecue, and cook
for about 10 minutes.

Transfer to warmed plates,
season to taste and serve at
once with wholemeal French
bread and a mixed salad.

Serves 2

Per Portion
about 220 calories
2 g carbohydrate
22 g protein · 12 g fat

Cook's Tip
The quantities will also
serve 4 as a starter.

Shellfish Specialities

Fish Paella

1 onion
2 cloves garlic
*4 tablespoons cold-pressed olive
 oil*
150 g/5 oz long-grain brown rice
*about 500 ml/17 fl oz freshly
 made vegetable stock
 (recipe page 38)*
salt
500 g/18 oz ripe tomatoes
1 red pepper
1 green pepper
500 g/18 oz red mullet fillets
*6 cooked Mediterranean prawns
 in shell*
1 lemon
*300 g/11 oz shelled fresh peas
 (about 750 g/1½ lb in shells),
 or frozen peas*
1 tablespoon butter
1 sachet saffron threads
*bunch of fresh parsley or handful
 of fresh chervil*
cayenne pepper

Peel and finely chop the onion
and garlic. Heat the olive oil in
a frying pan or wide saucepan
and fry the onion and garlic

over a moderate heat, stirring
continuously, until transparent.
Add the rice and stir until all
the grains are coated in oil.

Add the vegetable stock and
season to taste with salt if
necessary. Bring the stock to
the boil, cover the pan and
cook for 30 minutes over the
lowest possible heat. If the rice
becomes too dry, add a little
more stock.

Meanwhile, blanch the tomatoes in boiling water for 30
seconds and then rinse in cold
water. Peel and dice the tomatoes, removing the core and
the seeds. Quarter the peppers
and remove the stalks, white
pith and seeds. Rinse under
cold running water, wipe dry
and cut across into 0.5 cm/¼ in
strips.

Rinse the red mullet fillets
and prawns in cold water and
wipe dry. Cut the fish into
1 cm/½ in cubes. Halve the
lemon. Keep one half to garnish and squeeze the juice from
the other half over the fish and
prawns. Leave to stand while
the peppers are cooking.

Stir the peppers into the rice
and cook for a further 10 minutes. Then stir in the fish,
prawns, peas and tomatoes and
continue cooking for a further 5
to 10 minutes.

Melt the butter in a small
frying pan over a low heat until
hot but not brown. Rub the saffron threads between your finger and thumb into the butter
and stir to dissolve. (Saffron
should always be dissolved in
hot water or fat or it will not
mix evenly into the food.)

Wash the parsley, strip the
leaves from the stalks, pat dry
and finely chop. If using
chervil, wash, dry and chop
both the leaves and stems.

Stir the saffron butter into
the paella with a fork. Season
the paella with salt and a generous pinch of cayenne, and
sprinkle with the chopped parsley or chervil. Cut the reserved
lemon half into slices or wedges
and arrange on the rice.

Serve with Uncooked vegetable salad (recipe page 21).

Serves 6

Per Portion
about 380 calories
16 g carbohydrate
27 g protein · 13 g fat

Cook's Tip
Cubes of chicken meat
can be added to the
paella. Use 2 boneless
chicken breasts. Remove
the skin and cut the meat
into cubes. Fry the
chicken with the onion
and garlic, then continue
as above.

Saucy Meat Dishes

Lamb Ragoût with Yogurt

*600 g/1¼ lb boned shoulder of
  lamb*
1 onion
1 clove garlic
bunch of fresh parsley
1 tablespoon vegetable oil
150 ml/¼ pint natural yogurt
freshly ground black pepper
1 red pepper
1 tablespoon crème fraîche
50 g/2 oz walnuts, chopped

Dry the meat, remove any fat
and gristle and cut into 2 cm/
¾ in cubes. Peel and finely chop
the onion and garlic. Wash the
parsley in cold water, strip the
leaves off the stalks, pat dry
and finely chop. Keep one third
of the parsley in reserve to
garnish.

Heat the oil in a frying pan.
Seal the meat, in batches, over
a moderate to high heat. As
each batch is sealed, transfer it
to a sieve over a basin to collect
the juice.

When all the lamb is cooked,
fry the onion and garlic in the
fat until transparent, stirring
continuously.

Return the meat and juice to
the pan. Stir in the parsley and
yogurt and season to taste with
pepper. Stir the sediment on the
bottom of the pan into the
sauce. Cover and simmer over a
low heat for 1 hour.

Just before the end of the
cooking time, quarter the pepper lengthways and remove the
stalk, white pith and seeds.
Wash, wipe dry and finely
chop. Stir the red pepper and
crème fraîche into the ragoût
and heat through.

Serve at once, sprinkled with
walnuts and the remaining
parsley, with brown rice.

Serves 4

Per Portion
about 555 calories
10 g carbohydrate
24 g protein · 44 g fat

Lamb Stew with Quinces

*750 g/1½ lb boned shoulder of
  lamb*
1 large onion
2 cloves garlic
1–2 pieces preserved stem ginger
1 lemon
1 tablespoon vegetable oil
250 ml/8 fl oz dry white wine
300 g/11 oz quinces
250 ml/8 fl oz double cream
2 teaspoons mustard powder
½ teaspoon ground cinnamon
salt
cayenne pepper

Cut the meat into cubes. Peel
and finely chop the onion and
garlic. Chop the ginger.

Cut a thin piece of rind from
the lemon and cut into very
thin strips. Squeeze the juice.

Heat the oil in a frying pan
and seal the meat, in batches,
over a moderate to high heat.
Fry the onion and garlic in the
fat until transparent.

Return the meat and juice to

the pan. Add the lemon juice
and white wine and stir the
sediment on the bottom of the
pan into the sauce. Add the ginger and lemon rind. Cover and
simmer for 1 hour.

Quarter, peel and core the
quinces and cut into 1-cm/½-in
wedges. Add to the meat and
simmer, covered, for a further
30 minutes.

Remove the meat and
quinces from the pan to a serving dish and keep hot. Add the
cream to the sauce and boil to
reduce by about half over a
high heat. Season the sauce
with the mustard, cinnamon,
and salt and cayenne to taste
and pour over the meat.

Serves 6

Per Portion
about 560 calories
16 g carbohydrate
19 g protein · 41 g fat

Fried Lamb with Tomatoes

600 g / 1¼ lb boneless lamb from
*   the leg*
500 g / 18 oz ripe tomatoes
1 onion
3 cloves garlic
bunch of fresh basil
4 tablespoons sunflower oil
pinch of caster sugar
salt
freshly ground black pepper
125 ml / 4 fl oz double cream

Remove any fat or gristle from the lamb and cut across the grain into 2 cm/¾ in slices, then into strips.

Blanch the tomatoes in boiling water for 30 seconds, rinse in cold water and peel. Finely dice the tomatoes, removing the core and the seeds. Peel and finely chop the onion and garlic. Wash the basil, strip the leaves off the stems, pat dry and cut into strips.

Heat 1 tablespoon oil in a frying pan and fry the lamb, in batches, over a high heat for about 30 seconds. Add only enough lamb in each batch to cook without overlapping in the pan, and use more oil as necessary. As each batch of lamb is cooked transfer it to a sieve over a basin to catch the juice; this will prevent the meat continuing to cook in the juice and keep it tender.

Add the remaining oil, reduce the heat and fry the onion and garlic over a moderate heat until transparent. Add the tomato, stir until warmed through and season with the sugar and salt and pepper to taste.

Return the meat and juice to the pan and stir until heated through. Stir in the cream and heat through. Stir in the basil and serve at once, with brown rice or just with bread.

Serves 4

Per Portion
about 545 calories
10 g carbohydrate
25 g protein · 43 g fat

Lamb Cutlets in Thyme Sauce

bunch of fresh thyme
3 cloves garlic
1 lemon
4 double lamb cutlets, about
  180 g/6 oz each
2 tablespoons sunflower oil
salt
freshly ground white pepper
125 ml/4 fl oz double cream

Wash the thyme under cold running water and shake dry. Strip the leaves off the stalks. Peel and very finely chop the garlic. Squeeze the lemon and keep the juice in reserve for the sauce.

Wipe the lamb cutlets with a damp cloth to remove any splinters of bone. Using a sharp knife, cut through the fat around the edge at 2 cm/¾ in intervals to prevent the chops curling up during cooking. Make sure you do not cut into the meat itself.

Heat the oil in a frying pan.

Seal the chops on both sides over a high heat. Reduce the heat and cook the chops for a further 2 to 3 minutes on each side.

Transfer the chops to warmed plates, season to taste and keep hot.

Add the thyme leaves and garlic to the pan and stir over a low to moderate heat until the garlic is transparent. Add the lemon juice and stir in the sediment from the bottom of the pan.

Stir in the cream and boil over a high heat, stirring, until the sauce is creamy. Season to taste with pepper and pour over the cutlets. Serve with wheatgerm rolls or potatoes and salad.

Serves 4

Per Portion
about 705 calories
3 g carbohydrate
23 g protein · 63 g fat

Lamb Medallions with Rosemary Potatoes

750 g/1½ lb small new potatoes
salt
4 cloves garlic
4 sprigs of fresh rosemary
4 tablespoons cold-pressed olive
  oil
12 medallions of lamb, about 2–
  3 cm/1 in thick
freshly ground black pepper

Scrub the potatoes well under cold running water and boil in the skins in salted water until tender. This will take 20 to 30 minutes depending on size.

Peel the garlic. Rinse the rosemary in cold water, strip the leaves off the stalks and pat dry.

Drain the potatoes, evaporate some of the steam and peel.

Heat 3 tablespoons olive oil in a frying pan. Fry 1 garlic clove over a low to moderate

heat until transparent, then remove from the pan and discard. (The garlic is used only to flavour the oil.)

Add the potatoes and rosemary to the oil and over a moderate heat brown the potatoes, stirring frequently. Transfer the potatoes to a heated plate and keep hot.

Wipe the lamb medallions dry. Heat the remaining oil and fry the 3 remaining garlic cloves until transparent, then remove from the pan and discard. Increase the heat and fry the medallions over a moderate to high heat on both sides, for 5 to 6 minutes in all. They should remain pink on the inside.

Serve the medallions on heated plates with the rosemary potatoes. Season to taste. Serve with green beans in butter and tomatoes.

Serves 4

Per Portion
about 480 calories
28 g carbohydrate
26 g protein · 27 g fat

Herby Lamb Steaks

4 lamb leg steaks, about 1.5 cm/ ½ in thick
4 sprigs of fresh thyme
sprig of fresh rosemary
5 cloves garlic
5 tablespoons cold-pressed olive oil
750 g/1½ lb spinach beet (stalks with leaves)
1 shallot
1 large lemon
salt
freshly ground black pepper

Rub the lamb steaks on each side with a damp cloth to remove any splinters of bone.

Rinse the thyme and rosemary under cold running water and shake thoroughly dry. Strip the leaves from the stalks and coarsely chop on a board. Peel 2 cloves of garlic and either squeeze through a garlic press or chop to a pulp. Mix the garlic with the herbs and 2 tablespoons olive oil.

Brush the lamb steaks on both sides with the oil mixture, place one on top of the other and cover with foil or a bowl. Marinate in a cool place overnight or for 8 hours.

The following day, remove the coarse stalks from the spinach beet and separate the leaves. Wash the spinach beet well under cold running water, shake dry and cut into 1 cm/½ in pieces.

Peel the shallot and the remaining garlic and finely chop. Squeeze the juice from the lemon.

Heat 1 tablespoon oil in a frying pan and cook the shallot over a moderate to low heat until transparent. Add the garlic and stir until it begins to colour. Do not allow it to brown as this gives a bitter taste.

Add the spinach beet, pour on the remaining olive oil and the lemon juice and cook over a low heat for about 3 minutes until tender but still firm to bite. Season to taste and keep to one side. The spinach beet is served lukewarm.

Wipe the herbs and garlic off the lamb steaks with a cloth (they would burn during frying). Using a very sharp knife cut through the outer skin and fat at regular intervals to prevent the meat curling up as it cooks. Make sure you do not cut into the meat itself.

Heat a heavy frying pan without adding any fat. Fry the lamb steaks over a high heat, then over a moderate heat for about 5 minutes each side. You don't need any oil or fat in the pan as the lamb will have absorbed sufficient oil from the marinade. Do not turn the lamb when frying until a crust has formed on the underside, ie when it comes away easily from the pan.

Remove the fried lamb steaks to warmed plates and season to taste. Serve the spinach beet separately. You can also serve wheatgerm rolls or jacket-boiled potatoes and an uncooked vegetable salad.

Serves 4

Per Portion
about 460 calories
6 g carbohydrate
25 g protein · 35 g fat

Cook's Tip

Instead of spinach beet you can use dandelion leaves which are available in early summer.

Stuffed Shoulder of Lamb

1 (100 g/4 oz) piece celeriac
1 carrot
1 small leek
bunch of fresh parsley
3 sprigs of fresh thyme
50 g/2 oz each sesame and
  sunflower seeds
2 shallots
2 cloves garlic
4 tablespoons cold-pressed olive
  oil
1 kg/2¼ lb boned shoulder of
  lamb
salt
freshly ground black pepper
125 ml/4 fl oz dry white wine

Trim, peel and wash the celeriac and carrot. Cut the roots and about two thirds of the green leaves off the leek and then cut a cross in the leaves down to the white. Open the leaves and wash the leek to remove all the dirt. Cut the celeriac, carrot and leek into fairly large pieces.

Rinse the parsley under cold running water, strip the leaves from the stalks and pat dry. Keep a few stalks to go in the stock and finely chop the leaves for the stuffing. Wash the thyme, shake dry and strip off the leaves.

Crush the sesame seeds and coarsely chop the sunflower seeds. Peel the shallots and garlic and chop to a pulp. Stir the herbs, sesame seeds, sunflower seeds, shallots and garlic with 2 tablespoons olive oil to make a smooth spreadable paste.

Pat the shoulder of lamb dry with a cloth and place on the worktop with the fat side underneath. Remove as much fat as you can from the inside of the shoulder.

Mix salt with plenty of pepper in a small dish. Rub into the inside of the shoulder and spread with the herb paste. Starting at the long side, roll up the meat and tie into shape with cooking string. This keeps the meat in shape as it cooks and prevents the stuffing escaping. Season the outside of the joint

with pepper only and rub into the meat with the ball of your hand.

Heat the remaining oil in a large stewpan with a lid. Seal the lamb over a moderate to high heat to form a crust which will keep the meat moist as it cooks.

Add the celeriac, carrot, leek and parsley stalks and fry for a few minutes. Pour the white wine around the sides of the pan. The liquid will loosen the sediment from the bottom of the pan so that you can scrape it off with a wooden spatula. Cover the pan and braise the meat over a low heat for about 1 hour.

Remove the meat from the pan, wrap tightly in aluminium foil and leave in the warm place for about 10 minutes.

Meanwhile, strain the stock into a saucepan, pressing the vegetables and seasonings with a spatula to squeeze out the liquid. Discard the solids in the sieve. Skim any fat from the stock or soak it up with absorbent kitchen paper.

Unwrap the lamb, remove the string and, using a sharp knife, carve the meat into slices against the grain. Arrange the slices on a warmed plate and spoon on the stock, or serve the stock separately.

Serve with jacket-boiled potatoes or crispy wheatgerm rolls and salad.

Serves 6

Per Portion
about 590 calories
8 g carbohydrate
27 g protein · 44 g fat

Ways with Larger Cuts

Simmered Leg of Lamb with Vegetables

1 (2 kg/4½ lb) leg of lamb, boned
2.5 litres/4¼ pints cold water
1 leek
¼ celeriac
2 carrots
1 onion
2 cloves garlic
3 bunches of fresh parsley
2 sprigs of fresh thyme
3 black peppercorns
1 bay leaf
salt
300 g/11 oz each broccoli,
 courgettes and carrots
1 tablespoon wholemeal flour
freshly ground white pepper
125 ml/4 fl oz single cream
1 egg yolk
30 g/1¼ oz butter

Place the lamb bones in a large pan and pour on the water. Bring slowly to the boil and simmer gently for 30 minutes.
 Trim the lamb of fat and roll up with the skin to the outside. Tie neatly.
 Add the meat to the pan and simmer gently for a further 30 minutes. Make sure the stock does not bubble vigorously or it will be cloudy and the meat tough. Do not cover the pan completely.
 Trim, wash and coarsely chop the leek. Peel and coarsely chop the celeriac and carrots. Peel and halve the onion and garlic cloves. Rinse 1 bunch of parsley with the thyme in cold water.
 Add the herbs to the meat with the leek, celeriac, carrots, onion, garlic, peppercorns and bay leaf. Cook the lamb for a further 30 minutes. Season the stock to taste with salt.
 Meanwhile, trim and wash the broccoli and separate into florets. Wash and dry the courgettes, top and tail them and cut into sticks 5 cm/2 in long and 1 cm/½ in thick.
 Peel and wash the carrots and cut into similar sticks. Wash the remaining parsley, strip off the leaves, pat dry and finely chop.
 Transfer the lamb from the stock to a warmed serving plate and keep hot. Strain the stock through a sieve lined with muslin and discard all the solid ingredients. Measure scant 250 ml/8 fl oz stock for the sauce.
 Heat the flour in a saucepan until it gives off a slight aroma. Gradually whisk in the measured stock. (Whisking prevents the flour forming lumps.) Bring to the boil, still whisking until all the lumps of flour have dispersed. Simmer the sauce over a low heat for about 10 minutes.
 Bring the remaining stock to the boil and cook the broccoli and carrot for 5 minutes. Add the courgettes and cook for a further 3 minutes until all the vegetables are tender but still firm to bite.
 Stir the parsley into the sauce and season to taste with salt and pepper. Beat the cream with the egg yolk, add to the sauce and cook gently, stirring, until thickened. Do not allow to boil. Cut the butter into small pieces and whisk into the sauce.
 Carve the lamb into slices and arrange with the drained vegetables in a shallow dish. Spoon on a little of the stock used to cook the vegetables. Serve the sauce separately.
 Serve with jacket-boiled potatoes and freshly grated horseradish or creamed horseradish.

Serves 6

Per Portion
about 800 calories
10 g carbohydrate
55 g protein · 53 g fat

Mexican-style Breast of Lamb

$2\,kg/4\frac{1}{2}\,lb$ breast of lamb on the
  bone
freshly ground black pepper
$250\,g/9\,oz$ ripe tomatoes
2 tablespoons Worcestershire
  sauce
4 tablespoons honey
3 tablespoons olive oil
generous dash of red wine
  vinegar
1 tablespoon sweet paprika
Tabasco sauce or cayenne
  pepper
2 cloves garlic
1 tablespoon bottled green
  peppercorns

Cut the lamb's breast between
the bones into 6 large equal
pieces and wipe with a damp
cloth to remove any splinters of
bone. Rub all over with pepper.
    Blanch the tomatoes in boil-
ing water for 30 seconds, rinse
in cold water and peel. Dice the
tomatoes, removing the core
and the seeds. Tip the tomatoes
into a pan and stir over a high
heat until thick and smooth.
Remove the pan from the heat.
    Stir in the Worcestershire
sauce, honey and olive oil.
Season with the red wine vinegar, paprika and Tabasco
sauce or cayenne to taste to
make a sweet, fairly hot sauce.
    Peel the garlic and squeeze in
a garlic press. Crush the green
peppercorns with a fork. Add
both to the sauce.
    Place the breast of lamb
under a hot grill and cook for
25 to 30 minutes, turning frequently and brushing re-
peatedly with the sauce during
the last 10 minutes, until the
pieces are nice and brown.
Make sure that the meat does
not become too dark for the
honey and paprika in the sauce
burn easily.
    Serve with bread and salad.

Serves 6

Per Portion
about 910 calories
10 g carbohydrate
24 g protein · 81 g fat

Ways with Larger Cuts

Roast Leg of Lamb with Garlic

1 (2 kg/4½ lb) leg of lamb
5 cloves garlic
6 sprigs of fresh thyme or
  1 tablespoon dried thyme
2 tablespoons Dijon mustard
2 tablespoons olive oil
freshly ground black pepper
1 kg/2¼ lb potatoes
300 g/11 oz shallots or small
  onions
2 carrots
salt
250 ml/8 fl oz dry white wine

Wipe the lamb with a damp cloth to remove any splinters of bone.

Peel the garlic. Crush 2 cloves in a garlic press and cut the rest into thin sticks. (When the garlic is old the cloves produce green shoots. These should be removed as they give food an unpleasantly strong taste of garlic.)

Spike the leg of lamb with the sticks of garlic around the bone and between the separate sections of meat. To do this, free the meat carefully from the bone with the point of a knife and push in the garlic between meat and bone. Loosen the skin between the sections of meat and push in the garlic. Do not cut into the meat itself or you will lose the juice as the meat cooks.

Rinse the fresh thyme in cold water and shake thoroughly dry. Strip the leaves off the stalks. For dried thyme rub the leaves between finger and thumb.

Mix the crushed garlic with the thyme, mustard, olive oil and pepper to taste to make a paste. Spread over the leg of lamb, wrap in aluminium foil and marinate for 2 hours.

Peel, wash and dice the potatoes. Peel and halve or quarter the shallots or onions. Peel and wash the carrots and cut into fairly thick sticks. As the vegetables cook with the lamb you need fairly large pieces or they will cook too quickly.

Spread the potatoes, shallots and carrots over the bottom of a roasting tin and season with a little salt. Place the leg of lamb on the vegetables. Place the tin in a hot oven (220 C, 425 F, gas 7) and roast for 30 minutes.

Pour the white wine around the sides of the tin and roast for a further 60 minutes, turning the meat over halfway through. It is impossible to give a precise roasting time as this depends on your oven and how well done you like your meat. After 1½ hours the leg will still be pink inside. The only way to be sure is to use a meat thermometer which you stick into the meatiest part of the leg before it goes into the oven. The thermometer should not touch the bone as this conducts heat differently from the meat and the thermometer will not give a correct reading.

Wrap the lamb in aluminium foil and allow to stand for 15 minutes to allow the juice to settle. This will avoid you losing too much juice during carving.

Wrap a napkin or tea towel around the end of the bone. Place the lamb on a board, preferably one with a gully to catch the juice, hold the joint upright and carve with a sharp knife parallel to the bone. Arrange with the vegetables on warmed plates and serve at once.

Serves 6

Per Portion
about 905 calories
32 g carbohydrate
51 g protein · 51 g fat

Lamb Curry

500 g/18 oz boneless lamb
3 cloves garlic
300 ml/½ pint natural yogurt
3 tomatoes
piece of fresh root ginger, about
   2 cm/¾ in long
1 large onion
1 teaspoon each turmeric and
   cumin
½ teaspoon ground coriander
generous pinch of hot chilli
   powder
3 tablespoons vegetable oil
piece of cinnamon stick
2 cloves · 2 cardamom pods
salt · bunch of fresh parsley

Cut the lamb into 2.5-cm/1-in
cubes. Peel and finely chop the
garlic. Mix the lamb with the
garlic and yogurt, cover and
marinate for 2 hours.
   Blanch the tomatoes in boiling water for 30 seconds, rinse
in cold water and peel. Dice the
tomatoes, removing the seeds.
Peel the ginger and cut into thin
strips. Peel and finely chop the
onion.

In a bowl, mix together the
turmeric, cumin, coriander and
chilli powder.
   Heat the oil in a frying pan
and fry the cinnamon, cloves
and cardamoms for 1 minute,
stirring continuously. Add the
ginger and onion and fry until
the onion is transparent.
   Add the lamb and its
marinade and cook for about
10 minutes, stirring continuously. Stir in the tomatoes and
the turmeric mixture and
season to taste with salt. Cover
the pan and simmer the lamb
curry over a low heat for 1¼
hours.
   Chop the parsley and use to
garnish the curry.

Serves 4

Per Portion
about 390 calories
7 g carbohydrate
19 g protein · 28 g fat

Lamb Stew with Oranges

1 kg/2¼ lb boned shoulder of
   lamb
1 kg/2¼ lb small onions
4 juicy oranges
3–4 tablespoons olive oil
scant 1 tablespoon caster sugar
salt
freshly ground black pepper
piece of cinnamon stick
4 cloves
250 ml/8 fl oz dry white wine

Remove skin and gristle from
the lamb, pat dry and cut into
2.5 cm/1 in cubes. Peel the
onions. Wash and dry 1 orange
and thinly cut off half the rind;
set aside. Completely peel and
segment the orange, removing
all the white pith. Halve the
segments. Squeeze the remaining oranges and keep the juice
to one side for the stock.
   Heat 1 tablespoon of the
olive oil in a frying pan and seal
the lamb, in batches. As they
are sealed transfer them to a

sieve over a basin to catch the
juice, and add more oil to the
pan as necessary.
   Fry the onions in batches.
   Arrange the lamb and onions
in layers in a stewpan and top
with the pieces of orange. Add
the sugar, and season to taste
with salt and pepper. Add the
piece of orange rind, cinnamon
stick and cloves. Pour on the
orange juice and wine.
   Cover the pan and bring
slowly to the boil, then cook
over a low heat for about 1
hour. Remove the lid and simmer over a moderate heat for a
further 30 minutes to thicken
the sauce.

Serves 8

Per Portion
about 450 calories
16 g carbohydrate
18 g protein · 30 g fat

Full-flavoured Meat Dishes

Lamb with Tarragon

750 g/1½ lb boneless lamb from the leg
4 cloves garlic
3 sprigs of fresh tarragon
2 tablespoons olive oil
1 tablespoon butter
2 tablespoons dry white wine
salt
freshly ground black pepper

Cut any fat and gristle off the lamb and cut across the grain into even strips. Peel and finely chop the garlic. Wash the tarragon under cold running water, strip the leaves from the stalks, pat dry and coarsely chop.

Heat the olive oil in a frying pan. Fry the lamb, in small batches, stirring continuously, until it takes on a grey colour. Keep the batches small enough to allow the lamb to cook separately without the strips touching. This takes longer but keeps the meat beautifully tender. As each batch of lamb is cooked transfer it to a warmed plate, cover and keep hot.

When all the lamb is cooked, melt the butter in the frying pan without allowing it to brown. Add the garlic and tarragon leaves and stir over a low to moderate heat until the garlic is transparent. Add the white wine and stir in the sediment from the bottom of the pan.

Pour the tarragon sauce over the lamb. Season to taste and serve at once with wholemeal rolls and Spinach salad with pine nuts (recipe page 22).

Serves 4

Per Portion
about 405 calories
1 g carbohydrate
28 g protein · 29 g fat

Sesame Lamb Balls

125 g/4½ oz fresh spinach
½ bunch of fresh parsley
1 onion
2 cloves garlic
100 g/4 oz feta cheese
500 g/1¼ lb minced lamb
4 tablespoons sesame seeds
1 egg
herb salt
freshly ground black pepper
about 125 ml/4 fl oz sunflower oil

Pick over the spinach, remove any tough stalks and wash several times. Shake dry and finely chop. Wash the parsley, strip the leaves from the stalks, pat dry and finely chop. Peel the onion and garlic and chop to a pulp.

Crush the cheese with a fork until smooth or blend in a liquidiser.

Mix the minced lamb with the spinach, parsley, onion, garlic, cheese, sesame seeds and egg. Season to taste with herb salt and pepper. Using wet hands, shape the meat mixture into walnut-sized balls.

Heat the oil a little at a time in a frying pan and fry the meat balls in batches over a moderate heat for about 8 minutes.

Serve the balls very hot, garnished with lemon wedges and parsley, if liked. Serve with potatoes and/or Uncooked vegetable salad with plenty of fresh herbs.

Serves 6

Per Portion
about 450 calories
3 g carbohydrate
21 g protein · 32 g fat

Cook's Tip

In spring you can replace the spinach with young nettle or dandelion leaves.

83

Stuffed Peppers

750 ml/1¼ pints water
1–2 teaspoons instant vegetable
*   stock granules*
150 g/5 oz long-grain brown rice
1 kg/2¼ lb ripe tomatoes
6 green peppers of similar size
1 red pepper
1 large onion
4 cloves garlic
bunch each of fresh parsley and
*   basil*
few sprigs of fresh salad burnet
sprig of fresh rosemary
2 tablespoons olive oil
500 g/18 oz minced lamb
salt
freshly ground black pepper
pinch of cayenne pepper

Bring the water and vegetable stock granules to the boil in a saucepan and add the rice. Reduce the heat, cover the pan and cook the rice over a low heat for 30 minutes.

Meanwhile, blanch the tomatoes in boiling water for 30 seconds, rinse in cold water and peel. Halve the tomatoes so that you can remove the seeds with a teaspoon. Remove the core. Finely chop about one-third of the tomatoes, then purée the rest and keep in reserve for the sauce.

Wash and dry the peppers. Cut round the green peppers about 1 cm/½ in below the stalk to make a lid. Carefully twist off the lid. Most of the seeds should come out with it. Remove the white pith and rinse the peppers in cold water to remove any remaining seeds. Dry well inside and out.

Halve the red pepper lengthways and remove the stalk, pith and seeds. Rinse the halves, wipe dry and chop very finely. Peel and finely chop the onion and garlic.

Wash the parsley, basil, burnet and rosemary and shake dry. Strip the parsley and basil leaves from the stalks and finely chop with the burnet. Strip the rosemary leaves from the stalk.

Heat the olive oil in a frying pan. Fry the onion and garlic until transparent. Add the minced lamb and stir until it is crumbly in texture and grey in colour.

Mix the lamb with the rice, chopped tomato, red pepper, parsley, basil and burnet. Season with salt and pepper to taste and a generous pinch of cayenne.

Season the insides of the green peppers with salt and fill with the lamb stuffing. Replace the lids on top.

Pour the puréed tomato into a saucepan large enough to take all the stuffed peppers side by side. Stir the rosemary leaves into the tomato. Stand the stuffed peppers in the pan and cover.

Bring the tomato to the boil, then reduce the heat to low and cook the peppers for about 40 minutes.

Lift the peppers carefully out of the tomato sauce and arrange on a warmed plate. Season the sauce to taste and reduce slightly over a high heat. Pour the sauce over the peppers before serving.

Serves 6

Per Portion
about 440 calories
37 g carbohydrate
21 g protein · 20 g fat

Cook's Tip

For a creamier sauce stir in about 125 ml/4 fl oz crème fraîche after the peppers have cooked and stir until reduced.

Supper-party Specials

Chicken Breasts in Savoy Cabbage

8 chicken breasts
8 large Savoy cabbage leaves
salt
freshly ground white pepper
100 g/4 oz Parmesan cheese, grated
bunch of fresh parsley
250 ml/8 fl oz crème fraîche

Skin and bone the chicken breasts and wipe dry.

With a knife trim the thick stalks of the cabbage leaves to flatten them, without damaging the leaves. Wash the leaves and blanch in plenty of boiling salted water for 3 to 4 minutes to make them easier to roll up. Lift the leaves out of the pan on a slotted spoon and plunge into iced water so that they keep their fresh green colour.

Sprinkle the chicken breasts with pepper to taste and the Parmesan. Put the breasts together in pairs and wrap each pair in 2 cabbage leaves. Tie up with cooking string.

Wash the parsley, strip the leaves off the stalks, pat dry and finely chop. Mix the crème fraîche with the parsley and season to taste.

Place the cabbage parcels on a sheet of extra-strong aluminium foil and bend up the edges. Pour the crème fraîche mixture over the parcels and seal the foil together firmly at the top and sides.

Cook the chicken breasts in a moderately hot oven (200 C, 400 F, gas 6) for about 40 minutes.

Open the foil, lift the parcels carefully out of the sauce and remove the string. Arrange the chicken breasts on a warmed plate and serve topped with the sauce.

Serves 4

Per Portion
about 500 calories
5 g carbohydrate
68 g protein · 24 g fat

Chicken Rissoles

1 rye or wholemeal bread roll
300 g/11 oz chicken meat
1 onion
handful of fresh chervil or bunch of fresh parsley
75 g/3 oz shelled walnuts
1 egg
1 teaspoon grated lemon rind
salt
freshly ground white pepper
2 tablespoons sunflower oil

Soak the bread roll in lukewarm water, then squeeze out well and fluff up with a fork.

Remove any skin, fat or gristle from the chicken. Wipe dry and finely dice. On a board, finely chop the diced chicken using a large, heavy knife, forming it into a pile and chopping repeatedly.

Peel and finely chop the onion. Wash the chervil or parsley and shake dry. You can chop the chervil on the stalks but parsley leaves should be stripped from the stalks first.

Finely chop the walnuts.

Mix the chicken with the onion, chervil or parsley, walnuts, egg, bread and lemon rind. Season to taste. Using wet hands, shape the mixture into rissoles of similar size.

Heat the oil in a frying pan. Seal the rissoles on either side over a high heat, then reduce the heat to moderate and fry the rissoles for about 7 minutes longer.

Serve with wholemeal French bread and potato salad with herbs.

Serves 4

Per Portion
about 330 calories
31 g carbohydrate
21 g protein · 22 g fat

Stuffed Chicken

3 bunches of fresh parsley
2 cloves garlic
1 large lemon
1 tablespoon pine nuts
100 g/4 oz Emmental cheese, grated
100 g/4 oz low fat Quark or other soft cheese
3 tablespoons single cream
salt
freshly ground black pepper
1 chicken, about 1.4 kg/3 lb
1 tablespoon olive oil
1½ teaspoons ground ginger
3 tablespoons dry white wine

To make the stuffing, wash the parsley under cold running water. Strip the leaves from the stalks, wipe thoroughly dry and finely chop. Peel and finely chop the garlic. Wash the lemon well in hot water, wipe dry and grate the rind. Then halve the lemon and squeeze the juice. Keep the juice in reserve to brush over the chicken.

Mix together the parsley, garlic, lemon rind, pine nuts, Emmental, Quark and cream and season to taste.

Remove the giblets from the chicken, if any, and use for some other dish. Rinse the chicken well inside and out under cold running water, making sure you remove any bits of lung or blood from the inside for these have a bitter taste. Drain the chicken and wipe dry inside and out. Mix salt and pepper in a bowl. Sprinkle it over the chicken inside and out and rub into the skin.

Stuff the chicken with the cheese mixture, but do not overfill as the stuffing expands during cooking and could split the skin if too tightly packed. Close the opening with four wooden cocktail sticks, or skewers, threading them horizontally through the skin. Wind a piece of cooking string around the sticks like a shoelace and tie in a knot.

Mix the lemon juice with the olive oil and ginger. Brush the chicken all over with the oil mixture. Place the chicken breast uppermost in a roasting tin and pour 2 tablespoons cold water around it.

Place in a moderately hot oven (200 C, 400 F, gas 6) and roast for about 1 hour, turning once and basting repeatedly with the juices in the tin to make the skin brown and crisp.

Remove the chicken from the oven, transfer to a roasting rack and return to the oven with the roasting tin beneath to catch the juices. Brown the chicken on the rack for a further 15 minutes.

To make the sauce, soak up the fat from the top of the cooking juices with absorbent kitchen paper. Add the white wine and stir over a low heat to work in the sediment from the bottom of the tin.

Remove the string and sticks from the chicken. Carve either in the kitchen or at the table, as preferred. Arrange the chicken on a warmed plate and serve with the stuffing and gravy. Serve with mixed salad and wholemeal French bread or brown rice.

Serves 4

Per Portion
about 595 calories
6 g carbohydrate
65 g protein · 30 g fat

Cook's Tip

For a different stuffing, halve the amount of Quark and add 1 large fairly tart apple, peeled, cored and finely diced, and a generous pinch of dried marjoram.

Chicken with Sage

1 young chicken, about 1 kg/
*   2¼ lb*
salt
freshly ground white pepper
1 lemon
2 cloves garlic
2 sprigs of fresh sage
1 tablespoon butter
1 tablespoon olive oil

Remove the giblets, if any. Wash the chicken well and remove any bits of lung or blood from the inside. Wipe thoroughly dry. Mix salt and pepper on a saucer, sprinkle over the chicken inside and out and rub into the skin.

Wash the lemon in hot water and wipe dry. Grate the rind and keep in reserve. Halve the lemon and squeeze the juice from one half. Peel the remaining half and dice the flesh. Peel and finely chop the garlic.

Wash the sage, shake dry, strip the leaves off the stalks and mix with the chopped lemon and garlic. Use to stuff the chicken. Close the opening as described in the recipe on the opposite page.

Melt the butter over a low heat and mix with the olive oil and lemon rind. Brush the chicken with half the seasoned butter and place breast uppermost in a roasting tin. Place the tin in a moderately hot oven (200 C, 400 F, gas 6), on the second shelf from the bottom. Roast for about 1 hour, turning once and basting with the remaining seasoned butter.

Transfer the chicken to a roasting rack, replace in the tin, brush with the lemon juice and roast for a further 15 minutes.

Serve with mixed salad.

Serves 2

Per Portion
about 645 calories
2 g carbohydrate
76 g protein · 33 g fat

Duck with Spring Onions

1 (1.5–2 kg/3–4½ lb) oven-
  ready duckling
salt
freshly ground black pepper
5 sprigs of fresh parsley
125 ml/4 fl oz hot water
2 bunches of spring onions
125 ml/4 fl oz stout

Wash the duck inside and out under cold running water, removing any bits of lung or blood from the inside. Drain the duck and then wipe dry inside and out. Mix salt and pepper in a saucer and rub into the duck inside and out.

Rinse the parsley in cold water, shake dry and place in the cavity in the duck. Place the duck, breast down, in a roasting tin. Place in a moderately hot oven (200 C, 400 F, gas 6) and roast for 35 minutes.

Turn the duck so that it lies in the tin with legs uppermost. Prick the skin below the legs with a skewer several times so that the fat can drain away from the fatty layer beneath the skin. Make sure that you do not prick the meat itself or it will become dry. Pour the hot water around the duck.

Roast the duck for a further 35 minutes, skimming off the fat that collects in the tin and basting the duck with the juices about every 10 minutes. This will remove almost all the fat from the duck and make the skin nice and crisp.

Cut the roots off the spring onions. Wash the onions well under cold running water and shake dry. Remove any limp leaves. Place the whole onions alongside the duck and season lightly.

Roast the duck for a further 30 minutes, brushing with the stout and juices every 10 minutes. Remember to remove as much fat from the juices as you can at the same time.

Transfer the duck to a roasting rack and return to the oven over the roasting tin to catch the juices. Roast for a further 10 minutes, brushing frequently with the stout to make the skin brown and crisp.

Remove the spring onions from the roasting tin, arrange on a warmed plate and keep hot. Skim the cooking juices thoroughly. Carve the duck or serve whole. Arrange on a warmed serving platter with the spring onions. Serve the juices separately.

Serve with wheatgerm rolls and mixed salad. Of course you can also serve potatoes with duck, but always accompany it with something fresh such as salad or uncooked vegetables.

Serves 4

Per Portion
about 705 calories
4 g carbohydrate
59 g protein · 43 g fat

Cook's Tip

If you would prefer to serve the duck jointed instead of having to carve the bird at the table, then it is a good idea to cut it into joints before cooking. Use a heavy cook's knife or meat cleaver and a pair of kitchen scissors. Split the duck in half down the middle, from head to tail, then use the scissor to cut each half into two portions. Make the cuts between the joints, leaving an equal amount of meat on each portion. Use the knife or cleaver to break the bones. You may have to tap the top of the knife very firmly with a wooden mallet or rolling pin to break the bones cleanly. Remove any small pieces of bone before cooking the joints.

Braised Chicken with Vegetables

1 (200 g/7 oz) leek
1 (250 g/9 oz) fennel bulb
3 sticks celery
200 g/7 oz carrots
bunch of fresh parsley
1 young chicken, about 1.6 kg/
    3½ lb
salt
freshly ground white pepper
25 g/1 oz butter
250 ml/8 fl oz dry white wine
1 bay leaf

Cut the roots and limp green leaves off the leek. Cut a cross into the leaves down as far as the white so that you can open the leaves and wash to remove all the dirt. Cut the leek into 2 cm/¾ in lengths.

Halve the fennel and cut out the wedge-shaped stalk with a sharp knife. Wash and dry the fennel and cut across into 1 cm/½ in slices. Peel off any tough threads from the celery, wash and cut into 1 cm/½ in lengths.

Peel and wash the carrots and cut into sticks or cubes. Wash the parsley and shake dry. Remove the stalks and finely chop them, keeping the leaves in reserve to sprinkle over the chicken later.

Remove the giblets from the chicken, if any, and use in another dish. Wash the chicken well inside and out under cold running water and remove any bits of lung or blood from the inside. Wipe dry. Place the chicken, breast uppermost, on a wooden board and with a large, heavy knife joint into the drumsticks, thighs, wings and breasts. You can use the backbone which has little meat to make a stock. Rub the chicken pieces all over with salt and pepper.

Heat the butter in a large pan without allowing it to brown. Seal the drumsticks, thighs and wings over a moderate heat for about 10 minutes until the skin is nice and brown. Add the breasts and brown for 5 minutes. Remove the chicken from the pan.

Add the vegetables and stir until coated in fat. Add the wine and stir in the sediment from the bottom of the pan.

Arrange the chicken pieces over the vegetables, add the bay leaf and cover the pan. Braise the chicken and vegetables over a low heat for about 30 minutes. Test both a leg and a breast by pricking with the point of a knife to check if they are cooked. If the juice runs clear the chicken is cooked.

Coarsely chop the parsley. Arrange the braised chicken and vegetables on a warmed plate, spoon on the cooking liquid and serve sprinkled with the parsley. Serve with rice, wheatgerm rolls or wholemeal French bread and Sprouted salad (recipe page 26).

Serves 4

Per Portion
about 580 calories
13 g carbohydrate
62 g protein · 25 g fat

Cook's Tip
This recipe is just as good made with lamb leg steaks instead of chicken. The meat is sealed for about 5 minutes on each side and then braised over the vegetables with a little garlic and the grated rind and juice of ¼ lemon.

89

Chicken and Duck

Chicken with Apricots

250 ml/9 oz dried apricots
250 ml/8 fl oz dry white wine
1 young chicken, about 1.3 kg/
   2¾ lb
salt
freshly ground black pepper
2 onions
2 cloves garlic
1 tablespoon vegetable oil
sprig of fresh rosemary

Wash the apricots well in hot
water, drain and soak in the
white wine in a covered bowl
for about 5 minutes.
   Cut the chicken into 8 pieces.
Rinse in cold water and dry.
Rub all over with salt and
pepper.
   Peel and finely chop the
onions and garlic.
   Heat the oil in a shallow
flameproof casserole. Brown
the chicken in batches over a
moderate to high heat and
transfer each batch to a plate as
it is done. When you have
browned all the chicken, pour
off the fat to leave only a thin
film on the base of the casserole. Add the onion and garlic
and fry for a few minutes, stirring continuously.
   Drain the apricots, reserving
the soaking wine. Pour the wine
into the casserole and stir in the
sediment from the bottom.
   Return the chicken to the
casserole with the juice that has
collected on the plate.
   Wash the rosemary, strip the
leaves from the stalk and add to
the chicken. Cover the casserole
and braise in a moderately hot
oven (200 C, 400 F, gas 6) for
about 30 minutes.
   Add the drained apricots and
cook for a further 20 to 25 minutes, uncovered, to brown the
chicken.
   Serve with brown rice.

Serves 4

Per Portion
about 620 calories
49 g carbohydrate
52 g protein · 17 g fat

Chicken and Duck

Exotic Chicken

1 young chicken, about 1.25 kg/
  2½ lb
salt
1 onion
5 cloves garlic
2 tomatoes
3 tablespoons vegetable oil
4 tablespoons water
5 tablespoons soy sauce
1 tablespoon honey
2 tablespoons lemon juice
cayenne pepper

Joint the chicken, rinse, wipe dry and rub with salt.

Peel and finely chop the onion and garlic. Blanch the tomatoes in boiling water for 30 seconds, rinse in cold water, then peel and quarter. Remove the core and the seeds.

Heat the oil in a shallow flameproof casserole. Brown the chicken joints in batches over a moderate to high heat, placing each batch on a plate as it is done. When you have browned all the chicken pour off the fat to leave only a thin film.

Fry the onion and garlic for a few minutes in the fat over a moderate heat. Add the water and stir in the sediment from the bottom of the casserole.

Return the chicken to the casserole. Add the tomatoes. Cover and place in a moderate oven (180 C, 350 F, gas 4). Cook the chicken for about 45 minutes.

Stir the soy sauce, honey and lemon juice together in a saucepan to warm them until the honey is fluid. Season to taste with cayenne and pour over the chicken. Cook for a further 30 minutes, turning the chicken frequently and basting with the sauce.

Serves 4

Per Portion
about 455 calories
14 g carbohydrate
48 g protein · 20 g fat

Chinese-style Chicken

4 chicken breasts
2 tablespoons dry sherry
2 tablespoons soy sauce
1 clove garlic
3 sticks celery
200 g / 7 oz mushrooms
1–2 bunches of fresh basil
1 tablespoon vegetable oil
3 tablespoons chopped walnuts
gomasio

Skin and bone the chicken breasts. Cut the meat across the grain into thin strips. Pour the sherry and soy sauce over the chicken and leave to marinate for 15 minutes, stirring occasionally.

Peel and finely chop the garlic. Wash and dry the celery. Pull off any tough threads and cut across into thin slices. Trim the mushrooms, rinse under cold running water and thinly slice. Wash the basil, strip the leaves from the stalks, pat dry and cut into strips.

Take the chicken out of the marinade, drain and pat dry. Reserve the marinade.

Heat the oil in a wok or frying pan and fry the garlic over a moderate heat until transparent. Add the strips of chicken and stir-fry for about 2 minutes. Remove the meat from the pan and keep to one side.

Add the celery and mushrooms to the fat and stir-fry for about 2 minutes. Pour on the sherry marinade and cook the vegetables over a low heat for a further 4 minutes.

Return the chicken to the pan and stir to heat through. Stir in the basil and walnuts. Sprinkle with gomasio to taste and serve at once with brown rice.

Serves 4

Per Portion
about 240 calories
8 g carbohydrate
24 g protein · 10 g fat

Aubergines with soya milk and the burning hot, wonderfully flavoursome spices of Indian cooking is just one of the many dishes in this chapter. Spoil yourself with these wonderful treats made with vegetables and cereals, pulses and tofu. Even non-vegetarians will enjoy the rye rissoles which taste just as good as hamburgers, the wholesome herby cheese Spätzle or asparagus with elegant Béarnaise sauce. Wholemeal pasta with roasted sesame seeds, wheat baked with fresh vegetables, and Tofu balls in caper sauce provide everything one needs for a healthy diet. If you want to find out how delicious pulses can be try the black beans with sun-ripened tomatoes and crispy garlic croûtons or lentils in a creamy chive sauce. There are unusual dishes like bulgur and buckwheat au gratin or cashew nut curry to provide special culinary delights.

Vegetarian Main Courses and Side Dishes

Cabbage Rolls with Buckwheat

4 tablespoons vegetable oil
100 g/4 oz buckwheat grain
500 ml/17 fl oz freshly made
  vegetable stock (recipe
  page 38)
salt
1 (1 kg/2¼ lb) white cabbage
600 g/1¼ lb tomatoes
1 onion
bunch of fresh chives
bunch of fresh parsley
150 g/5 oz tofu
1 tablespoon soy sauce
1 tablespoon dried oregano
1 egg
freshly ground black pepper
125–250 ml/4–8 fl oz crème
  fraîche or double cream

Heat 1 tablespoon oil in a saucepan and fry the buckwheat, stirring continuously. Add about one-third of the vegetable stock and bring to the boil, then tightly cover the pan and simmer over a low heat for 15 minutes. Remove from the

heat and leave the buckwheat to swell for 15 minutes in the covered pan.

Meanwhile, bring a large pan of salted water to the boil. Trim the cabbage, remove any limp outer leaves and cut out as much of the stalk as you can. Drop the cabbage into the fast-boiling water and boil for 5 to 6 minutes until the outer leaves are soft enough to be peeled off and rolled up. Take the cabbage out of the pan and remove 12 outside leaves.

Return the head of cabbage to the boiling water and cook for a further 5 minutes. Drain.

Trim the thick ribs of the loose cabbage leaves to make them flat. Spread the 6 largest leaves side by side on the worktop and cover with the smaller leaves. If you prefer a thinner covering of cabbage use all 12 leaves separately.

Blanch the tomatoes in boiling water for 30 seconds, rinse in cold water, peel and chop, removing the core and seeds as you go.

Halve the head of cabbage

and cut out all the stalk. Cut first into strips and then into small pieces.

Peel and finely chop the onion. Wash the chives and parsley and shake dry. Cut up the chives. Strip the parsley leaves from the stalks and chop half of them for the filling. Keep the remaining leaves in reserve.

Drain the tofu, crush with a fork and mix with the soy sauce. Mix the buckwheat with the chopped cabbage, about one-third of the chopped tomato, the onion, chives, parsley, crushed tofu, the oregano and egg. Season generously with salt and pepper.

Spread the buckwheat filling on the cabbage leaves. Fold over the sides, roll up and secure with string.

Heat the remaining oil in a shallow pan and fry the cabbage rolls on a moderate heat until golden on all sides. Add the remaining vegetable stock and tomatoes. Cover the pan and cook over a low heat for about 30 minutes.

Arrange the rolls in a

warmed shallow dish and keep hot. Stir the crème fraîche into the cooking sauce and boil to reduce over a high heat until thick.

Finely chop the remaining parsley. Pour the sauce over the cabbage rolls, sprinkle with the parsley and serve at once, with jacket-boiled potatoes.

Serves 6

Per Portion
about 285 calories
24 g carbohydrate
10 g protein · 17 g fat

Light Main Dishes

Stuffed Vine Leaves

*about 350 ml/12 fl oz freshly
 made vegetable stock (recipe
 page 38)*
100 g/4 oz long-grain brown rice
20–25 vine leaves, in brine
3 bunches of fresh dill
30 g/1¼ oz sunflower seeds
freshly ground white pepper
salt (optional)
250 ml/8 fl oz crème fraîche
250 ml/8 fl oz double cream
½ lemon

Bring the stock to the boil in a
saucepan, add the rice and
cover the pan. Cook over the
lowest possible heat for about
40 minutes until tender.

Meanwhile, rinse the vine
leaves in cold water to remove
excess salt. (Vine leaves in oil
are not as good for this dish.)
Drain the vine leaves well.

Wash the dill, shake dry and
finely chop.

Mix the rice with half the dill
and the sunflower seeds and
season to taste with pepper and
salt, if liked.

Spread the vine leaves out on
the worktop and place 1 heaped
teaspoon of the rice mixture on
each. Fold in the sides of the
leaves and roll up carefully into
small packets. You need to proceed very carefully for the
leaves tear easily. If any leaves
do tear you can chop them and
use them in the sauce.

Boil the crème fraîche and
cream over a moderate to high
heat until reduced to about
one-third the original volume.

Heat the stuffed vine leaves
in the cream mixture over a
moderate to low heat.

Stir the remaining chopped
dill and any chopped vine
leaves into the sauce. Squeeze
the juice from the lemon and
add to the sauce. Serve hot with
wheatgerm rolls and salad.

Serves 4

Per Portion
about 530 calories
24 g carbohydrate
7 g protein · 45 g fat

Aubergines in Soya Milk

400 g/14 oz aubergines
salt
300 g/11 oz ripe tomatoes
1 green pepper
1 large onion
2 cloves garlic
piece of fresh root ginger
125 ml/4 fl oz sunflower oil
1 tablespoon lemon juice
½ teaspoon turmeric
1 teaspoon mustard seeds
7 tablespoons soya milk
pinch of caster sugar

Wash, dry and top and tail the aubergines. Cut lengthways into slices 1 cm/½ in thick. Sprinkle with salt and leave to sweat.

Blanch the tomatoes in boiling water for 30 seconds, rinse in cold water and peel. Slice the tomatoes downwards into 1 cm/½ in slices, removing the core and seeds.

Remove the stalk from the pepper, cut in half and remove all the white pith and the seeds. Rinse the pepper halves in cold running water to get rid of all the seeds, then wipe thoroughly dry and cut into very thin strips.

Peel and finely chop the onion and garlic. Peel the ginger and thinly slice it.

Dab off the moisture which has formed on the aubergines to prevent the oil spitting too much when you fry them.

Heat about 2 tablespoons oil in a frying pan. Brown the aubergines on both sides, in batches, over a high to moderate heat. You will need to keep adding oil and this should be spooned in at the side of the pan so that it heats before reaching the aubergines.

As the aubergines are browned remove them from the pan and drain on a thick layer of absorbent kitchen paper. When all the aubergines are browned, remove the pan from the heat to cool slightly otherwise the garlic will burn and taste bitter.

Pour the remaining oil into the pan and fry the green pepper, onion, garlic and ginger over a low to moderate heat until the onion and garlic are transparent, stirring continuously.

Fill the pan with layers of aubergine and tomato. Sprinkle with the lemon juice and season with a little salt, the turmeric and mustard seeds. Pour the soya milk around the sides of the pan. Cover and cook over a low heat for about 10 minutes.

Sprinkle with the sugar and serve at once, with brown rice or flat breadcakes (recipe page 19).

You can serve the aubergines as a vegetarian main course or as part of an Indonesian rice table.

Serves 4

Per Portion
about 360 calories
13 g carbohydrate
4 g protein · 29 g fat

Cook's Tip
Soya milk is made from yellow soya beans. It is a pure vegetable product and rich in valuable protein. You can buy it in healthfood shops.

The reason for salting aubergines before cooking them is to remove any bitter juices which they may contain.

Sweet and Sour Vegetables

*225 g/8 oz each broccoli, cauli-
    flower, green beans and
    carrots*
1 fairly tart apple
1 orange · 1 banana
1 onion
1 clove garlic
2 tablespoons vegetable oil
*250 ml/8 fl oz freshly made vege-
    table stock (recipe page 38)*
bunch of fresh parsley
freshly ground white pepper
1–2 tablespoons cider vinegar
gomasio for sprinkling

Trim and wash all the vegetables. Separate the broccoli and
cauliflower into florets, top and
tail the beans; peel the carrots
and cut into sticks.

Peel and core the apple and
cut into wedges. Peel the
orange, removing all the white
pith, then separate into segments. Peel and slice the banana. Peel and finely chop the
onion and garlic.

Heat the oil in a saucepan.
Fry the onion and garlic, until
transparent. Add the vegetables
and stir well. Add the vegetable
stock and bring to the boil. Reduce the heat, cover and simmer for about 5 minutes.

Stir in the fruit and cook
over a low heat for a further 5
to 7 minutes.

Meanwhile, wash the parsley,
strip the leaves from the stalks,
pat dry and coarsely chop.
Season the sweet and sour vegetables to taste with pepper and
cider vinegar. Stir in part of the
parsley. Serve sprinkled with
the remaining parsley.

Serve the gomasio separately.

Serves 4

Per Portion
about 200 calories
26 g carbohydrate
6 g protein · 6 g fat

Vegetables with Soy Sauce and Sesame

*750 g/1½ lb vegetables (carrots,
    kohlrabi, fennel, celery and
    spring onions)*
*piece of fresh root ginger, about
    2 cm/¾ in long*
1 clove garlic
200 g/7 oz mung bean sprouts
2 tablespoons sunflower oil
*7 tablespoons freshly made vege-
    table stock (recipe page 38)*
1 tablespoon dry sherry
*3 tablespoons soy sauce
sambal oelek*
4 tablespoons sesame seeds

Peel or trim the vegetables and
then wash them. Cut the carrots
and kohlrabi into sticks. Halve
the fennel, cut out the wedge-
shaped stalk and then cut
across the grain into thin slices.
Cut off the celery leaves and
keep in reserve. Cut the celery
and spring onions into 1-cm/
½-in lengths.

Peel the ginger and garlic.
Thinly slice the ginger; chop the
garlic.

Tip the bean sprouts into a
sieve and rinse in cold water.

Heat the oil in a frying pan.
Fry the ginger and garlic over a
moderate heat until the garlic is
transparent. Add the vegetables
and stir until completely coated
in oil. Add the vegetable stock,
sherry and soy sauce and bring
to the boil. Reduce the heat,
cover the pan and cook over a
low heat for 3 to 4 minutes.

Season to taste with sambal
oelek and stir in the sesame
seeds. Scatter with the reserved
celery leaves and serve at once.

Serves 4

Per Portion
about 180 calories
15 g carbohydrate
7 g protein · 8 g fat

97

Light Main Dishes

Light Main Dishes

Vegetarian Main Courses and Side Dishes

Dried Winter Vegetables

100 g/4 oz dried vegetables (carrots and/or leeks)
1 onion or 2 shallots
1 tablespoon butter
herb salt
freshly ground white pepper
200 ml/7 fl oz double cream
bunch of fresh parsley or dill, or handful of fresh chervil

Tip the vegetables into a bowl, cover with lukewarm water and soak for 4 hours.

Drain the soaked vegetables (which now weigh around 300 g/11 oz) very thoroughly. You can use the soaking water in a soup, although carrot water is very sweet and will need to be highly seasoned.

Peel and finely chop the onion or shallots. Melt the butter in a saucepan without allowing it to brown. Fry the onion or shallot until transparent, stirring frequently.

Add the soaked vegetables and stir until completely coated in fat. Season to taste with herb salt and pepper. Add the cream. Bring to the boil, then cover the pan and cook over a low heat for 10 to 15 minutes.

Meanwhile, wash the herbs, shake dry and finely chop. If using parsley, it should be stirred in a few minutes before the end of the cooking time. Chervil and dill should be sprinkled on at the end for they lose some of their flavour if cooked.

Serve with fried meat or with rice and salad for a vegetarian main course, in which case you should increase the amount of cream.

Serves 4

Per Portion
about 225 calories
10 g carbohydrate
2 g protein · 20 g fat

98

Vegetable Rissoles with Tofu

350 g/12 oz celeriac
200 g/7 oz carrots
200 g/7 oz leeks
1 onion
2 cloves garlic
bunch of fresh parsley
100 g/4 oz tofu
2 eggs
5 tablespoons wholemeal
* breadcrumbs*
salt
freshly ground white pepper
about 6 tablespoons vegetable oil
* for frying*

Peel the celeriac and carrots and wash under cold running water. Dry them and then finely grate. Trim the leek, cut a cross down through the green leaves to the white part and wash. Cut across the leek into thin slices including about two thirds of the green leaves. Place the prepared vegetables in a tea towel and squeeze well.

Peel and finely chop the on-ion and garlic. Wash the pars-ley, strip the leaves from the stalks, pat dry and finely chop. Drain and dice the tofu or crush with a fork.

Place all the prepared ingre-dients in a bowl and mix with the eggs and breadcrumbs to make a firm, smooth and mal-leable mixture. Season to taste, cover and leave to stand for 10 minutes.

With moist hands shape the mixture into rissoles. Heat about half the oil in a frying pan. Fry the vegetable rissoles over a high to moderate heat for about 10 minutes, turning once. Add a little more oil to the side of the pan as and when necessary.

Serve hot, with mixed salad with sunflower seeds.

Serves 4

Per Portion
about 295 calories
16 g carbohydrate
8 g protein · 20 g fat

Vegetable Omelette

200 g/7 oz courgettes
salt
1 clove garlic
2 sprigs of fresh thyme or
* 5 leaves fresh sage*
250 g/9 oz potatoes
4 eggs
1 tablespoon wholemeal flour
75 g/3 oz Parmesan cheese,
* grated*
freshly ground white pepper
1 tablespoon vegetable oil
25 g/1 oz butter

Wash, dry, top and tail the courgettes. Grate them, place in a bowl and sprinkle with salt to get rid of excess moisture. Leave to sweat for about 30 minutes.

Peel and finely chop the gar-lic. Rinse the thyme in cold water, strip off the leaves and pat dry. If you use sage, wash and dry the leaves and cut into fine strips.

Peel, wash and grate the po-tatoes. Place the grated pota-toes and courgettes in a tea towel and squeeze well.

Beat the eggs with a fork. Stir the courgettes, potatoes, garlic, herbs, flour and cheese into the egg and season to taste.

Divide the oil and butter be-tween two heavy frying pans and heat. Pour the egg mixture into the pans, cover and cook over a low to moderate heat for 10 minutes, until set. When the omelettes are brown under-neath, turn them and fry on the other side for about 5 minutes.

Serves 2

Per Portion
about 570 calories
29 g carbohydrate
29 g protein · 37 g fat

Stuffed Vegetables

Tomatoes Stuffed with Wheat

350 ml/12 fl oz water
200 g/7 oz whole wheat grains
    (wheat berries)
8 large, firm tomatoes (about
    2 kg/4½ lb)
1 onion
3 cloves garlic
bunch of fresh parsley
2 sprigs of fresh thyme
½ tablespoon butter
salt
freshly ground black pepper
200 g/7 oz Emmental or Gruyère
    cheese
pinch of caster sugar
150 g/5 oz mozzarella cheese

Bring the water to the boil in a saucepan, add the wheat, cover and cook over a low heat for 1 hour. Remove from the heat and leave to soak, covered, for 1 further hour.

Meanwhile, wash and dry the tomatoes. Cut a lid from each tomato and cut out the core with a sharp knife. Remove the insides of the tomatoes with a teaspoon, trying to get rid of all the seeds. Finely chop the flesh you have removed and the lids and place in a sieve lined with muslin to drain.

Peel and finely chop the onion and garlic. Rinse the parsley and thyme in cold water. Strip the parsley leaves from the stalks, pat dry, finely chop and keep for the filling. Strip the thyme leaves from the stems and dry.

Drain the soaked wheat.

Melt the butter in a frying pan over a moderate heat until slightly frothy but not brown. Fry the onion and garlic until transparent. Add the thyme and fry for a few minutes: the hot fat will bring out its full flavour. Add the wheat and stir in well.

Add half the chopped tomato and cook over a high heat until the liquid has completely evaporated. Remove the pan from the heat and season to taste. Leave to cool slightly.

Meanwhile, finely dice the Emmental or Gruyère cheese.

Stir the diced cheese and chopped parsley into the wheat mixture.

Lightly salt the inside of the tomatoes and fill with the wheat mixture.

Season the remaining chopped tomato with the sugar and salt and pepper to taste and tip into a baking dish large enough to take all the tomatoes side by side. Place the filled tomatoes in the dish.

Drain and thinly slice the mozzarella and place on top of the tomatoes. Place the dish in a hot oven (220 C, 425 F, gas 7), on the second shelf from the bottom, and bake the stuffed tomatoes for 15 to 20 minutes, or until the mozzarella is melted and slightly browned. Serve with fresh rye or wholemeal bread.

Serves 4

Per Portion
about 610 calories
50 g carbohydrate
34 g protein · 30 g fat

Cook's Tip

Whole wheat grain takes quite a long time to prepare. To save time you can use a pressure cooker. If you often serve cooked wheat it is worth boiling and soaking double the quantity. In a container with a tight lid, cooked wheat will keep in the fridge for up to 1 week.

Stuffed Vegetables

Stuffed Onions

300 g/11 oz floury potatoes
1 litre/1¾ pints freshly made vegetable stock (recipe page 38)
8–10 equal sized onions
1 clove garlic
150 g/5 oz hard cheese (Emmental, Gruyère or mature Gouda)
¼ bunch each of fresh parsley, dill and chives
handful of fresh chervil
sprig of fresh thyme
few leaves fresh marjoram
salt
freshly ground white pepper
freshly grated nutmeg
30 g/1¼ oz butter

Wash the potatoes and cook in a little boiling water, in the skins, until very soft. This will take 30 to 40 minutes depending on size.

Bring the vegetable stock to the boil in a saucepan. Trim and peel the onions and add to the fast-boiling stock. Return to the boil, then reduce the heat and cook for 12 to 15 minutes until the onions are soft enough for you to remove the inside.

Lift the onions out of the pan on a slotted spoon, drain and leave to cool. Keep the stock to use in some other dish such as soup.

Cut off the top quarter of each onion and gently squeeze out the centres. Do not damage the two or three outer layers of the onion; set these onion shells aside. Finely chop the onion from the insides and the lids.

Drain the potatoes, evaporate some of the steam and peel. Mash the potatoes. Mix the chopped onion with the mashed potato.

Peel and finely chop the garlic. Grate the cheese. Wash and dry the herbs. Finely chop the parsley and dill and finely snip the chives. Pick over and finely chop the chervil. Strip the thyme leaves from the stalks. Chop the marjoram.

Mix the garlic, cheese and herbs into the onion and potato mixture. Season to taste with salt, pepper and nutmeg.

Grease an ovenproof dish large enough to take all the onions side by side with a little of the butter. Season the inside of the onions and place in the dish. Fill with the stuffing. Cut the remaining butter into flakes and dot over the onions.

Place the dish in a hot oven (220 C, 425 F, gas 7), on the second shelf from the bottom, and bake the onions for 20 minutes. Reduce the temperature to moderate (180 C, 350 F, gas 4) and bake for a further 15 minutes.

Serve with Bean salad with tomato vinaigrette (recipe page 23) or another fresh salad.

Serves 4

Per Portion
about 340 calories
29 g carbohydrate
14 g protein · 18 g fat

Cook's Tip

For the best flavour, use Spanish onions for this dish. You will only need 4 of these. You may have some filling left over depending on the size of the onions. This can either be spread in the bottom of the dish and topped with onions, or you can make it into small burgers to be fried on both sides in oil and served with the onions.

Vegetable Side Dishes

Courgette Vegetable Dish

500 g/18 oz small young
  courgettes
300 g/11 oz potatoes
1 onion
2 cloves garlic
3 tablespoons vegetable oil
3 tablespoons vegetable stock,
  preferably freshly made
  (recipe page 38)
¼ lemon
2 carrots
pinch of caster sugar
salt
freshly ground black pepper
1 tablespoon chopped fresh
  parsley

Wash and trim the courgettes.
Cut lengthways into thick slices
and then into large cubes. Peel,
wash and dry the potatoes. Cut
into small cubes (they take
longer to cook than the
courgettes). Peel and finely
chop the onion and garlic.

Heat 2 tablespoons oil in a
frying pan and fry the potato
over a moderate heat for about
5 minutes, stirring continuously. Add the onion and garlic
and fry until transparent. Add
the courgette and fry until
lightly browned all over.

Add the stock, reduce the
heat, cover the pan and cook
over a low heat for 5 to 7
minutes.

Meanwhile, squeeze the juice
from the lemon. Peel the carrots, rinse in cold running
water, dry and coarsely grate.
Sprinkle at once with the lemon
juice and season with the sugar,
and salt and pepper to taste.
Stir in the remaining oil.

Season the courgette mixture
to taste. Stir in the grated carrots and serve at once,
sprinkled with the parsley. This
is delicious with lamb chops or
just with rice if you prefer a
vegetarian dish.

Serves 4

Per Portion
about 180 calories
22 g carbohydrate
4 g protein · 7 g fat

Kohlrabi with Walnuts

750 g/1½ lb young, tender
  kohlrabi
2 shallots
1 tablespoon vegetable oil
herb salt
freshly ground white pepper
freshly grated nutmeg
125 ml/4 fl oz double cream
50 g/2 oz fresh chervil
4 tablespoons coarsely chopped
  walnuts

Trim the kohlrabi, cutting off
the feathery leaves and keeping
in reserve to sprinkle over the
vegetables later. Peel the kohlrabi, cut out any tough parts,
wash and halve. Cut the halves
first into 1 cm/½ in slices and
then into sticks. Peel and finely
chop the shallots.

Heat the oil in a frying pan
and fry the shallots over a moderate heat until transparent,
stirring continuously. Add the
kohlrabi and stir until completely coated in oil.

Season with herb salt, pepper
and nutmeg to taste. Add the
cream, reduce the heat, cover
the pan and cook over low heat
for 5 to 8 minutes until the
kohlrabi is tender but still firm
to bite.

Meanwhile, pick over and
wash the chervil, shake dry and
coarsely chop. Rinse the kohlrabi leaves, pat dry and finely
chop.

Stir the chervil into the
cooked vegetables. Transfer to
a warmed dish and serve
sprinkled with the kohlrabi
leaves and walnuts. Serve with
grilled lamb chops.

Kohlrabi with walnuts also
makes an excellent vegetarian
main course served with jacket-
boiled new potatoes or brown
rice.

Serves 4

Per Portion
about 255 calories
14 g carbohydrate
7 g protein · 19 g fat

Asparagus with Two Sauces

3 kg/6½ lb asparagus
2 shallots
4 white peppercorns
bunch of fresh tarragon
handful of fresh chervil
2 tablespoons dry white wine
3 tablespoons tarragon vinegar
200 g/7 oz butter
2 egg yolks
2 tablespoons hot water
salt
cayenne pepper
pinch of caster sugar
250 ml/8 fl oz crème fraîche
750 ml/1¼ pints natural yogurt
2 tablespoons chopped mixed
    fresh herbs (eg parsley, dill,
    nettles, salad burnet, cress,
    borage and lemon balm)
1 teaspoon chive mustard
2 tablespoons lemon juice
1 teaspoon sunflower oil
freshly ground white pepper

Thinly peel the bottom end of the asparagus stalks and cut off any woody parts. Wash the as-paragus and wrap in a tea towel.

To make the Béarnaise sauce, peel and very finely chop the shallots. Crush the peppercorns in a mortar. Rinse the tarragon and chervil in cold water and shake dry. Strip the leaves from the stalks and keep in reserve. Coarsely chop the stalks.

Put the white wine into a saucepan and add the vinegar, shallots, crushed peppercorns and herb stalks. Bring to the boil. Reduce over a moderate heat, stirring continuously, un-til you have about 1 tablespoon of liquid left. Strain the liquid, squeezing or pressing the shallots and herbs before dis-carding them. Keep the liquid hot.

Melt the butter over a low heat until liquid but not on any account brown. Skim off the white foam that forms. Pour the clear or clarified butter into another pan leaving the white sediment behind. Keep the butter hot.

Fill a saucepan with hot water and keep hot on the hob without allowing it to boil. Put the egg yolks and hot water into a heatproof bowl and place in the pan of hot water. Whisk to a thick, frothy cream.

Whisk in the warm clarified butter, a teaspoon at a time ini-tially and then in a thin trickle. The butter should be warm but not hot or the egg yolks will separate.

Whisk in the warm herb liq-uid a teaspoon at a time. Finely chop the tarragon and chervil leaves and stir in. Season the sauce to taste with salt and cay-enne and keep lukewarm until ready to serve.

Fill a large frying pan three quarters full with water. (The pan must be large enough to take the asparagus flat.) Add the sugar and a pinch of salt and bring the water to the boil. Place the asparagus in the boil-ing water and cook over a mod-erate heat for 8 to 10 minutes until tender but still firm to bite.

Meanwhile, mix the crème fraîche with the yogurt. Stir in the chopped herbs, mustard, lemon juice and sunflower oil. Season to taste with pepper.

Gently lift the asparagus out of the water on a skimmer, drain and serve with the Béarnaise and herb sauces, and with jacket-boiled new potatoes.

Serves 8

Per portion
about 425 calories
18 g carbohydrate
12 g protein · 33 g fat

Cauliflower Curry with Potatoes

1 (800 g/1¾ lb) cauliflower
500 g/18 oz floury potatoes
1 onion
1 clove garlic
1 green pepper
piece of fresh root ginger
2 teaspoons turmeric
1 teaspoon ground ginger
1½ teaspoons ground anise or
  cumin
1 teaspoon ground coriander
hot chilli powder
3 tablespoons sunflower oil
5 cloves
4 cardamom seeds
about 350 ml/12 fl oz soya milk
salt
bunch of fresh parsley

Trim the cauliflower, separate into florets, wash well in cold water and drain thoroughly. Peel and wash the potatoes and cut into cubes. Peel and finely chop the onion and garlic. Cut the green pepper in half and re-move the stalk, pith and all the

seeds. Wash in cold water to make sure you have got rid of all the seeds and cut into fine strips. Peel the ginger and finely chop.

Mix the turmeric, ground ginger, anise or cumin and cori-ander with chilli powder to taste in a bowl.

Heat the sunflower oil in a saucepan. Fry the onion, garlic, green pepper, root ginger, cloves and cardamom seeds over a moderate heat, stirring continuously, until the onion and garlic are transparent.

Increase the heat. Add the potatoes and cauliflower and fry, stirring, until completely coated in oil. Sprinkle with the spice mixture and stir well. Add the soya milk, season to taste with salt and bring to the boil. Cover the pan and cook over a low heat for 15 to 20 minutes, stirring frequently for soya milk burns easily.

Wash the parsley, strip the leaves from the stalks, pat dry and finely chop.

Sprinkle the cauliflower curry with the parsley and

transfer to a warmed dish. Serve with mixed or Sprouted salad (recipe page 26).

Serves 4

Per Portion
about 260 calories
33 g carbohydrate
11 g protein · 9 g fat

Variation
Leek and Carrot Curry
Trim and wash 750 g/1½ lb leeks and cut into 0.5 cm/¼ in slices, including about one-third of the green leaves. Scrape and wash 400 g/14 oz young carrots and cut into sticks 0.5 cm/¼ in thick. Peel and finely chop 1 clove garlic. Make up the spice mixture as described. Heat 3 tablespoons sunflower oil in a saucepan and fry the garlic with 3 cardamom seeds and 4 cloves. Add the vegetables and con-tinue frying. Stir the spices into the vegetables, add 300 ml/½ pint soya or coconut milk and bring to the boil. Season to taste with salt, cover the pan and cook over a low heat for 10

to 15 minutes. Squeeze the juice from ½ lemon. Flavour the curry with the lemon juice and serve sprinkled with 1 table-spoon cut fresh chives. Serve with brown rice.

Cook's Tip

The curry is delicious made with coconut milk, which is easy to make, in-stead of soya milk. Instructions for coconut milk are included in the Nut curry recipe on page 125.

Broccoli and Potatoes with Cheese Sauce

600 g/1¼ lb floury potatoes
salt
100 g/4 oz Cheddar cheese
1 kg/2¼ lb broccoli
250 ml/8 fl oz double cream
20 g/¾ oz butter
freshly ground white pepper
freshly grated nutmeg
3 tablespoons chopped mixed
  fresh herbs

Scrub the potatoes well under cold running water and cook in the skins in a little boiling salted water until soft. This will take 30 to 40 minutes depending on size.

Meanwhile, finely dice the cheese. Wash the broccoli. Cut off large leaves and the tough ends of the stalks. Using a small pointed knife peel off the skin from the bottom of the stalks towards the top. Cut off the florets for they cook quicker than the stalks.

Bring a large pan of salted water to the boil. Add the broccoli stalks and cook for about 3 minutes. Then add the florets and cook for a further 3 minutes. Remove from the pan with a slotted spoon. Drain well and keep hot in a warmed dish.

Drain the potatoes, evaporate some of the steam and peel. Cut into slices or cubes and add to the broccoli.

Bring the cream to the boil with the butter. Over a moderate heat stir the diced cheese into the cream until melted. The cream should not be too hot or it will not bind with the cheese and will be lumpy. Also the sauce burns easily if it is not stirred continuously.

Season the sauce with a little salt – the cheese already contains salt – and pepper and nutmeg to taste. Stir the herbs into the sauce.

Pour the cheese sauce over the broccoli and potatoes and serve at once.

Serves 4

Per Portion
about 695 calories
47 g carbohydrate
20 g protein · 40 g fat

Versatile Potatoes

Potatoes in Herb Sauce

1 kg/2¼ lb floury potatoes
1 large onion
3 cloves garlic
2 tablespoons olive oil
150 ml/¼ pint freshly made vegetable stock (recipe page 38)
150 ml/¼ pint natural yogurt
30 g/1¼ oz butter
4 tablespoons chopped mixed fresh herbs (eg parsley, chervil, sorrel, salad burnet, chives)
gomasio for sprinkling

Peel and wash the potatoes and cut into 1-cm/½-in cubes. Dry the potatoes to prevent the oil spitting when you fry them. Peel and finely chop the onion and garlic.

Heat the olive oil in a frying pan. Fry the onion and garlic over a moderate heat until transparent, stirring continuously. Add the potatoes and stir until completely coated in oil. Add the vegetable stock, bring to the boil and then reduce the heat. Cover the pan and cook over a low heat for about 15 minutes until the potatoes are tender.

During the last 5 minutes of the cooking time make the sauce. Pour the yogurt into a heatproof bowl and place in a pan of hot, but not boiling water. Cut the butter into flakes, add to the yogurt and whisk in to make a thick, frothy sauce. Stir in the herbs.

Transfer the potatoes to a warmed dish and pour on the herb sauce. Sprinkle with gomasio and serve at once, with Carrots with nut vinaigrette (page 25) or Sprouted salad (page 26).

Serves 4

Per Portion
about 400 calories
50 g carbohydrate
11 g protein · 14 g fat

Jacket Potatoes with Quark

1.5 kg/3 lb floury potatoes
4–6 tablespoons sunflower oil
4 tablespoons caraway seeds
1 large beef tomato
bunch of radishes
bunch of spring onions
500 g/18 oz low-fat Quark or other soft cheese
125 ml/4 fl oz crème fraîche or soured cream
2 tablespoons chopped fresh mixed herbs
herb salt
freshly ground black pepper
1 teaspoon cold-pressed olive oil

Scrub the potatoes well in cold water since they are to be cooked in their skins. Halve the potatoes lengthways.

Brush a baking sheet with the sunflower oil and scatter with the caraway seeds. Place the potatoes, cut side down, on the baking sheet. Bake in a moderately hot oven (200 c, 400 f, gas 6), on the second shelf from the bottom, for 30 to 40 minutes until tender.

Meanwhile, wash, dry and chop the beef tomato, removing the core and the seeds. Trim, wash, dry and chop the radishes. Trim and wash the spring onions, shake dry and cut into thin rings, including about one-third of the green leaves.

Stir the Quark and crème fraîche together until smooth. Stir in the tomato, radishes, spring onions and herbs and season to taste with herb salt and pepper. Add the olive oil.

Season the potatoes to taste with salt and serve with the Quark sauce. Accompany with a mixed salad in a herb and garlic vinaigrette.

Serves 6

Per Portion
about 415 calories
47 g carbohydrate
17 g protein · 18 g fat

Potato Fingers with Sage Butter

1 kg/2½ lb floury potatoes
6 tablespoons wholemeal flour
4 tablespoons cornflour
salt
freshly grated nutmeg
freshly ground white pepper
handful of fresh sage leaves
100 g/4 oz butter

Scrub the potatoes well in cold running water. Cook in the skins, in a little boiling water until soft, then drain. Evaporate some of the steam, peel and mash well until smooth. Add the flour, cornflour, and salt, nutmeg and pepper to taste and work in to give a uniform mixture.

Sprinkle the worktop with flour and tip out the potato mixture. Shape the mixture into long rolls about the thickness of your thumb. Cut into 1 cm/½ in lengths and shape into fingers.

Drop the potato fingers into a large pan of boiling salted water and simmer gently over a moderate heat until they rise to the surface. Remove from the pan on a slotted spoon, rinse in cold water and drain thoroughly. Leave the fingers to dry for about 3 hours.

Rinse the sage leaves in cold water, pat dry and cut into narrow strips.

Melt the butter in a large frying pan. Fry the sage over a low to moderate heat to bring out its full flavour. Add the potato fingers and brown all over, turning them continuously.

Serve hot with a mixed salad.

Serves 4

Per Portion
about 460 calories
59 g carbohydrate
7 g protein · 21 g fat

Potato Tortilla

250 g/9 oz floury potatoes
1 large onion
4 tablespoons vegetable oil
salt
freshly ground black pepper
4 eggs
½ bunch of fresh chives

Peel, wash and dry the potatoes. Cut into slices about 2 mm/⅛ in thick. Dry the slices well on absorbent kitchen paper. Peel and halve the onion and cut into thin rings.

Heat the oil in a heavy frying pan and fry the onions over a moderate heat until transparent, stirring frequently.

Reduce the heat, add the potatoes and spread them evenly. Season to taste and cook over a low heat for about 10 minutes, turning them frequently, until they are tender and brown.

Meanwhile, beat the eggs until frothy.

Pour the eggs over the potatoes and shake the pan to distribute the mixture evenly. Cook over a low heat for about 10 minutes until the egg has set.

Loosen the tortilla from the pan with a spatula, slide on to a plate and return to the pan the other way up. Cook on the second side for a further 5 minutes.

Rinse the chives in cold water, pat dry and snip.

Halve the tortilla and serve at once on warmed plates, sprinkled with chives. Serve with tomato salad with spring onions and chopped fresh herbs.

Serves 2

Per Portion
about 470 calories
27 g carbohydrate
18 g protein · 30 g fat

Versatile Potatoes

Boiled Potatoes with Mushroom Sauce

20 g/¾ oz dried cèpes or morels
250 ml/8 fl oz lukewarm water
750 g/1½ lb small new potatoes
salt
1 tablespoon wholemeal flour
75 g/3 oz hard cheese
  (Emmental, mature Gouda or
  Gruyère)
¼ bunch of fresh parsley
125 ml/4 fl oz double cream
1 tablespoon butter
freshly ground white pepper
freshly grated nutmeg
1–2 tablespoons lemon juice
salt or gomasio

Soak the dried mushrooms in the water in a covered bowl for 2 hours.

Tip the soaked mushrooms into a sieve, reserving the soaking water, and wash well under cold water to remove any grit or soil (sand tends to collect in the caps of morels). Never wash dried mushrooms before soaking as this loses some of the flavour.

Strain the soaking water through a coffee filter paper to remove any bits of dirt. Set aside.

Scrub the potatoes well under cold running water. Cook, in the skins, in a little boiling salted water until tender. This will take 20 to 30 minutes depending on size.

Meanwhile, heat the flour in a dry pan over a high to moderate heat, stirring continuously, until it gives off a slight aroma. Gradually add the mushroom soaking water, whisking vigorously to avoid lumps. Bring to the boil and continue whisking to form a smooth, velvety sauce. Reduce the heat, cover the pan and simmer over a low heat for 5 minutes, stirring frequently for the sauce burns easily.

While the sauce is cooking, grate the cheese. Wash the parsley, strip the leaves from the stalks, pat dry and finely chop. Add the drained mushrooms, cream and cheese to the sauce and stir to melt the cheese. Whisk in the butter. Finally, stir in the parsley and season to taste with pepper, nutmeg, lemon juice and salt. (If you prefer to use gomasio instead of salt, sprinkle it over the potatoes at the end.) Keep the sauce hot until ready to serve.

Drain the potatoes, evaporate some of the steam, peel and serve in the mushroom sauce with a wild herb or mixed salad.

Serves 4

Per Portion
about 385 calories
35 g carbohydrate
11 g protein · 19 g fat

Cook's Tip

Cèpes: a prized mushroom found in woods in spring and autumn. They are the size of a large common mushroom, with a shiny brown top and spongy gills. They are collected all through the summer in France and they are dried for use in soups and sauces. Morels: these have either a yellowish or black cap (smaller varieties) and some are pointed. They are gathered in the woods in the spring and used fresh or they can be dried for winter use.

Versatile Potatoes

Potato Gnocchi in Herb Sauce

500 g / 18 oz floury potatoes
salt
150 g / 5 oz wholemeal flour
50 g / 2 oz wholemeal semolina
1 egg
1 egg yolk
freshly ground white pepper
freshly grated nutmeg
125 ml / 4 fl oz crème fraîche
125 ml / 4 fl oz double cream
40 g / 1½ oz Parmesan cheese,
* grated*
4 tablespoons chopped mixed
* fresh herbs (eg parsley,*
* chervil, little thyme)*
cayenne pepper

Scrub the potatoes well in cold running water. Cook, in the skins, in a little boiling salted water until tender. This will take 30 to 40 minutes depending on size.

Peel the potatoes and mash while still hot. Mix the potato with the flour, semolina, egg, egg yolk, salt to taste and a generous pinch each of pepper and nutmeg to make a fairly soft malleable mixture. If the mixture is too soft, work in a little more semolina. If it is too dry add 1 more egg yolk.

To make the sauce, boil the crème fraîche and cream over a high heat to reduce by about one-third. Add the grated cheese and stir over a low heat until melted. Do not have the heat too high or the sauce will separate. Stir in the herbs and season to taste with nutmeg and a generous pinch of cayenne. Cover the sauce and keep hot.

To make the gnocchi, shape the potato mixture into balls using 2 teaspoons dipped in water. Cook in a large pan of boiling salted water until they rise to the surface. Lift out on a slotted spoon, drain, cover with the herb sauce and serve.

Serves 4

Per Portion
about 380 calories
53 g carbohydrate
15 g protein · 15 g fat

Wholemeal Spaghetti with Cheese and Cream Sauce

salt
400 g/14 oz wholemeal spaghetti
250 ml/8 fl oz double cream
100 g/4 oz pecorino cheese,
  grated
freshly ground white pepper
freshly grated nutmeg
5 leaves fresh sage

Bring about 4 litres/7 pints salted water to the boil. Allow to boil for about 30 seconds, then add the spaghetti. Stir to avoid it sticking together, then cook until *al dente* (tender but still firm to bite), making sure that the water boils throughout and stirring the spaghetti frequently.

Meanwhile, make the sauce. Pour the cream into a saucepan, bring to the boil and reduce by half on a moderate heat, stirring continuously.

Reduce the heat and stir in the pecorino until melted. You need a really low temperature here or the cheese will form lumps and not bind with the sauce. Make sure you stir throughout for the cheese sauce will burn easily. Season the sauce to taste with salt, pepper and nutmeg.

Wash and dry the sage leaves and cut into strips. Stir into the sauce.

Tip the pasta into a sieve, drain well and stir into the cream sauce. Serve at once on warmed plates with mixed salad in herb vinaigrette.

Serves 4

Per Portion
about 655 calories
66 g carbohydrate
23 g protein · 34 g fat

Variation
Wholemeal Macaroni with Garlic Oil
Cook 400 g/14 oz wholemeal macaroni in a large pan of boiling salted water until *al dente*.

Meanwhile, wash a bunch of fresh parsley, strip the leaves from the stalks, pat dry and chop very finely. Peel and thinly slice 4 cloves garlic. Heat 125 ml/4 fl oz olive oil and fry the garlic over a low to moderate heat until transparent, stirring often. Rub a dried red chilli pepper between your fingers and add to the garlic oil with the parsley. Drain the cooked pasta and stir into the garlic oil at once.

Wholemeal Pasta with Uncooked Tomato Sauce
Cook 400 g/14 oz wholemeal short cut macaroni in a large pan of boiling salted water until *al dente*. Meanwhile, blanch 750 g/1½ lb tomatoes in boiling water for 30 seconds and rinse in cold water. Peel and finely chop the tomatoes, removing the core and the seeds. Peel and very finely chop 1 clove garlic. Wash a bunch of fresh basil, strip the leaves from the stalks, pat dry and cut into fine strips. Mix the chopped tomato with the herbs, garlic, 2 tablespoons

cold-pressed olive oil, a pinch of caster sugar and salt and freshly ground black pepper to taste. Drain the pasta and mix with the tomato sauce while very hot.

Cook's Tip
Wholemeal pasta comes in a wide variety of shapes and they can all be substituted for the spaghetti. Children in particular, prefer to eat smaller shapes and find them more attractive.

Ravioli with Herbs and Ricotta

400 g/14 oz wholemeal or
wheatmeal flour
salt
4 eggs
1 tablespoon vegetable oil
1–3 egg yolks
about 500 g/18 oz mixed fresh
herbs and wild leaves (eg
parsley, basil, nettle, dandelion leaves, wild garlic and
wild marjoram)
1 onion
1 clove garlic
125 g/4½ oz butter
500 g/18 oz ricotta cheese
freshly ground white pepper
freshly grated nutmeg
cayenne pepper
6 sprigs of fresh thyme

To make the dough, mix the
flour with a pinch of salt, the
eggs, oil and 1 of the egg yolks.
The dough should be firm and
smooth and not at all crumbly.
If necessary, work in the other
egg yolks or a few drops of cold

water. It is a good idea to mix
pasta doughs made with refined
wheat flour with your hands so
that you can feel the
consistency. Wrap the dough in
foil and allow to stand for at
least 1 hour.

For the filling, pick over the
herbs, wash, shake dry and
coarsely chop. Peel and finely
chop the onion and garlic. Heat
1 tablespoon butter in a frying
pan without allowing it to
brown. Fry the onion and garlic
over a moderate heat until
transparent, stirring often. Add
the herbs and stir until they
produce juice. Remove the pan
from the heat and allow to cool
slightly.

Tip the herb mixture into a
liquidiser or food processor and
add the ricotta. Blend until
smooth. Season to taste with
salt, pepper, nutmeg and a generous pinch of cayenne.

Cut the pasta dough into
portions and roll out very
thinly on a floured worktop.
Cover every other sheet of pasta
with teaspoons of filling at
5-cm/2-in intervals. Brush

between the piles with water to
stick the layers of pasta together.
Cover with a second sheet of
dough and press down well
between the piles of filling with
your fingertips. Then cut out
the ravioli with a pastry wheel.

Bring a large pan of salted
water to the boil. When the
water has been boiling for
about 2 minutes, add the ravioli
and cook for 3 to 6 minutes until *al dente* (tender but still firm
to bite). It is impossible to give
the time exactly for it depends
on the consistency of the pasta
and how long the ravioli has
stood around and dried before
cooking. Moist doughs cook
quickest, but if the dough has
become dry it will take longer.

While the ravioli is cooking,
wash the thyme, shake dry and
strip the leaves from the stalks.

Heat the remaining butter in
a small pan until slightly
brown. Add the thyme to the
butter and fry slightly.

Scoop the ravioli out of the
water on a slotted spoon and
drain well. Mix at once with the
thyme butter.

Serves 6

Per Portion
about 660 calories
58 g carbohydrate
27 g protein · 34 g fat

Cook's Tip
Pasta machines usually
have ravioli-making at-
tachments. These ma-
chines can be used to roll
the dough, then the ravi-
oli attachment can be
used to fill and cut the
dough. Alternatively, a
ravioli tin similar to the
one shown in the picture
can be used. Lift a sheet
of pasta over the tin, eas-
ing it into the hollows.
Put the filling in the hollows, brush between with
water and top with pasta.
Press down and cut be-
tween the hollows. Cook
as above.

111

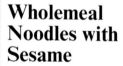

Wholemeal Noodles with Sesame

150 g/5 oz wholemeal or
*   wheatmeal flour*
salt
1 egg
1–3 egg yolks
1 tablespoon sunflower oil
2 cloves garlic
½ bunch of fresh parsley
4 tablespoons olive oil
4 tablespoons sesame seeds

To make the pasta, work the flour with a pinch of salt, the egg, 1 egg yolk and the sunflower oil. If the dough is too dry, gradually work in the remaining yolks and keep checking the consistency. If it is too soft add a little more flour.

Wrap the dough in foil and leave to rest for 30 minutes.

Thinly roll out the dough on a floured worktop or in a pasta machine and cut into noodles. Spread on a tea towel and leave to dry for about 1 hour.

Peel and finely chop the garlic. Wash the parsley, strip the leaves from the stalks, pat dry and finely chop.

Heat the olive oil in a frying pan. Fry the sesame seeds over a moderate heat, stirring continuously, until golden brown. Add the parsley and garlic and cook until the garlic is transparent. Remove the pan from the heat to prevent the garlic browning and becoming bitter.

Cook the noodles in a large pan of boiling salted water, stirring frequently, for 2 to 4 minutes until *al dente* (tender but still firm to bite). Drain well and mix at once with the sesame mixture.

Serves 4

Per Portion
about 370 calories
28 g carbohydrate
11 g protein · 20 g fat

Herb Spätzle

100 g/4 oz mixed young dande-
*   lion and nettle leaves*
3 bunches of fresh parsley
500 g/18 oz wheatmeal flour
salt
5 eggs
1–3 egg yolks
400 g/14 oz onions
300 g/11 oz Emmental cheese
75 g/3 oz butter

Wash the dandelion, nettle and parsley leaves, shake dry and finely chop.

Mix the flour with the herbs, a pinch of salt, the eggs and 1 egg yolk to give a batter thick enough for marks made with a wooden spoon to disappear only slowly. If the batter is too thick, work in more egg yolk; if it is too runny, work in a little more flour. Cover and leave to stand for 30 minutes.

Meanwhile, peel the onions and cut into thin rings. Grate the Emmental.

Melt the butter in a frying pan and fry the onions until soft and golden brown. Remove from the heat and keep warm.

Bring a large pan of salted water to the boil. Scrape the herb batter off a board into the boiling water, in batches to make squiggly noodles. Remove the noodles or spätzle from the water as soon as they rise to the surface, drain and place in a warmed dish. Sprinkle with a layer of grated cheese and keep hot.

Cook the next batch, transfer to the bowl and sprinkle with cheese. Continue in this way until you have used all the batter and cheese.

Serve topped with the onion rings.

Serves 6

Per Portion
about 720 calories
65 g carbohydrate
33 g protein · 35 g fat

Pancakes to Dumplings

Wholemeal Pancakes with Vegetables

bunch of fresh parsley
250 g/9 oz wholemeal flour
salt
250 ml/8 fl oz milk
250 ml/8 fl oz mineral water
2 eggs
250 g/9 oz celery
1 shallot
250 g/9 oz mung bean sprouts
about 6 tablespoons vegetable oil
 for frying
25 g/1 oz butter
250 ml/8 fl oz crème fraîche or
 soured cream
2 tablespoons lemon juice
1 tablespoon dry sherry
freshly ground white pepper
handful of fresh chervil

Wash the parsley, shake dry and finely chop.

Whisk the flour with a pinch of salt, the milk and mineral water. Whisk in the eggs and parsley. Cover and leave to stand for 20 minutes.

Meanwhile, wash and trim the celery and cut into 1 cm/½ in lengths. Keep the leaves to sprinkle over the vegetables. Peel and finely chop the shallot. Wash and drain the bean sprouts.

Heat 1 tablespoon oil in a heavy frying pan. Tip 1 ladle of batter into the pan and cook the first pancake. Keep hot. Heat more oil and add more batter. Continue in this way until you have used all the batter. Keep the pancakes hot.

To cook the vegetables, melt the butter in a frying pan without allowing it to brown. Fry the shallot on a moderate heat, stirring continuously. Add the celery and bean sprouts and fry for 2 minutes. Stir in the crème fraîche, lemon juice and sherry. Season to taste, cover and cook gently for about 4 minutes.

Meanwhile, pick over and wash the chervil, shake dry and finely chop. Scatter over the vegetables with the celery leaves.

Fill the pancakes with the vegetables and serve at once.

Serves 4

Per Portion
about 685 calories
49 g carbohydrate
18 g protein · 44 g fat

Mushrooms with Corn Fritters

40 g/1½ oz wheatmeal flour
salt
225 g/8 oz sweetcorn
2 tablespoons snipped chives
2 eggs, beaten
3 tablespoons water
vegetable oil for cooking
450 g/1 lb mushrooms
½ lemon
2 sprigs of fresh thyme
1 small onion
small bunch of parsley
25 g/1 oz butter
150 ml/¼ pint double cream
freshly ground white pepper

Put the flour in a bowl with salt to taste. Stir in the sweetcorn and chives. Beat in the eggs, adding the water if necessary, to make a thick batter.

Heat a little oil in a large frying pan. Drop in spoonfuls of the batter and fry over a moderate heat until golden underneath. Turn and cook the second side until golden.

Drain the cooked fritters on absorbent kitchen paper, then keep hot until all the batter is cooked.

Wash the mushrooms only if necessary, but never leave standing in water. Dry and finely slice the mushrooms. Squeeze the lemon juice over the mushrooms at once to keep them white.

Meanwhile, rinse the thyme in cold water, shake dry and strip the leaves from the stalks. Peel and finely chop the onion. Reserve a small sprig of parsley for garnish, then chop the rest.

Heat the butter in a frying pan without allowing it to brown. Fry the onion over a moderate heat until transparent. Add the thyme leaves and mushrooms and stir over a high heat until the liquid produced by the mushrooms has completely evaporated. Gradually add the cream and heat gently without boiling. Season to taste.

To serve, arrange the corn fritters on four warmed plates. Add the creamed mushrooms

and sprinkle with the parsley. Garnish with the reserved sprig of parsley. Serve with tomato salad with chives or Uncooked vegetable salad (recipe page 21).

Serves 4

Per Portion
about 610 calories
64 g carbohydrate
17 g protein · 32 g fat

Variation
If you like you can pep up the corn fritters by adding a little spice and using natural yogurt instead of the cream to give the meal an unusual and exotic flavour.

Use 2 tablespoons chopped fresh coriander instead of the chives and add 1 teaspoon ground coriander to the corn mixture. If you like spicy food, add a good pinch of chilli powder to the fritter mixture. Make the fritters as in the main recipe.

Heat the butter for the mushrooms and add a crushed clove

of garlic. Add the mushrooms and 2 tablespoons finely chopped cucumber instead of the thyme. Add natural yogurt instead of the cream and heat very gently without allowing the mixture to boil. Sprinkle a little chopped mint over the mushrooms and serve.

A tomato salad would be suitable as an accompaniment for the spicy variation. Instead of sprinkling chopped chives on the tomatoes, substitute a finely chopped green chilli. Cut a small, mild green chilli in half and remove the seeds. Rinse well, then cut away the stalk and finely chop the chilli. Sprinkle the chilli over the salad just before it is served.

Pancakes to Dumplings

Rye Rissoles

1 onion
3 tablespoons vegetable oil
200 g/7 oz rye grain, crushed
 medium-fine
375 ml/13 fl oz cold water
2 eggs
1–2 tablespoons chopped fresh
 parsley
salt

Peel and finely chop the onion. Heat 1 tablespoon oil in a saucepan and fry the onion until transparent, stirring continuously. Add the rye and stir until completely coated in fat. Add the water, cover the pan and simmer over a low heat for 10 minutes.

Remove from the heat and leave the rye to soak in the covered pan for 50 minutes. Then uncover the pan and allow to cool to lukewarm.

Beat the eggs with a fork and mix into the rye with the parsley. Season to taste with salt.

Using wet hands, shape the mixture into 8 equal rissoles.

Heat the remaining oil in a frying pan and fry the rissoles over a moderate heat for about 10 minutes until golden brown, turning once.

Serves 4

Per Portion
about 305 calories
36 g carbohydrate
10 g protein · 13 g fat

Cook's Tip
If you can't get rye grain, cook 300 g/11 oz coarsely crushed whole wheat (wheat berries) in about 750 ml/1¼ pints boiling water, stirring frequently to prevent it burning. Leave the wheat to soak and cool as in the recipe. Mix 1 chopped onion and 2 eggs into the wheat and season. Shape and cook as above.

Buckwheat Dumplings in Gorgonzola Cream

300 ml/½ pint water
150 g/5 oz buckwheat grain,
 coarsely crushed
150 g/5 oz wholemeal or
 wheatmeal flour
50 g/2 oz wholemeal semolina
2 eggs
2 tablespoons soured cream
3 tablespoons chopped fresh
 parsley
3 tablespoons snipped fresh
 chives
salt
freshly ground white pepper
freshly grated nutmeg
30 g/1¼ oz butter
150 g/5 oz gorgonzola cheese
250 ml/8 fl oz double cream

Bring the water to the boil in a saucepan, add the buckwheat, cover the pan and simmer for 20 minutes. Remove from the heat and soak for 1 hour.

Mix the buckwheat with the flour, semolina, eggs, soured cream and herbs to a fairly soft but malleable dough. Season to taste with salt, pepper and nutmeg.

Using 2 wet teaspoons, shape the mixture into dumplings and cook in a large pan of boiling salted water until they rise to the surface. Remove them from the water with a slotted spoon, drain well and arrange in a buttered baking dish. Crumble the gorgonzola. Tip into a saucepan and add the cream. Stir over a low heat until the cheese has melted. Season to taste with pepper and nutmeg and pour over the dumplings. Dot with the remaining butter.

Place the dish in a hot oven (220 C, 425 F, gas 7), and cook for 12 to 15 minutes.

Serves 4

Per Portion
about 780 calories
60 g carbohydrate
24 g protein · 50 g fat

Braised Wheat

about 450 ml/¾ pint water
200 g/7 oz whole wheat grain
  (wheat berries)
400 g/14 oz aubergines
salt
400 g/14 oz ripe tomatoes
1 onion
2 cloves garlic
5–6 tablespoons olive oil
125 ml/4 fl oz dry red wine
1 teaspoon vegetable stock
  granules
1 tablespoon fresh thyme leaves
  or 1 teaspoon dried oregano
freshly ground black pepper
100 g/4 oz Emmental cheese
bunch of fresh basil

Bring the water to the boil in a saucepan, add the wheat, cover and simmer gently over a low heat for 1 hour. Remove the pan from the heat and leave the wheat to soak in the open pan for a further hour.

Wash and dry the aubergines. Cut off the stalks and then cut into 1 cm/½ in cubes. Sprinkle with salt and leave to sweat for about 10 minutes.

Meanwhile, blanch the tomatoes in boiling water for 30 seconds, rinse in cold water and peel. Chop the tomatoes, removing the core and the seeds. Peel and finely chop the onion and garlic.

Dry the aubergines. Heat the olive oil a little at a time in a frying pan and fry the aubergines until golden brown. Add the onion and garlic and cook until transparent, stirring continuously. Add the wheat with any water that has not yet been absorbed and stir thoroughly. Add the red wine and bring to the boil.

Reduce the heat and season with the stock granules, thyme or oregano and pepper to taste. Cover the pan and cook over a low heat for 10 minutes.

Stir in the tomatoes, re-cover the pan and cook for a further 10 minutes.

Meanwhile, coarsely grate the cheese. Wash the basil, strip the leaves from the stalks, pat dry and coarsely chop.

Season the cooked wheat to taste with salt and arrange in layers with the grated cheese in a warmed dish. Sprinkle with the basil and serve at once.

Variation
Buckwheat Gratin
Peel and finely chop 1 onion and 1 clove garlic. Heat 1 tablespoon butter and fry the onion and garlic until transparent, stirring continuously. Add 200 g/7 oz roasted buckwheat grain (kasha) and fry. Add 1 litre/1¾ pints freshly made vegetable stock (recipe page 38), bring to the boil and simmer for 5 minutes on a low heat. Remove the pan from the heat, cover and leave the buckwheat to swell and form a thick paste, about 15 minutes. Wash 500 g/ 18 oz young courgettes. Top and tail them and cut into sticks. Peel 300 g/11 oz tomatoes and dice, removing the core and the seeds. Fry the courgettes and tomatoes with 2 tablespoons dried oregano in 2 tablespoons olive oil until the juice that forms has evaporated.

Season the buckwheat paste to taste with salt, freshly ground black pepper and the juice of 1 lemon. Stir the vegetables into the buckwheat with 100 g/4 oz grated mature Gouda cheese. Transfer to a baking dish, smooth the top and scatter with a further 150 g/ 5 oz grated Gouda cheese. Place the dish in a moderately hot oven (200 c, 400 f, gas 6) and bake for about 30 minutes.

Serves 4

Per Portion
about 505 calories
40 g carbohydrate
15 g protein · 25 g fat

Wholesome Ways with Grains

Vegetable Pilau

50 g/2 oz dried chickpeas
1 onion
2 cloves garlic
350 g/12 oz long-grain brown rice
5 tablespoons vegetable oil
1 litre/1¾ pints freshly made vegetable stock (recipe page 38)
1 aubergine
1 courgette
1 large carrot
herb salt
freshly ground black pepper
2 tablespoons chopped fresh parsley

Soak the chickpeas overnight in cold water. Drain well.

Peel and finely chop the onion and garlic. Rinse the rice under cold running water and drain.

Heat 1 tablespoon oil in a saucepan over a moderate heat, add the rice and stir until transparent. Stir in the chickpeas, onion and garlic and fry for a few minutes, stirring continu-

ously. Add the vegetable stock. Bring to the boil, cover the pan and cook gently for about 50 minutes.

Wash, trim and dice the aubergine and courgette. Peel and wash the carrot and cut into sticks.

Heat the remaining oil in a frying pan. Fry the aubergine until golden, then add the other vegetables and fry until tender but still firm to bite. Season to taste with herb salt and pepper.

Mix the vegetables gently into the rice. Cover and cook for 5 minutes. Serve sprinkled with parsley.

Serves 4

Per Portion
about 540 calories
83 g carbohydrate
12 g protein · 15 g fat

Risotto with Peas and Saffron

1 onion
1 clove garlic
2 tablespoons olive oil
400 g/14 oz round-grain brown rice
1–1.25 litres/1¾–2¼ pints freshly made vegetable stock (recipe page 38)
herb salt
freshly ground white pepper
300 g/11 oz shelled peas, fresh or frozen
125 ml/4 fl oz double cream
1 tablespoon butter
1 sachet saffron threads
100 g/4 oz Parmesan cheese, grated

Peel and finely chop the onion and garlic. Heat the olive oil in a saucepan and fry the onion and garlic over a moderate heat until transparent. Stir in the rice.

Add half the vegetable stock and season to taste with herb salt and pepper. Bring to the

boil over a high heat, then reduce the heat to low and cook for about 50 minutes, adding the remaining stock as the rice soaks up the liquid. Stir the rice often with a fork as it cooks to keep the risotto nice and velvety. Stir in the peas and cream and cook for 5 minutes.

Meanwhile, melt the butter in a small pan without allowing it to brown. Rub the saffron threads between finger and thumb into the butter and allow to dissolve.

Fold the saffron butter and Parmesan into the cooked risotto with a fork. Serve at once in a warmed bowl.

Serves 4

Per Portion
about 705 calories
87 g carbohydrate
22 g protein · 27 g fat

Buckwheat Pancake with Scorzonera

250 g/9 oz buckwheat flour
250 ml/8 fl oz sour milk or
   buttermilk
250 ml/8 fl oz mineral water
3 tablespoons sunflower oil
salt
1–2 tablespoons vinegar
500 g/18 oz scorzonera
1 tablespoon lemon juice
1 tablespoon butter
3 tablespoons crème fraîche or
   soured cream
freshly ground black pepper
2 tablespoons chopped fresh
   parsley

Whisk the buckwheat flour
with the sour milk or buttermilk, mineral water, 2 tablespoons oil and a little salt to
make a smooth batter. Leave to
stand for 45 minutes.

Fill a bowl with cold water
and add the vinegar. Peel and
wash the scorzonera. Cut into
2 cm/$\frac{3}{4}$ in pieces and place at
once in the acidulated water to
keep them white.

Bring about 600 ml/1 pint
water to the boil with the lemon
juice and a little salt. Add the
scorzonera to the boiling water
and cook over a moderate heat
for about 15 minutes until
tender but still firm to bite.
Drain. Keep the cooking water
to use in some other dish such
as soup.

Heat the remaining oil in a
heavy frying pan. Pour in the
buckwheat batter and cook
over a moderate heat until solid
around the edge. Turn the pancake and cook on the other
side. Break into pieces using
two forks and cook the pancake pieces for a further 2 minutes, stirring often. Remove
from the pan and keep hot.

Heat the butter in the pan
without allowing it to brown.
Stir in the scorzonera over a
moderate heat until coated in
fat. Stir in the crème fraîche
and season to taste. Stir in the
chopped parsley, and serve with
the buckwheat pancake.

Serves 4

Per Portion
about 485 calories
69 g carbohydrate
11 g protein · 17 g fat

Variation
*Wholemeal Pancakes
with Leeks*
Beat 250 g/9 oz wholemeal flour
with salt and 250 ml/8 fl oz each
milk and uncarbonated mineral
water until smooth. Beat in
2 eggs and leave the batter to
stand for 30 minutes to allow
the flour to swell. Meanwhile,
cut the roots and any limp
leaves from 500 g/18 oz leeks.
Cut a cross in the leaves down
as far as the white. Open the
leaves, wash well and shake
dry. Cut the leeks, including
about two thirds of the pale
green leaves into 1 cm/$\frac{1}{2}$ in
lengths. Peel and finely chop 2
cloves garlic. Pick over, wash
and dry 2 handfuls of fresh
chervil. Heat 2 tablespoons
vegetable oil in a frying pan,
pour in the batter and cook the
pancake as described above.

Keep hot. Heat another tablespoon oil in the pan and fry the
leeks for 2 minutes, stirring
continuously. Add the garlic
and fry for a few more minutes.
Add scant 125 ml/4 fl oz vegetable stock, bring to the boil,
then cover and cook over a low
heat for 8 to 10 minutes until
the leek is tender but still firm
to bite. Meanwhile, finely chop
the chervil. Stir the chervil into
the leeks with 2 tablespoons
cream and season with salt and
freshly ground white pepper.
Serve the leeks with the pancake pieces.

Wholesome Ways with Grains

Polenta Slices with Tomato Sauce

1.25 litres/2¼ pints water
250 g/9 oz cornmeal
salt
300 g/11 oz spinach beet
700 g/1½ lb ripe tomatoes
250 g/9 oz mushrooms
1 onion
1 clove garlic
bunch of fresh basil or parsley
3 tablespoons olive oil
pinch of caster sugar
freshly ground black pepper

Bring the water to the boil in a saucepan, add the cornmeal and a pinch of salt and leave to swell over the lowest possible heat in the open pan for about 45 minutes until the mixture comes away from the sides of the pan.

Meanwhile, strip the beet leaves off the stalks (use the stalks in another dish). Wash, dry and coarsely chop.

When the semolina has been cooking for 30 minutes, stir in the beet leaves.

Spread out the polenta on a baking sheet and leave to dry for about 20 minutes until firm enough to cut. Then cut into pieces about 2 × 5 cm/¾ × 2 in.

Wash and halve the tomatoes, remove the seeds and purée. Trim and slice the mushrooms. Peel and finely chop the onion and garlic. Wash and finely chop the basil or parsley.

Heat 2 tablespoons oil in a frying pan and fry the polenta slices until golden brown on both sides. Remove from the pan and keep hot.

Heat the remaining oil in the pan and fry the onion and garlic until transparent, stirring often. Add the mushrooms and fry for 2 minutes, stirring continuously. Add the puréed tomatoes and season with the sugar and salt and pepper to taste. Cover the pan and heat through.

Stir in the basil or parsley and serve the sauce with the polenta slices.

Serves 5

Per Portion
about 305 calories
50 g carbohydrate
9 g protein · 7 g fat

Chickpeas with Savoy Cabbage

1 small (750 g/1½ lb) Savoy
  cabbage
2 shallots
1 (2 cm/¾ in) piece of fresh root
  ginger
300 g/11 oz sprouted chickpeas
  (instructions page 26)
30 g/1¼ oz butter
250 ml/8 fl oz double cream
salt
freshly ground white pepper

Remove any limp outer leaves
from the cabbage. Remove two
more leaves and keep in reserve. Quarter the cabbage and
cut out the stalk. Wash the
quarters well under cold running water and dry. Coarsely
chop the cabbage.
   Peel and finely chop the
shallots. Peel and thinly slice
the ginger. Tip the chickpea
sprouts into a sieve, rinse well
and drain.
   Heat the butter in a saucepan
and fry the shallots and ginger
over a moderate heat until the
shallots are transparent, stirring
often. Add the cabbage and
chickpeas and fry for a few
more minutes.
   Add the cream and bring to
the boil. Reduce the heat to
low, cover the pan and cook for
about 10 minutes, stirring
occasionally.
   Meanwhile cut the thick ribs
out of the two reserved cabbage
leaves. Rinse, dry and finely
chop.
   Season the cooked vegetables
to taste, transfer to a warmed
dish and serve sprinkled with
the chopped cabbage. Serve
with buttered wholemeal rolls
sprinkled with gomasio, or
brown rice.

Serves 4

Per Portion
about 425 calories
27 g carbohydrate
12 g protein · 30 g fat

Sweetcorn with Tomatoes

500 g/18 oz ripe tomatoes
1 onion
2 cloves garlic
2 (325 g/11½ oz) cans sweetcorn
  kernels
1 tablespoon sunflower oil
125 ml/4 fl oz double cream
1 teaspoon turmeric
1 teaspoon ground anise or
  cumin
½ teaspoon ground coriander
hot chilli powder
salt
bunch of fresh parsley

Blanch the tomatoes in boiling
water for 30 seconds, rinse in
cold water and peel. Chop the
tomatoes, removing the core
and all the seeds. Peel and
finely chop the onion and garlic. Drain the sweetcorn.
   Heat the oil in a saucepan
and fry the onion and garlic
over a low to moderate heat until transparent, stirring continuously. Stir in the tomatoes and
sweetcorn. Add the cream.
Season with the turmeric, anise
or cumin, coriander, and chilli
powder and salt to taste. Bring
to the boil. Reduce the heat to
low, cover the pan and cook for
5 minutes.
   Meanwhile, wash the parsley,
strip the leaves from the stalks,
dry and chop medium fine.
   Serve the vegetables
sprinkled with the parsley, with
wholemeal pasta or brown rice
and a salad of uncooked
vegetables.

Serves 4

Per Portion
about 355 calories
44 g carbohydrate
8 g protein · 16 g fat

Wholesome Ways with Grains

Bulgur with Vegetables

250 g/9 oz bulgur
1 onion
2 cloves garlic
2 tablespoons vegetable oil
about 550 ml/18 fl oz freshly
  made vegetable stock (recipe
  page 38)
250 g/9 oz ripe tomatoes
250 g/9 oz broccoli
salt
freshly ground black pepper
bunch of fresh parsley

Tip the bulgur into a fine-meshed sieve, wash well under cold running water and drain. Peel and finely chop the onion and garlic.

Heat the oil in a saucepan and fry the onion and garlic until transparent, stirring often. Add the bulgur and cook over a low to moderate heat for about 5 minutes, stirring continuously.

Add half the vegetable stock, bring to the boil, cover the pan

and simmer over a low heat for 20 minutes, adding more stock and stirring from time to time.

Meanwhile, blanch the tomatoes in boiling water for 30 seconds, rinse in cold water and peel. Cut into wedges, removing the core and the seeds. Wash the broccoli, cut off large leaves and the woody ends of the stalks. Peel the stalks from the bottom towards the top. Cut off the florets for they cook quickly.

Bring a large pan of salted water to the boil and cook the broccoli stalks for 3 minutes. Add the florets and cook for a further 3 minutes. Drain and rinse in ice-cold water to keep the broccoli nice and green.

Arrange the tomato wedges on top of the bulgur and cook for a further 5 minutes in the covered pan.

Add the broccoli, stir in and season to taste. Heat the broccoli through, stirring gently from time to time to prevent the bulgur sticking to the pan.

Wash the parsley, strip the leaves from the stalks, dry and

finely chop. Serve the bulgur sprinkled with the parsley.

Serves 4

Per Portion
about 305 calories
51 g carbohydrate
10 g protein · 6 g fat

Variation
Bulgur Side dish
Wash 300 g/11 oz bulgur in cold running water and add to 1 litre/1¾ pints boiling water with a little salt. Boil vigorously for 5 minutes, then drain. Place 1 tablespoon butter in the pan and melt without browning. Cover the bottom of the pan with a 2 mm/⅛ in layer of sliced brown bread. Arrange the bulgur in the pan in a pyramid and dot 20 g/¾ oz butter around the edge. Wrap the lid of the pan in a tea towel, place on the pan and weight down. Cook the bulgur over the lowest possible heat for about 1 hour until completely dry. To serve, stand the bottom of the pan in cold water to loosen the bread. Turn

the bulgur into a shallow dish and top with the toasted bread slices.

Cook's Tip

Bulgur is eaten mainly in the Near and Middle East. It is made from wheat which is first soaked, then boiled for a few hours in a little water and finally dried. After being treated in this way the wheat is coarsely ground to the consistency of semolina. You can buy bulgur in health food shops.

Fried Rice

500 ml/17 fl oz water
250 g/9 oz long-grain brown rice
1 onion
2 cloves garlic
100 g/4 oz mushrooms
1 tablespoon lemon juice
500 g/18 oz broccoli
2 tablespoons vegetable oil
1 tablespoon soy sauce
2 tablespoons dry sherry
salt
freshly ground white pepper
2 eggs

Bring the water to the boil in a saucepan. Add the rice, reduce the heat, cover the pan and cook the rice over the lowest possible heat for about 40 minutes until fluffy. Allow to cool.

Peel and finely chop the onion and garlic. Trim the mushrooms, wash if necessary and thinly slice. Sprinkle at once with the lemon juice. Trim and wash the broccoli and separate into florets and stalks.

Heat half the oil in a frying pan and fry the onion and garlic until transparent, stirring often. Add the broccoli stalks and cook for about 3 minutes, stirring continuously. Add the mushrooms and broccoli florets and cook, stirring often, until the vegetables are tender but still firm to bite and the liquid that forms has evaporated. Remove the vegetables from the pan and keep hot.

Heat the remaining oil in the pan and fry the rice until lightly browned. Stir in the vegetables. Season with the soy sauce, sherry, and salt and pepper to taste.

Beat the eggs with a fork, pour over the rice and stir in until the egg sets. Serve the rice in a warmed dish with Sprouted salad (recipe page 26).

Serves 4

Per Portion
about 385 calories
55 g carbohydrate
14 g protein · 9 g fat

Tempting Tofu Ideas

Tofu Schnitzel with Green Rye and Mushrooms

300 g/11 oz tofu
4 tablespoons soy sauce
200 ml/7 fl oz freshly made vege-
  table stock (recipe page 38)
100 g/4 oz rye grain
1 slice stale rye or wholemeal
  bread (about 40 g/1½ oz)
2 bunches of fresh parsley
1 onion
400 g/14 oz fresh mushrooms
  (button, oyster or mixed)
2 tablespoons wholemeal flour
freshly grated nutmeg
1 egg
5 tablespoons sunflower oil
salt
freshly ground white pepper

Drain the tofu and cut into slices scant 1 cm/½ in thick. Place the slices side by side in a shallow dish, sprinkle with the soy sauce and marinate for 2 hours, turning frequently so that they soak up the soy sauce.

Bring the stock to the boil in a saucepan. Add the rye, reduce the heat to low, cover the pan and simmer gently for 25 minutes. Remove the pan from the heat and leave the rye to soak in the open pan for 1 hour.

Finely grate the rye or wholemeal bread or whizz to crumbs in a liquidiser. Wash the parsley, strip the leaves from the stalks, dry well and finely chop. Peel and finely chop the onion. Trim the mushrooms, rinse, if necessary, and thinly slice.

Transfer the tofu slices from the bowl to a thick layer of absorbent kitchen paper. If they are too wet the coating will not stick.

To make the coating, put the wholemeal flour into a shallow dish and mix in nutmeg to taste. Beat the egg with a fork in a second dish and tip the breadcrumbs into a third dish.

First dip the tofu slices in flour, then in egg and finally in breadcrumbs.

Heat 4 tablespoons oil in a frying pan. Fry the tofu slices

over a moderate heat for about 5 minutes until golden brown on each side. Keep hot in the oven.

Heat the remaining oil in the pan and fry the onion until transparent. Add the mushrooms and rye and heat through over a high heat, stirring continuously. You need the temperature really high to prevent the mushrooms producing juice. Stir in the chopped parsley and season to taste.

Serve the tofu schnitzel and rye and mushrooms separately. Serve with a mixed salad with sunflower or pumpkin seeds in a garlic and herb vinaigrette.

Serves 4

Per Portion
about 380 calories
37 g carbohydrate
16 g protein · 17 g fat

Cook's Tip

If you can't get rye, use whole wheat grain (wheat berries) which you boil for 1 hour and leave to soak for 1 further hour.

You can, if you like, add some sesame seeds to the breadcrumbs which coat the tofu. Alternatively add some poppy seeds or very finely chopped nuts to vary the flavour and texture.

Tofu Balls in Caper Sauce

1 onion
bunch of fresh parsley
300 g / 11 oz tofu
2 tablespoons soy sauce
1 egg
3 tablespoons finely grated walnuts
2 tablespoons fine wholemeal breadcrumbs
1–2 tablespoons grated Parmesan cheese
freshly ground white pepper
2 tablespoons wholemeal flour
scant 450 ml / ¾ pint cold freshly made vegetable stock (recipe page 38)
1 tablespoon butter
4 tablespoons cream
1 tablespoon capers
2 tablespoons chopped fresh chervil
1 teaspoon lemon juice
salt

Peel and finely chop the onion. Wash and finely chop the parsley. Crush the tofu.

Mix the tofu with the onion, parsley, soy sauce, egg, nuts, breadcrumbs and Parmesan. Knead by hand to bind together and season to taste with white pepper. Shape the mixture into walnut-sized balls.

Tip the flour into a saucepan and stir over a high heat until it gives off a pleasant smell. Gradually whisk in the vegetable stock. Continue whisking until the sauce comes to the boil and thickens to a smooth, velvety consistency.

Add the tofu balls and simmer gently for 10 minutes. Lift out the balls on a slotted spoon and keep hot in a warmed serving dish.

Whisk the butter into the sauce. Stir in the cream, capers, chervil and lemon juice and season the sauce to taste with salt. Pour over the tofu balls.

Serves 4

Per Portion
about 220 calories
10 g carbohydrate
10 g protein · 15 g fat

Fried Tofu with Vegetables

300 g / 11 oz tofu
4 tablespoons soy sauce
1 tablespoon dry sherry
250 g / 9 oz each leeks, celeriac and sprouted chickpeas
1 clove garlic
1½ tablespoons wholemeal flour
3 tablespoons oil
125 ml / 4 fl oz freshly made vegetable stock (recipe page 38)
freshly ground white pepper
2 tablespoons chopped fresh parsley
gomasio for sprinkling

Drain the tofu and cut into 1-cm/½-in cubes. Pour the soy sauce and sherry over the tofu and marinate for at least 30 minutes, turning frequently.

Trim and wash the leeks, shake dry and cut into 1-cm/½-in lengths. Peel and wash the celeriac. Slice and then cut into sticks about 0.5 cm/¼ in wide. Wash the chickpea sprouts. Peel and finely chop the garlic.

Drain the tofu, reserving the marinade, and coat in the flour. Heat 2 tablespoons oil in a frying pan and fry the tofu until brown and crisp, stirring frequently. Remove and keep hot.

Heat the remaining oil in the pan and fry the leeks, celeriac, chickpea sprouts and garlic over a moderate to high heat until the vegetables are coated in oil. Add the stock and tofu marinade. Bring to the boil, cover and simmer for 5 to 7 minutes.

Season to taste with pepper. Arrange the tofu on the vegetables and serve sprinkled with parsley and gomasio.

Serves 4

Per Portion
about 195 calories
24 g carbohydrate
13 g protein · 5 g fat

Nuts and Pulses

Black Beans and Sweetcorn

300 g/11 oz dried black beans
2 leeks
½ celeriac
3 carrots
bunch of fresh parsley
bunch of fresh savory
1 bay leaf
4 white peppercorns
2 shallots
2 (325 g/11½ oz) cans sweetcorn
  kernels
2 tablespoons vegetable oil
salt
freshly ground white pepper
250 ml/8 fl oz crème fraîche or
  double cream
hot chilli powder

Wash the beans then soak in cold water for 12 hours.

The following day, trim and wash the leeks. Peel and wash the celeriac and carrots. Chop these vegetables coarsely. Wash the herbs and shake dry. Strip the parsley leaves from the stalks and chop.

Tip the beans and soaking water into a saucepan and add the leeks, celeriac, carrots, parsley stalks, savory, bay leaf and peppercorns. Bring to the boil, cover and simmer for about 1¼ hours until the beans are tender.

Drain the beans and discard the vegetables, herbs and peppercorns.

Peel and finely chop the shallots. Drain the sweetcorn.

Heat the oil in a saucepan and fry the shallots until transparent. Add the beans and sweetcorn and season to taste. Stir in the crème fraîche, bring back to the boil, cover and cook gently for 5 minutes. Season with a pinch of chilli powder and garnish with chopped parsley.

Serves 4

Per Portion
about 665 calories
84 g carbohydrate
23 g protein · 26 g fat

Nut Curry

300 g/11 oz cashew nuts
250 g/9 oz fresh peeled coconut
350 ml/12 fl oz warm water
1 onion
1 clove garlic
1 red pepper
1 teaspoon turmeric
½ teaspoon ground ginger
½ teaspoon ground anise or
  cumin
pinch of ground cinnamon
salt
3 tablespoons sunflower oil

Tip the cashew nuts into a bowl, cover with warm water and soak for 4 hours.

Break the coconut into pieces and blend with the water in a liquidiser. Pour the puréed coconut through a muslin-lined sieve placed over a bowl, pressing it well with a wooden spoon. Discard the coconut in the sieve and keep the milk in reserve for the curry.

Peel and finely chop the onion and garlic. Halve the red pepper and remove the stalk, pith and seeds. Rinse in cold water, dry and cut into fine strips.

In a bowl mix the turmeric, ginger, anise or cumin, cinnamon and salt to taste.

Drain the nuts.

Heat the oil in a frying pan and fry the onion and garlic until transparent. Add the nuts and red pepper and fry until the liquid has evaporated.

Sprinkle the spices over the nuts and pour on the coconut milk. Stir well, bring to the boil, cover the pan and cook over a low heat for 5 minutes.

Serve with brown rice.

Serves 4

Per Portion
about 755 calories
30 g carbohydrate
16 g protein · 63 g fat

Black Beans with Tomatoes

300 g / 11 oz dried black beans
3 cloves garlic
sprig of fresh rosemary
1 dried chilli pepper
1 bay leaf
500 ml / 17 fl oz freshly made
  unsalted vegetable stock
  (recipe page 38)
250 ml / 8 fl oz dry red wine
500 g / 18 oz tomatoes
2 wheatgerm or wholemeal rolls
bunch of fresh basil
5 tablespoons olive oil
pinch of caster sugar
salt
freshly ground black pepper

Rinse the beans in cold water and then soak in cold water for 12 hours.

The following day, peel 1 clove garlic. Rinse the rosemary. Rub the chilli pepper between finger and thumb to crumble it.

Put the drained beans in a saucepan and add the peeled garlic, rosemary, chilli pepper, bay leaf, vegetable stock and wine. Bring to the boil, cover and cook for 1½ hours.

Meanwhile, blanch the tomatoes in boiling water for 30 seconds, rinse in cold water and peel. Coarsely chop the tomatoes, removing the core and the seeds. Dice the rolls. Wash the basil, shake dry and coarsely chop. Peel and finely chop the remaining garlic.

Heat 1 tablespoon oil in a saucepan. Add the tomatoes and cook until soft, stirring.

Heat the remaining oil in a frying pan and fry the bread cubes until golden brown. Add the garlic and fry briefly.

Mix the beans with the tomato and basil and season with the sugar and salt and pepper to taste. Scatter over the fried bread cubes.

Serves 4

Per Portion
about 485 calories
59 g carbohydrate
20 g protein · 13 g fat

Russian-style Lentils

1 leek
¼ celeriac
2 carrots
1 shallot
1 clove garlic
400 g / 14 oz red lentils
1 tablespoon butter
about 1 litre / 1¾ pints water
2 cloves
1 bay leaf
3 white peppercorns
2 bunches of fresh chives
250 ml / 8 fl oz soured cream
salt
freshly ground white pepper

Trim and wash the leek. Peel and wash the celeriac and carrots. Dice these vegetables. Peel and finely chop the shallot and garlic. Rinse the lentils in cold water.

Heat the butter in a saucepan. Fry the leek, celeriac, carrots, shallot and garlic until the shallot and garlic are transparent, stirring frequently. Add the lentils and cook for a few minutes. Add the water, then the cloves, bay leaf and peppercorns. Bring to the boil, cover the pan and cook over a low heat for 10 to 15 minutes until the lentils are tender but still with some bite. If the mixture becomes too dry, add a little more water.

Rinse the chives in cold water, dry and finely snip.

Stir the soured cream into the lentils and reheat but do not boil. Season to taste. Stir about two-thirds of the chives into the lentils and scatter the rest on top. Serve with wholemeal pasta or brown rice and a salad.

Serves 4

Per Portion
about 435 calories
62 g carbohydrate
26 g protein · 10 g fat

Nuts and Pulses

White Beans Provençal

300 g / 11 oz dried white haricot
beans
sprig of fresh rosemary
2 sprigs of fresh thyme
1 bay leaf
400 g / 14 oz ripe tomatoes
1 onion
3 cloves garlic
6 tablespoons olive oil
salt
freshly ground black pepper
1–2 tablespoons raspberry
vinegar
3 tablespoons chopped fresh
parsley
2 tablespoons capers

Wash the beans and soak in cold water for 12 hours.

The following day, wash the rosemary and thyme and shake dry. Tip the beans and soaking water into a saucepan and add the herbs and bay leaf. Bring to the boil, then reduce the heat to low, cover the pan and cook for 1¾ hours.

Blanch the tomatoes in boiling water for 30 seconds, rinse in cold water and peel. Dice the tomatoes, removing the core and the seeds. Peel and finely chop the onion and garlic.

Heat 2 tablespoons olive oil in a saucepan and fry the onion and garlic until transparent. Add the tomatoes and the beans with their cooking water. Discard the bay leaf and herbs. Cover the pan and cook over a low heat for a further 15 minutes until the beans are tender.

Season to taste with salt, pepper and raspberry vinegar and mix with the remaining olive oil, the parsley and capers.

Transfer the beans to a warmed dish and serve with lamb chops or wholemeal bread and butter.

Serves 4

Per Portion
about 440 calories
50 g carbohydrate
18 g protein · 17 g fat

Red Beans with Apple

400 g / 14 oz dried red kidney
beans
400 g / 14 oz fairly tart apples
250 g / 9 oz onions
2 cloves garlic
2 tablespoons vegetable oil
250 ml / 8 fl oz cider
1 teaspoon dried marjoram
salt
freshly ground black pepper
cayenne pepper

Tip the beans into a sieve and rinse in cold water. Soak in cold water for 12 hours.

The following day, tip the beans and soaking water into a saucepan and bring to the boil. Boil hard for 3 minutes. Cover the pan, reduce the heat and simmer gently for 1½ hours.

Peel, core and coarsely chop the apples. Peel the onions and cut into rings. Peel and chop the garlic.

Heat the oil in a saucepan. Fry the apples, onions and gar-lic until transparent, stirring often.

Drain the beans, add to the apples and cook for a few minutes, stirring continuously. Add the cider and marjoram. Bring to the boil, cover the pan and simmer over a low heat for about 30 minutes or until the apples are very soft.

Season the beans to taste with salt, black pepper and a pinch of cayenne and transfer to a warmed dish. Serve with lamb or poultry, or for a vegetarian meal, serve with brown rice.

Serves 4

Per Portion
about 485 calories
74 g carbohydrate
23 g protein · 7 g fat

Puddings, Desserts and Drinks

The rich strudel made with a healthy refined flour and with a delicious filling of soft cheese and cherries is sure to delight both children and adults alike. Even those with the sweetest tooth will find that wholefood cooking has much to offer. There are baked desserts like the savarin with dried fruit and cream or an unusual boiled pudding with nuts and sprouts. Apple pancakes; Quark balls with cinnamon and wholemeal breadcrumbs fried in butter; or Millet and rice cakes served with stewed fruit – a selection of tempting and unusual puddings. Or perhaps you prefer a lighter dessert. Our Honey ice cream on orange salad, flavoured with orange liqueur, peaches topped with nut meringue or fresh plums with a tasty custard will delight even the most refined palate. The chapter ends with a selection of milk shakes made with fruit and nuts which make satisfying and refreshing drinks for between meals and savoury drinks which can be served as a vitamin-rich starter before a heavy main course. You can use our suggestions as a basis for your own creations.

Wholemeal Savarin with Stewed Fruit

300 g/11 oz wheatmeal flour
30 g/1¼ oz fresh yeast
scant 125 ml/4 fl oz lukewarm
  milk
90 g/3½ oz butter
3 tablespoons honey
½ lemon
2 eggs
1 egg yolk
1 teaspoon vanilla sugar
salt
250 g/9 oz prunes
  (unsulphurised)
2 liqueur glasses plum brandy
250 ml/8 fl oz dry white wine
2 tablespoons orange marmalade
½ cinnamon stick
butter and flour for the tin
250 g/9 oz cooking apples
2 teaspoons ground cinnamon
250 ml/8 fl oz double or whipping
  cream

To make the savarin, put the flour into a mixing bowl. Make a well in the centre and crumble in the yeast. Stir the yeast with 2 tablespoons milk and a little of the flour in the bowl. Cover the bowl and leave to stand in a warm place for 15 minutes.

Meanwhile, pour the remaining milk into a pan and add the butter and 1 tablespoon honey. Warm over a low heat until the butter and honey have melted.

Wash the lemon in hot water, dry and then grate the rind. Squeeze the juice and keep to one side for the stewed apple.

Add the butter and honey mixture, the grated lemon rind, the eggs, egg yolk, vanilla sugar and a pinch of salt to the yeast mixture and mix until smooth, beating the mixture with a wooden spoon until light and airy and coming away from the sides of the bowl.

Cover and leave to rise in a warm place for 30 minutes.

Rinse the prunes under hot running water and drain. Put into a bowl and pour on the plum brandy.

Keeping 2 tablespoons in reserve for the stewed apple, heat the white wine with the marmalade, 1 tablespoon honey and the cinnamon stick over a low heat until the honey is fluid. Pour over the prunes, cover and leave to soak until the savarin is cooked.

Grease and flour a savarin or ring tin. Fill with the dough, cover and leave to rise again until it has more or less doubled in volume. This takes around 30 minutes.

Bake the savarin in a moderately hot oven (200 C, 400 F, gas 6), on the second shelf from the bottom, for 30 to 35 minutes.

Meanwhile, peel and core the apples and cut into thick slices. Put the apples in a saucepan with the lemon juice and the remaining wine. Bring to the boil, then cover and cook over a low heat until tender but not mushy. Stir in the remaining honey and the ground cinnamon.

Drain the prunes, reserving the juice; discard the cinnamon stick. Gently mix the prunes with the apple.

Turn the savarin out on to a plate and prick all over with a cocktail stick. Using a teaspoon, spoon the juice from the prunes over the savarin so that it is absorbed evenly. Leave until lukewarm.

Whip the cream and fold into the prunes and apple. Spoon into the centre of the savarin before serving.

Serves 6

Per Portion
about 700 calories
79 g carbohydrate
12 g protein · 32 g fat

Cook's Tip

The savarin is just as delicious filled with fresh fruit.

Hearty Puddings

Pudding with Nuts and Sprouts

100 g/4 oz mixed dried fruit
40 g/1½ oz unsalted shelled
    pistachios
2 tablespoons orange liqueur
butter and fine wholemeal bread-
    crumbs for the basin
1 tablespoon sprouted chickpeas
½ orange
100 g/4 oz butter, softened
1 tablespoon honey
generous pinch each of ground
    cloves, cardamom and nutmeg
½ teaspoon ground cinnamon
salt
2 tablespoons vanilla sugar
4 eggs, separated
1 tablespoon sprouted whole
    wheat grain (wheat berries)
50 g/2 oz cornflour

Finely chop the dried fruit and
pistachios. Put into a bowl, stir
in the orange liqueur, cover and
leave to soak for 30 minutes.

Butter a 900-ml/1½-pint pudding basin or mould and sprinkle with breadcrumbs. Crush
the chickpea sprouts. Grate the
orange rind.

Cream the butter with the
honey until light and fluffy. Stir
in all the spices, orange rind, a
pinch of salt and the vanilla sugar. Beat the egg yolks a little
at a time into the butter mixture. Stir in the dried fruit and
pistachio mixture, chickpeas
and wheat grain sprouts.

Whisk the egg whites until
very stiff. Spoon on to the pudding mixture, sprinkle on the
cornflour and fold in gently.
Pour the mixture into the pudding basin and cover with a lid
or greaseproof paper and foil
tied on with string. Place the
basin in a saucepan and pour in
boiling water to come two
thirds of the way up the sides of
the basin. Cover and steam for
about 70 minutes or until a
skewer inserted into the middle
comes out clean.

Lift the basin out of the
water and leave to stand,
covered, for 10 minutes. Serve
hot, with custard flavoured
with finely chopped orange
rind.

Serves 6

Per Portion
about 735 calories
130 g carbohydrate
4 g protein · 20 g fat

Quark and Cherry Strudel

250 g/9 oz wheatmeal flour
salt
125 ml/4 fl oz lukewarm water
5 tablespoons vegetable oil
1 egg yolk
1 kg/2¼ lb Morello cherries or
  600 g/1¼ lb bottled or canned
  Morello cherries
3 slices stale wholemeal bread
1 orange
500 g/18 oz low-fat Quark or
  other soft cheese
125 ml/4 fl oz crème fraîche or
  soured cream
2 eggs
3 tablespoons maple syrup
2 tablespoons vanilla sugar
75 g/3 oz butter for coating
flour for rolling

Strudel dough should always be left to stand in a warm place for a while to make it smooth enough to stretch. The best way is to bring a little water to the boil in a pan. Then tip away the water, cover the empty pan

and leave it in a warm place so that it is warm rather than hot.

To make the dough, mix the flour with a pinch of salt, the water, oil and egg yolk. The dough should be soft and smooth but not sticky. If necessary you can add a few more drops of lukewarm water or a little more flour to give the right consistency. Wrap the dough in greaseproof paper and stand in the warm pan for about 30 minutes.

To make the filling, wash and drain the cherries. Remove the stalks and stones. If you are using bottled or canned cherries they should be thoroughly drained.

Grate the wholemeal bread in a nut mill, or make into fine crumbs in a liquidiser or food processor. Set aside.

Grate about half the orange rind and squeeze out the juice.

Beat the Quark with the orange rind and juice, the crème fraîche or soured cream, eggs, maple syrup and vanilla sugar. Stir in the prepared cherries.

Place the butter in a baking tin large enough to take two strudels side by side and place the tin in a hot oven (220 C, 425 F, gas 7) to melt the butter.

Halve the strudel dough. Roll out one portion on a floured worktop and then place on a floured tea towel and stretch as thin as possible by hand. The easiest way to do this is to drape the dough like a cloth over the backs of your lightly clenched fists and to stretch it gently from the centre. Then spread it on the tea towel again and stretch the edges between your fingertips.

Brush the stretched dough with a little of the melted butter. Sprinkle with half the breadcrumbs and cover with half the filling, making sure you leave 1–2 cm/½–¾ in clear around the edge to prevent the filling spilling out as you roll the strudel. Fold the shorter sides of the dough in a little way. Lift the edge of the tea towel and roll up the strudel away from you. Lift the rolled strudel on the cloth and gently

slide it into the baking tin. Repeat the whole process with the second portion of strudel dough.

Brush the strudels well with melted butter. Pour the remaining butter into a small pan and keep warm.

Place the tin on the second shelf from the bottom of the oven and bake for about 25 minutes, brushing frequently with the remaining melted butter to make it nice and brown.

Serves 6

Per Portion
about 635 calories
70 g carbohydrate
22 g protein · 29 g fat

Hearty Puddings

Millet and Rice Griddle Cakes

200 g / 7 oz millet flakes
200 g / 7 oz brown rice flour
40 g / 1½ oz fresh yeast
scant 375 ml / 13 fl oz lukewarm
  milk
3 eggs
100 g / 4 oz butter, softened
2 tablespoons maple syrup
1 tablespoon vanilla sugar
salt
grated rind of ½ orange
vegetable oil for frying

Bring all the ingredients to room temperature.

In a food processor or liquidiser, grind the millet flakes to a fine flour. Mix with the rice flour in a bowl. Make a well in the middle. Add the crumbled yeast, the milk, eggs, butter, maple syrup, vanilla sugar, a pinch of salt and the orange rind. Gradually work in the flour, then beat to a smooth batter. Cover and leave to stand for 1 hour.

Lightly grease and heat a griddle or frying pan. Using 2 tablespoons batter for each, fry small cakes over a moderate to low heat until the underside is brown and coming away from the pan. Turn and cook gently on the second side. Don't have the pan too hot or the cakes will break as you turn them. When the temperature is right the cakes will puff up as they cook. Keep the cooked cakes hot.

Add more batter to the pan and continue in this way until all the cakes are cooked. Keep the pan lightly greased as you cook the batter.

Serve with stewed blackberries, Morello cherries or plums.

Serves 6

Per Portion
about 600 calories
60 g carbohydrate
13 g protein · 33 g fat

Apple Pancakes

250 g / 9 oz wholemeal flour
salt
3 eggs
500 ml / 17 fl oz buttermilk
½ lemon
500 g / 18 oz cooking apples
4 tablespoons sugar
2 tablespoons ground hazelnuts
2 teaspoons ground cinnamon
about 75 g / 3 oz butter for frying

Beat the flour with a pinch of salt, the eggs and buttermilk to make the pancake batter. Cover and leave to stand for 30 minutes.

Meanwhile squeeze the juice from the lemon. Peel and core the apples and cut into thin wedges. Sprinkle with the lemon juice. Mix the sugar with the hazelnuts and cinnamon.

Stir the batter. If it is too thick add a little mineral water.

Heat 1 tablespoon butter in a frying pan. Pour scant 1 ladleful batter into the pan, tilting the pan so that the bottom

is evenly covered. Cover the pancake with apple slices and sprinkle with the sugar mixture. Cook over a moderate heat until the pancake comes easily away from the bottom of the pan.

Reduce the heat, turn the pancake carefully and cook on the other side until fully cooked, keeping the heat low to avoid burning the sugar. Keep the cooked pancakes hot, and cook the remaining pancakes in the same way.

Serves 6

Per Portion
about 400 calories
50 g carbohydrate
9 g protein · 15 g fat

Dinner Party Desserts

Cheese Dumplings

*500 g/18 oz home-made curd
  cheese (recipe page 29)*
120 g/4½ oz wholemeal semolina
*25 g/1 oz wholemeal or
  wheatmeal flour*
1 egg
1 teaspoon caster sugar
salt
grated rind of ¼ lemon
50 g/2 oz butter
*1 tablespoon stale wholemeal
  breadcrumbs*
*1 tablespoon caster sugar mixed
  with 1 teaspoon ground
  cinnamon*

For these dumplings you need
dry, well-drained curd cheese.

Mix the cheese with the
semolina, flour, egg, sugar, a
pinch of salt and the grated
lemon rind to make a dough.
Cover and leave to stand for 30
minutes.

Bring a large pan of salted
water to the boil. Using 2 tablespoons, make a test dumpling
and drop into the fast boiling
water. If it does not fall apart

the dough is the right consistency and you can make and
cook the remaining dumplings.
If it does fall apart the dough is
too soft and needs a little more
semolina added. Reduce the
heat and cook the dumplings
gently for 10 to 15 minutes.

Heat the butter in a frying
pan and fry the breadcrumbs
until crisp.

Remove the dumplings from
the water, drain and arrange on
a warm plate. Sprinkle with the
cinnamon-sugar and pour on
the buttered crumbs.

Serves 4

Per Portion
about 380 calories
36 g carbohydrate
25 g protein · 13 g fat

Peaches with Nut Meringue

*4 ripe peaches (preferably
  white)*
2 tablespoons lemon juice
*2 tablespoons Cassis
  (blackcurrant liqueur)*
3 egg whites
pinch of salt
*75 g/3 oz shelled hazelnuts,
  finely ground*
3 tablespoons maple syrup

Blanch the peaches in boiling
water for 30 seconds, rinse in
cold water and peel. Halve,
stone and slice the peaches.
Cover the bottom of a shallow
baking dish with the peaches
and sprinkle with the lemon
juice and Cassis.

Whisk the egg whites with
the salt until very stiff. Fold the
hazelnuts and maple syrup
gently into the whites using a
metal spoon or a spatula.
Mix very gently at this stage for
if you beat vigorously the
meringue will lose air.

Spoon the meringue over the
peaches and smooth the top.
Bake in a hot oven (220 C, 425 F,
gas 7) for about 10 minutes until the meringue is lightly
browned. Serve hot or the
meringue will become soft.

Serves 4

Per Portion
about 225 calories
24 g carbohydrate
6 g protein · 12 g fat

Plums with Custard

250 g/9 oz plums
½ orange
2 tablespoons caster sugar
½ vanilla pod
250 ml/8 fl oz milk
salt
1 egg yolk
2 teaspoons cornflour
2 slices (about 80 g/3 oz) stale wholemeal bread
2 tablespoons white rum
125 ml/4 fl oz double or whipping cream
2 tablespoons coarsely chopped walnuts

Halve and stone the plums. Cut off a very thin piece of orange rind about 3 cm/1¼ in long. Squeeze out the juice.

Cook the plums with the orange juice and 1 tablespoon sugar in a covered pan for about 2 minutes until they begin to soften. Set aside.

Slit the vanilla pod open lengthways. Scrape out the seeds and add to the milk with a pinch of salt and orange rind. Bring to just below boiling point.

Meanwhile, beat the egg yolk with the remaining sugar until frothy. Stir in the cornflour. Whisking continuously, add the hot milk, then return to the pan. Cook gently, stirring, until the custard thickens. Leave the custard to cool, stirring from time to time to prevent a skin forming.

Coarsely grate or grind the bread and moisten with the rum.

Whip the cream until stiff and fold into the cooled custard.

Fill 4 glasses with the plums and their juice, then add the breadcrumb mixture and finally the custard. Top with the walnuts.

Serves 4

Per Portion
about 360 calories
40 g carbohydrate
7 g protein · 18 g fat

Honey Ice with Orange Salad

100 g/4 oz honey
2 eggs
pinch of ground ginger
grated rind of ½ orange
250 ml/8 fl oz double or whipping cream
1 kg/2¼ lb oranges
2 liqueur glasses orange liqueur
3 tablespoons unsalted shelled pistachios

Fill a saucepan with hot water and place over a low heat. Tip the honey into a heatproof basin and warm in the water until fluid.

Add the eggs, ginger and orange rind and whisk until thick and frothy.

Tip away the hot water and fill the pan with cold water and a few ice cubes. Place the bowl in the iced water and, stirring continuously, allow to cool. This prevents the ingredients separating out again.

Whip the cream until stiff and fold gently into the honey mixture. Cover the bowl and leave to set in the freezer until firm taking it out and whisking from time to time to prevent ice crystals forming and to keep the ice cream nice and smooth.

Peel the oranges, removing all the white pith, and thinly slice lengthways, removing the pips as you go and catching the juice. Arrange the sliced orange on plates. Stir the liqueur into the orange juice and sprinkle over the oranges. Coarsely chop the pistachios and scatter over the oranges.

Serve with the honey ice cream.

Serves 6

Per Portion
about 330 calories
37 g carbohydrate
6 g protein · 17 g fat

Bilberry Pudding

250 g/9 oz bilberries
250 ml/8 fl oz lukewarm milk
3 eggs
pinch of salt
1 teaspoon caster sugar
20 g/¾ oz fresh yeast
175 g/6 oz wholemeal or
  wheatmeal flour
50 g/2 oz butter
125 ml/4 fl oz double or whipping
  cream
2 tablespoons honey

Pick over the bilberries, rinse under cold running water if necessary and drain very well.

Beat the milk with the eggs, salt and sugar. Crumble in the yeast. Gradually whisk in the flour and continue whisking until completely smooth.

Place the butter in a shallow baking dish and place in a moderate oven (180 C, 350 F, gas 4) to melt.

Pour the batter into the dish and scatter with the bilberries. Bake in the oven for 10 minutes.

Whip the cream with the honey and pour over the bilberry pudding. Bake for a further 10 minutes until the top is nice and brown.

Serves 4

Per Portion
about 540 calories
50 g carbohydrate
13 g protein · 30 g fat

Cook's Tip
The pudding is delicious made with fresh Morello cherries, or in winter with frozen berries.

Strawberries with Dates

400 g/14 oz strawberries
100 g/4 oz fresh dates
100 g/4 oz shelled walnuts
1 tablespoon lemon juice
250 ml/8 fl oz double or whipping
  cream
½ tablespoon maple syrup
2 tablespoons rum

Wash the strawberries well, pat dry, remove the stalks and cut into slices. Arrange decoratively on six plates.

Stone the dates and halve or quarter them. Coarsely chop the walnuts on a board using a heavy knife.

In a basin, mix the walnuts and dates with the lemon juice. Cover and leave to stand at room temperature for 15 minutes.

Whip the cream until stiff. Whisk in the maple syrup and rum.

Scatter the date and walnut mixture over the strawberries

and serve the rum cream separately.

Serves 6

Per Portion
about 330 calories
20 g carbohydrate
4 g protein · 24 g fat

Cook's Tip
The strawberries are delicious with a wine sauce instead of cream: place 2 egg yolks in a heatproof basin with ½ tablespoon maple syrup and 125 ml/ 4 fl oz dry white wine. Whisk over hot water with a hand or electric whisk until light and frothy. Arrange the prepared strawberries in glass dishes, cover with the wine sauce and serve at once.

Dinner Party Desserts

Elderflowers in Batter

12 sprigs elderflowers
150 g/5 oz wheatmeal flour
pinch of salt
125 ml/4 fl oz milk
2 eggs
600 ml/1 pint corn oil
3 tablespoons honey
1 teaspoon ground cinnamon

You can pick elderflowers during May and June. Never pick them from road-side trees because they could be full of harmful substances.

Rinse the flowers well to get rid of any insects, then shake well and dry on absorbent kitchen paper.

For the batter, beat the flour with the salt and milk until smooth.

Separate the eggs. Beat the yolks into the batter, which should then be quite thin. Leave the batter to stand for 15 minutes to allow the flour to swell. If it becomes too thick add a little mineral water.

Whisk the egg whites until stiff and fold gently into the batter.

Heat about one third of the oil in a small pan into which a whole flower head will fit. Take one elder sprig by the stalk, dip in the batter and cook in the oil over a moderate to high heat until golden brown.

As they are cooked keep the sprigs warm in a low oven.

Heat more oil and fry the remaining flowers in the same way.

Gently warm the honey until fluid and stir in the cinnamon.

Arrange the elder flowers on 4 plates, pour on the honey and serve at once. Delicious with honey ice cream (recipe page 135).

Serves 4

Per Portion
about 425 calories
39 g carbohydrate
6 g protein · 27 g fat

Drinks, Sweet and Savoury

Milk Shakes

Serves 1

Peach

1 small ripe peach
1 tablespoon cranberry sauce
125 ml/4 fl oz each milk and sour
*   milk or buttermilk*

Blanch the peach in boiling
water for 30 seconds, rinse in
cold water and peel. Halve,
stone and slice the peach. Blend
in a liquidiser with the cranberry sauce, milk and sour milk
or buttermilk.

Per Portion
about 220 calories
26 g carbohydrate
9 g protein · 9 g fat

Pistachio

30 g/1¼ oz shelled, unsalted
*   pistachios*
small piece of candied ginger
250 ml/8 fl oz milk
½ tablespoon each maple syrup
*   and fluid honey*

Blend the pistachios and ginger
with the milk in a liquidiser.
Add the syrup and honey and
blend again briefly. Serve
chilled.

Per Portion
about 390 calories
28 g carbohydrate
14 g protein · 25 g fat

Almond

30 g/1¼ oz blanched almonds
1 tablespoon white rum
1 teaspoon honey
250 ml/8 fl oz milk

Stir the almonds in a pan without fat until golden brown.
Blend in a liquidiser with the

rum, honey and milk, until the
almonds have been finely
chopped.

Per Portion
about 385 calories
22 g carbohydrate
14 g protein · 23 g fat

Banana

1 small ripe banana
½ orange
1 tablespoon honey
250 ml/8 fl oz buttermilk

Peel the banana. Squeeze the
juice from the orange. Place
both in a liquidiser with the
honey and buttermilk and
blend well. If you like you can
serve sprinkled with finely
chopped orange rind.

Per Portion
about 265 calories
47 g carbohydrate
6 g protein · 2 g fat

Apple

1 small fairly tart apple
½ lemon
½ tablespoon maple syrup
180 ml/6 fl oz soya milk
pinch of ground cinnamon

Peel, core and slice the apple.
Squeeze the juice from the
lemon. Blend the apple with the
lemon juice, maple syrup and
soya milk in a liquidiser until
the apple is reduced to a pulp.
Flavour with the cinnamon and
serve well chilled – possibly
decorated with a sprig of
lemon balm.

Per Portion
about 135 calories
19 g carbohydrate
6 g protein · 3 g fat

Drinks, Sweet and Savoury

Grapefruit Juice with Apple

1 small apple
250 ml/8 fl oz grapefruit juice
few leaves of fresh marjoram,
   chopped
salt
pinch of caster sugar
freshly ground white pepper

Peel, quarter and core the apple. Blend the apple quarters with the grapefruit juice in a liquidiser. Stir in the marjoram and season to taste with salt, sugar and pepper.

Serves 1

Per Portion
about 120 calories
25 g carbohydrate
5 g protein · 0 g fat

Tomato Juice

250 g/9 oz ripe tomatoes
salt
freshly ground white pepper
Tabasco sauce
½ teaspoon vegetable oil

Blanch the tomatoes in boiling water for 30 seconds, rinse in cold water and peel. Halve the tomatoes, remove the core and the seeds and blend in a liquidiser. Season generously with salt, pepper and Tabasco sauce. Stir in the oil. If the drink is too thick add a little uncarbonated mineral water. Serve well chilled, garnished with a few fresh basil or cress leaves.

Serves 1

Per Portion
about 52 calories
10 g carbohydrate
2 g protein · 0 g fat

Orange and Carrot Juice

250 g/9 oz young carrots
2 juicy oranges
1 tablespoon lemon juice
½ teaspoon vegetable oil
1 teaspoon chopped fresh parsley

Trim, scrape and wash the carrots. Squeeze in an electric juice extractor. Squeeze the juice from the oranges. Mix together the orange, carrot and lemon juices. Stir in the oil and parsley.

Serves 1

Per Portion
about 280 calories
48 g carbohydrate
5 g protein · 3 g fat

Herb Drink

125 ml/4 fl oz uncarbonated
   mineral water
150 ml/¼ pint natural yogurt
3 tablespoons chopped mixed
   fresh herbs (eg parsley, dill,
   cress or watercress, borage
   and lemon balm)
1 teaspoon lemon juice
salt
freshly ground white pepper

Stir the mineral water into the yogurt and whisk thoroughly. Stir in the herbs and lemon juice and season to taste. If you like, serve garnished with a sprig of fresh herbs.

Serves 1

Per Portion
about 90 calories
10 g carbohydrate
7 g protein · 3 g fat

Fresh and crunchy, attractive and delicious – this is what we want our food to be. But there is more to it if we look beyond the culinary aspects and take our daily health into account. We need to know what we are eating and the best way of preparing it. You will find all you need to know in the following pages. You will find an A to Z of utensils for the modern, nutrition-conscious cook – be they pans for nutritious cooking, preserving equipment, cereal mills or germinating trays for fresh sprouts, special equipment for steaming and dehydrating.

The glossary includes all those terms which you may often have heard, but of which you want to know more. It includes information on alternative forms of agriculture, on meat, fish and poultry. It tells you what to look for when buying everyday products and how to avoid harmful substances wherever possible.

Eating with pleasure and enjoyment is the motto of this book. But for this you need not only recipes and photos to inspire you to try something new, but also the information which is presented here at a glance.

The Way to Healthy Eating

Wholefood Menu Suggestions

The Way to Healthy Eating

The rules for making up a menu have relaxed as much as those governing which wine to serve with which dish. Make the menu fit your own tastes and make sure that guests who normally eat mostly meat are not presented with a menu consisting almost entirely of cereal.

Try to vary the courses to include different ingredients. If you start with Clear vegetable soup with plaice, don't follow this by a fish course. Don't serve Artichokes with tofu sauce followed by Tofu balls in caper sauce.

Try and alternate between light and filling dishes; Cold tomato soup with herbs makes a good starter for Stuffed onions or Buckwheat dumplings in gorgonzola sauce. Yogurt or Quark with fruit are excellent to follow Braised wheat.

Naturally you can make up a complete menu around the same theme – for example vegetable dishes, herby dishes or curries. You will find a few suggestions in this section. In nutrition-conscious, modern cooking most foods are prepared *à la minute*, ie just before they are eaten, and should not be kept hot for too long, if at all. Many dishes take quite a long time to cook and you can make the starter or start the dessert while they cook.

Always plan your menus thoroughly (the details of preparation times given in the recipes will help here) and choose dishes which won't mean you have to disappear into the kitchen for half an hour after every course. This spoils the atmosphere and will cause you unnecessary stress.

An Introduction to Wholefoods
Mooli Salad with Cheese Dressing (recipe page 21)

Herby Lamb Slices (recipe page 77)

Cheese Dumplings (recipe page 134)

Make the mooli salad just before you eat. After marinating, the lamb takes only a few minutes to fry. The spinach beet is served lukewarm and so can be made in advance. The cheese dough for the dessert can be standing while you eat the main course.

For Experienced Cooks
Spinach Salad with Pine Nuts (recipe page 22)
or Potato Soup with Herbs (recipe page 45)

Braised Chicken with Vegetables (recipe page 89)

Strawberry or Cherry Quark (recipe page 31)

While the chicken is cooking, make the dessert first and then the salad or soup. Chill the dessert until ready to serve.

Spicy Curries
Fennel Salad with Sesame Dressing (recipe page 22)

Vegetable Soup with Tofu (recipe page 40)

Lamb Curry (recipe page 82)
Aubergines in Soya Milk (recipe page 96)
Cauliflower Curry with Potatoes (recipe page 104)
Leek and Carrot Curry (recipe page 104)
Nut Curry (recipe page 125)

Wait until the curries are cooked before starting on the fennel salad or vegetable soup because it won't hurt these to be kept hot. If you have room for four pans, cook the curries together, otherwise start with the nut curry. Naturally it is best to do all the preparatory work before you start on the cooking.

Spring Menu
Pickled Fillets of Trout (recipe page 14)

Asparagus with Two Sauces (recipe page 103)

Pudding with Nuts and Sprouts (recipe page 131)

The starter and main course are so light that you can afford to serve a filling dessert. The trout fillets are prepared in advance. Make the asparagus and sauces while the pudding is cooking.

Summer Menu
Salmon Carpaccio with Chervil (recipe page 15)

Fried Lamb with Tomatoes (recipe page 75)
with
Spinach Salad with Pine Nuts (recipe page 22)

Honey Ice with Orange Salad (recipe page 135)

Do as much of the fried lamb and salad as you can in advance so that they only need the final touches. Then serve the carpaccio. The dessert can be made in advance. In summer serve it with puréed strawberries and/or apricots.

Simple Homely Menu
Bean Salad with Tomato Vinaigrette (recipe page 23)

Barley Casserole (recipe page 53)

Boil the beans for the salad in advance. While the casserole is cooking make the vinaigrette and serve the salad.

Italian Menu
Fried Mozzarella (recipe page 16)
with
Uncooked Vegetable Salad, half quantity (recipe page 21)

Cannelloni with Tofu and Spinach (recipe page 58)

For dessert serve a mixed fruit salad with chopped nuts.

The vegetable salad and dessert can be made in advance. While the cannelloni is in the oven you can fry the cheese.

Using Fresh Herbs
Herb Drink aperitif (recipe page 139)

Stuffed Vine Leaves, half quantity (recipe page 95)

Herby Fish in Lemon Butter (recipe page 66)
with
new potatoes
mixed salad

fresh strawberries with cream

The vine leaves can be made in advance and kept hot. The aperitif is extremely quick to make and the main course also cooks quickly.

A Simple Supper
Fennel Salad with Sesame Dressing (recipe page 22)
or Carrot and Courgette Soup (recipe page 41)

Cheese and Semolina Bake (recipe page 54)

The bake will cook while you make the salad or soup.

For a Dinner Party
Onion and Mushroom Salad with Smoked Salmon (recipe page 26)

Simmered Leg of Lamb with Vegetables (recipe page 79)

Plums with Custard (recipe page 135)

You will have time to make the starter and dessert while the lamb is cooking.

Wholefood Menu Suggestions

For a Party Buffet

Pickled Fillets of Trout (recipe page 14)

Tomato Quiche (recipe page 18)

Flat Bread Cakes with Olive Cheese and Avocado Cream (recipe page 19)

Romanian-style Marinated Vegetables (recipe page 20)

Couscous Salad (recipe page 23)

Rice Salad with Chicken and Bean Sprouts (recipe page 24)

Potato Soup with Lamb Meatballs (recipe page 49)

or Chilli with Lamb (recipe page 50)

Sesame Lamb Meatballs (recipe page 83)

Quark and Cherry Strudel (recipe page 132)

Everything apart from the potato soup or chilli is made in advance and served cold.

Special Vegetarian Menu

Spinach Salad with Pine Nuts (recipe page 22)

Tofu Balls in Caper Sauce (recipe page 124)
with
Bulgur (recipe page 121)

Vanilla Quark with Grapes (recipe page 31; increase quantity to serve 4)

First put the bulgur on to cook; once it is left to cook in the covered pan you needn't worry about it. The dessert can be made in advance with only the oat-flake croquant made at the last minute. Make up the tofu balls in advance and cook them while you eat the salad.

Simple Vegetarian Menu

Beetroot with Apple (recipe page 25)

Cabbage Rolls with Buckwheat (recipe page 94)

Yogurt with Nuts (recipe page 34; double the quantities)

Fill the cabbage rolls and keep to one side. Then make the dessert and afterwards the salad. Serve the starter while the cabbage rolls are cooking.

A Dinner Party Menu

Beansprout Salad with Prawns (recipe page 27)

Buckwheat Dumplings in Gorgonzola Cream (recipe page 115)

Apple Yogurt (recipe page 34)

Cook the buckwheat dumplings and arrange in the dish ready for browning. Then prepare the starter and leave to marinate. Finally make the gorgonzola cream. Eat the salad while the dumplings are browning. The dessert can be made à la minute.

A Speedy Menu

Fish and Cucumber Stew (recipe page 71)
or Lamb Cutlets in Thyme Sauce (recipe page 76)

Cherry Quark (recipe page 31)

The dessert is made in advance, the main course à la minute.

Quick, Light and Easy

Uncooked Vegetable Salad (recipe page 21; adapt the recipe to the ingredients you have handy)

Wholemeal Pasta with Sesame (recipe page 112)

Yogurt with Nuts or Apple Yogurt (recipe page 34)

Make the vegetable salad and dessert first and then the pasta (ready-bought)

For Lunch or Supper

Clear Vegetable Soup with Plaice (recipe page 46)

Potato Fingers with Sage Butter (recipe page 107)

Sprouted Salad (recipe page 26)

For dessert serve fresh fruit

Make the vegetable soup in advance. Make up the potato fingers and leave to dry. Then make the sprouted salad. It can be left to marinate quite happily. The main course and dessert will have to be made à la minute.

Imaginative Wholefoods

Romanian-style Marinated Vegetables (recipe page 20)

Rye Dumpling Soup (recipe page 44)

Plaice Fillets in Herb Sauce (recipe page 64)

Pudding with Nuts and Sprouts (recipe page 131)

Make the starter and the stock for the plaice fillets in advance. Make the main course while the pudding is cooking.

Autumn Menu

Pumpkin Soup (recipe page 45)

Rye Rissoles (recipe page 115)
or Millet Pudding (recipe page 54)

Vanilla Quark with Grapes (recipe page 31; increase quantities to serve 4)

First mix the dessert, without the oat-flake croquant, and refrigerate until ready to serve. Make up the rye rissoles ready to fry after the soup. Prepare the millet and vegetables for the pudding. Bring the soup to the boil and keep it hot while you make up the pudding and get it into the oven.

Inexpensive Satisfying Dishes

Millet Soup with Vegetables (recipe page 43)

Apple Pancakes (recipe page 133)

The batter for the pancakes can be resting while you make the soup.

A Brunch Party Menu

Pickled Fillets of Trout (recipe page 14)
or Salmon Carpaccio with Chervil (recipe page 15)

Flat Bread Cakes with Homemade Curd Cheese (recipe page 19 and page 29)

Warm Leek Salad with Chicken Breasts and Almonds (recipe page 27)

Assorted Mueslis (recipe page 32 and 33)

Oat-Flake Waffles with Soft Fruit (recipe page 35)

Potato Tortilla (recipe page 107)

The trout fillets and cheese can be made in advance. Put out the muesli ingredients so that everyone can make up their own. If you are serving carpaccio, prepare it before the leek salad. The Potato tortilla and Flat bread cakes are best baked together and both taste good served lukewarm. Cook the oat-flake waffles at the table.

Useful Equipment

If you want to go in for healthy and nutritious cooking you need the right equipment. This will not only save time and trouble, but also give you the best possible results, preserving all the goodness, flavour and aroma of your food.

The basic rule is only to use saucepans and frying pans which allow you to cook with very little fat or liquid. These make food easier to digest and improve the flavour, for liquid washes the goodness out of vegetables and changes the flavour. You can get good quality pans in copper, stainless steel or cast iron, each of which is an excellent conductor of heat and will cook evenly while saving energy. Non-stick surfaces will often eliminate the need for fat in cooking.

Copper pans are the most expensive and need to be treated carefully. You should use only wooden spoons. You should not use pan scrubbers on copper, nor should it be put in a dishwasher.

Stainless steel pans are cheaper and easier to look after and give just as good results as copper pans. Top quality stainless steel pans have a so-called 'sandwich' base comprising at least three layers, for example two layers of chromium nickel steel enclosing a copper layer. This provides good and even distribution of heat.

When the pan is cold the base should curve inwards slightly, but lie flat on the hot plate once it becomes hot. An important point to watch is that the diameter of the pan base should be the same as that of the hot plate. With gas stoves the flame should not come up around the base of the pan or you are wasting energy.

When buying pans have a look at the lid, too. It should be tight enough to prevent most of the steam escaping during cooking. The best ones are those with an elongated rim which fits down inside the pan. With a lid like this you can cook with little or no liquid. The effect of the heat is to bring moisture out of the food which evaporates and then condenses forming a layer of water between the edge of the lid and the rim of the pan, making the seal on the lid even more efficient. The condensed water also drips back into the pan making extra water unnecessary. So foods cook in their own juices and all their goodness and flavour are preserved.

Any pan needs a firm handle which will remain cold or become only slightly warm. Plastic handles are impractical for they mean that you can't use the pan in the oven.

When buying pans always check for the qualities we have mentioned here. You can also buy pressure cookers which are excellent for vegetables, though if you flick through the recipes in this book you will see that vegetables take only a few minutes to cook in a conventional pan, so such pans provide little in the way of saving time and energy.

Frying pans must be suitable for frying and braising in little fat. This is again achieved by the use of a 'sandwich' base with the different metal layers conducting and distributing the heat well.

The advantage of cast iron pans is that they are also excellent in the oven. Since most of them are very attractive, you can serve straight from the pan so that food will stay hot much longer.

Equipment for steaming

In Chinese cooking, which is recognised as one of the healthiest in the world, foods are often cooked in the steam produced by a liquid. This method ensures maximum retention of flavour and nutritive food value. Professional chefs in the West have also adopted this method which is excellent for delicate foodstuffs, such as fish or young vegetables.

You can buy a matching base pan and perforated steamer, a steamer with graduated ridges round the base, which allow it to be used over saucepans of six different sizes, or a perforated basket which will expand to fit various saucepans. The steam rising from the boiling water below the perforated food container cooks the food, so that no nutritional value is lost by seepage into the cooking water. A tight-fitting lid is essential.

Special steamers with two or three steaming baskets are extremely practical. These stacking steamers save energy. In addition, free-standing electric, work-top steamers are available. These are fairly compact appliances which are thermostatically controlled to prevent overheating.

Equipment for dehydrating

Dehydrating or drying food is a means of preserving which is quicker and easier than bottling. You can dehydrate vegetables, fruit, mushrooms and herbs. Food is cut up – although herbs can be left whole – and then dried in the sun, on a radiator, or in the oven on the lowest possible setting and with the door wedged slightly open.

If you plan to dry large quantities of food regularly, it is worth buying a dehydrator with a built-in heating element and fan to distribute the heat evenly. Dried foods such as vegetables, fruit and mushrooms are soaked and then prepared in exactly the same way as fresh foods (see recipe for Dried Winter Vegetables, page 98).

Glossary

This concise glossary brings together the main terms and products used in wholefood cooking. It also includes explanations of more general cooking terms which may be unfamiliar to the inexperienced cook.

A

Aduki beans Small, reddish-brown beans also known as red soya beans. The germ forms a striking white 'strip' along the side. Aduki beans are easier to digest than other pulses. Since yield per plant is low they are quite expensive.

Al dente Degree of cooking for pasta and vegetables. Pasta no longer tastes doughy yet still has some bite; vegetables are tender but still crisp. It is unfortunately impossible to give precise cooking times and you will have to keep testing for the correct degree of cooking.

Almonds Come in sweet and bitter varieties. Bitter almonds are high in prussic acid and poisonous if eaten in large enough quantities (in children as few as seven bitter almonds can be lethal). Do not use bitter almonds in baking, but always use instead artificially produced bitter-almond oil which is harmless. Owing to the high fat content almonds soon go rancid, so where possible it is best to avoid buying ground almonds and to shell and blanch your own almonds ready for grinding as you need them.

Alternative agriculture Has been in existence for several decades involving a variety of cultivation methods (on this see the heading 'cultivation methods') but with the same main aims:
- Improvement and development of the soil by mainly organic fertilisers;
- non-specialised farming;
- minimum use of mineral fertilisers and chemical herbicides and pesticides;
- production of healthy and nutritious foodstuffs.

With alternative agriculture yields are often smaller and the end product may look less attractive than usual, but the quality surpasses that of traditionally grown fruit and vegetables in several respects: foodstuffs contain more essential nutrients such as vitamins, stay fresh longer and have a low nitrate content. While the products of alternative agriculture are not entirely free from chemical substances (pollution from the air and rain also falls on the fields of the wholefood farmer) tests have shown that fruit and vegetables from alternative agriculture generally contain fewer chemicals.

Aluminium foil Highly recommended in cooking from the health aspect. Products need little or no fat, no juice is lost and there is no burning. Those who are environmentally aware, however, should use as little foil as possible because, as yet, used foil (including the tops of yogurt and cream cartons) is not collected for recycling. Bear in mind that it is a waste to use foil just for wrapping and storing foods.

Apples If you buy eating apples in a supermarket you will usually be offered Golden Delicious or Granny Smiths, depending on whether you prefer a sweet or sour apple. Yet there are other home-grown varieties with more flavour which are regrettably less well known. The favourite English dessert apple is the Cox's Orange Pippin with its juicy, crisp and aromatic flesh; it is in season from September to May. Two apples with short seasons are Worcester Pearmain (September to November) and Egremont Russet (October to December). The former has a tough yet sweet white flesh, while the Russet, with its characteristic matt reddish-brown skin, has a crisp refreshing flesh. Laxton's Superb (November to April) is firm and juicy. Other varieties include Scarlet Pimpernel (July), George Cave (July/August), Discovery (August), James Grieve (August/September), Miller's Seedling (August/September), Tydeman's Early (September/October), Laxton's Fortune (September/October), Lord Lambourne (October), Ellison's Orange (October to April), Spartan (November to January) and Crispin (December to April). Home-grown cooking apples include Early Victory (July/August), Grenadier (August/September), Lord Derby (October on), Bramley's Seedling (October to July) and Newton Wonder (December to March). In all varieties the way the trees have been handled is important. It is best to avoid perfect-looking fruit and to go for apples with minor imperfections. They have probably been sprayed less and this improves both the flavour and keeping qualities of the apple as well as your own health.

B

Barley Type of cereal which was one of the earliest cultivated plants. Contains slightly less protein than wheat and very little gluten which makes it unsuitable for baking purposes. Like all cereals it provides us with essential linoleic acids and B-group vitamins. The best way to use barley is in a muesli or soup.

Barley seeds, peeled and polished to a round shape, are called pearl barley. They contain less protein than whole grain or pot barley, as well as less fat and minerals. Pearl and pot barley need to be stored in a dry, well-ventilated place.

Basil A herb used extensively in Mediterranean cooking, sweet basil is the perfect companion to tomatoes and mozzarella cheese in particular. It forms the basis of the famous Italian pasta sauce, Pesto Genovese. Basil can be used fresh or dried, and is easily obtained from supermarkets in its dried form. But the flavour of fresh basil is superior and this herb can be grown in pots and window boxes. Grow it indoors on a window sill in winter, and outdoors in summer.

Basting To spoon the mixture of cooking juices repeatedly over food as it cooks. The aim is to form a brown crusty coating and to keep the food moist or well flavoured in certain cases. Used when roasting meat and poultry, when grilling foods or when cooking in a limited quantity of liquid in an open pan on the hob.

Bean sprouts Bean sprouts are usually sprouted mung beans. Mung beans will take 3–5 days to sprout completely and are ready to eat when they are 2.5–5 cm/1–2 in long. Use a clean jam jar to sprout 50 g/2 oz beans. Put the beans in the jar, and cover with a piece of muslin or net, secured with a rubber band. Pour in sufficient water to cover the beans to three times their depth and leave them to stand at room temperature for eight hours, or overnight.

Drain the beans through the cloth, then lay the jar on its side. Cover with a tea-towel to protect the sprouts from light. Do not cover the jar top, as the sprouts need air to grow. Rinse the sprouts in tepid water three times a day, draining them thoroughly after each rinsing. Once the beans are completely sprouted, place in a large bowl of cool water and shake the sprouts by the handful to detach the seed coats if you dislike their bitter taste. Drain the sprouts and pat dry on absorbent kitchen paper. They are now ready to contribute a crunchy texture and fresh flavour to salads and stir-fry dishes.

Beans Pulse vegetables of which either the fleshy pods or seeds are eaten. Fresh green beans are available from around May onwards. You can distinguish between the varieties by the pods. Wide, flat runner beans have quite tough flesh and should be trimmed and sliced before cooking. Bush-grown beans, with their more rounded pods, can be served whole as a vegetable or salad. The butter bean is delicious in salads. French beans, also known as *haricots verts*, have tender pods and make an excellent vegetable. Seeds from the bean pods can also be used fresh at certain times of the year. Dried beans are available throughout the year. There are red, white, black and brown beans all of which can be served as a vegetable or main course or – cold or lukewarm in vinegar, oil and herbs – as a starter. Dried beans are always soaked in water initially and then boiled for about 2 hours. Neither the pods nor the beans themselves should be eaten raw for they contain a poisonous substance known as phasine which is made harmless by cooking.

Bind To hold ingredients together by means of a liquid. For example by the addition of a little water or egg yolk to pastry. Minced meat is bound by a mixture of egg or milk and breadcrumbs to make meatballs. Stuffing mixtures based on breadcrumbs can be bound by the addition of a little fat or by the use of a liquid such as milk.

Blanch Cooking method for delicate vegetables such as spinach or greens, or precooking of tougher vegetables. For blanching, bring a large pan of salted water to the boil and add the trimmed, washed vegetables. The water should boil briskly throughout the 2 to 5 minutes cooking time. Then the blanched vegetables have to be cooled very quickly – in a bowl of iced water for instance – to keep the colour and halt the cooking process. If you intend to freeze vegetables they should first be blanched. Fresh vegetables contain enzymes which can destroy vitamin C and colour even when the food is frozen. Blanching destroys these enzymes and helps preserve the vitamins and colour. Blanching also describes the brief scalding in boiling water given to fruits like tomatoes and peaches before peeling them.

Boil To cook in plenty of water at around 100c/212f. Boiling point is reached when the cooking liquid bubbles vigorously. However, the term is applied to foods which are cooked gently in large quantities of liquid; in this case the liquid is brought to the boil initially, then the temperature is reduced to *simmer* the food until cooked.

Boiling point The point at which the liquid in which the food is cooked begins to bubble. The temperature can be reduced earlier when the surface of the liquid is ruffled, that is,

when the liquid begins to simmer.

Borlotti beans reddish brown beans spotted like pinto beans.

Braise Cooking foods in their own juice, sometimes with a little additional liquid and/or fat. Needs a pan with a close-fitting lid to prevent the liquid evaporating.

Bread There are many different types of bread on the market. Depending on the type of grain and fineness of the flour, there is bread made from a mixture of wheat and rye, white bread and wholemeal bread. The mixed and white breads are eaten in the largest quantities. Yet 'grainy', highly flavoured bread is no longer available only from health food shops; many supermarkets and bakers are now responding to consumer demand with wholemeal French bread and pitta bread, wheatgerm rolls and wholemeal toasting loaves. Don't be afraid to ask your baker for wholemeal products. The more people ask for the more healthy types of bread, the greater will be the choice available. The term 'wholemeal bread' does not mean that the bread has been made with whole grains, but with flour that contains all the goodness of the whole grain. See also Flour.

Broad beans Large, fairly flat beans, available fresh, frozen or dried.

Buckwheat Not a cereal but a kind of knotgrass, but treated as a cereal as far as cooking is concerned. Buckwheat is unsuitable for baking since it contains no gluten. Buckwheat with its triangular fruits can be bought whole, as flakes, crushed or ground. It is also available roasted as kasha. It has a savoury, slightly bitter flavour and can be used in sweet or savoury dishes. Best known in Blinis, small Russian pancakes made with buckwheat flour, eaten with soured cream and caviar.

Bulgur Also spelt bulghur or burghul. Precooked crushed wheat. See recipe Bulgur with vegetables, page 121.

Butter see Fat.

C

Cannellini beans Oval, white beans, a member of the haricot family.

Capers Capers are sold pickled in small jars in many supermarkets and delicatessens. Dull green in colour, these small flower buds from a Mediterranean shrub have a piquant flavour.

Cardamom Green, white or black cardamom pods are available. The green variety is the most common, the white pods are expensive and the large, hairy black pods are used in certain Indian recipes. The pods can be used whole to flavour dishes or the small black seeds can be removed and used either whole or ground. Ground cardamom can be purchased from specialist shops, however it is an expensive alternative to the whole pods. The spice is one of those that make up curry powder.

Cashew nuts Oily seeds of the cashew tree with a slightly sweet, almondy flavour. Can be served in muesli or cooked in a curry (see recipe page 25).

Cayenne Made from dried chilli peppers. It is a burning hot red-brown pepper and should be used sparingly.

Cereal Cultivated form of wild grasses, providing almost everything the body needs. The germ contains vitamins, minerals and fat with the essential linoleic acids and high-value protein. The outer layer of the grain provides minerals and plenty of indigestible roughage. The body of the grain consists mainly of starch, but also has gluten which is important in baking. For thousands of years cereal has been the basic human foodstuff and is today the staple diet of most of the world's population. The industrialised nations get most of their cereal in the form of bread. But it can also be served in muesli or soup, boiled, braised or gratinéed. When ground, the oxygen in the air takes out some of the vital nutrients, so it is extremely important to use really freshly ground or crushed cereal. Individual types of cereal such as wheat, rye, barley, oats,

millet, rice and maize can be found under their own names.

Cereal flakes Cereal grain is heated in steam, crushed and dried. Unlike whole grain, it can be eaten uncooked with no soaking. Serve in mueslis, add to bread or use in other baked items.

Cereal, milled Obtained by grinding whole grain.

Chervil Chervil contributes a subtle aniseed flavour to the *fines herbes* of French cuisine. (*Fines herbes* are traditionally a mixture of chopped parsley, tarragon, chives and chervil, used to flavour omelettes, salads, and herb butter.) Chervil's delicate aroma is destroyed by cooking, so add it to hot dishes at the last stage of cooking, or use it fresh. Roast chicken and fish flavours in particular are enhanced by chervil.

This herb will grow as easily in a window box or pot as in a garden, as long as it is not in direct sunlight. Remove the flower stalks, otherwise chervil will dry up and die after flowering.

Chick-peas Pulse vegetable with yellow to reddish, irregularly shaped seeds, eaten mainly in the Mediterranean area and the Middle East. Can be boiled or ground into a flour to make dumplings or even sweets. Sprouted chick-peas are also delicious. Dried chick-peas need soaking and then boiling for about 2 hours.

Chilli Available fresh, dried, pickled, or ground into a powder. A range of chillies are available, from fiery hot types to mild green ones. Dried red chillies are particularly hot. The seeds inside the pods are very hot and should be removed before cooking. Take care not to rub your eyes after handling chillies because the juices irritate the skin. Chilli powder varies in strength and quality depending on the brand.

Chives Chives are a delightful herb because they are so easy to grow – in a light position – in a garden, window box, or pot on the window sill, and perfectly amenable to year-round snipping of the fine, bright green stems. A cousin of the onion, chives merely suggest an oniony flavour. They complement scrambled eggs and omelettes and baked and boiled potatoes especially. For an appetising garnish, cut and sprinkle over salads and puréed soups just before serving.

Citrus fruits Usually sprayed to protect against mould and/or treated with synthetic wax to keep longer. I have used only unsprayed fruit for the recipes in this book.

Coconuts Extremely fatty fruit of the coconut palm which can grow up to 30 m tall. Coconut milk (see recipe for Nut curry, page 125) gives curries a delicious aroma.

Coriander Spice plant with peppercorn-like fruits, used in a variety of recipes, both savoury and sweet. Used as a flavouring for pickles.

Corn oil Obtained from the germ of the maize or corn grain. Contains several unsaturated fatty acids and linoleic acids (essential fatty acids). See also Oil.

Cornmeal Maize ground to varying grades which is used in the same way as wheat semolina. Used to make the popular Italian dish Polenta, which is a thick, boiled cornmeal, cut into pieces when cold and then fried. See recipe for Polenta Slices with Tomato Sauce, page 119.

Couscous Couscous is prepared from fine semolina which is sprinkled with flour to keep the grains separate. The mixture is moistened with a little water and worked with the fingers to produce a grainy result similar in size to rice. The couscous is cooked by steaming. A *Couscousier* is a specially designed French steamer. Couscous is extensively eaten in North Africa where it is steamed over meat or poultry stews. It is available from healthfood shops and supermarkets prepared ready for steaming.

Crème fraîche Thick, slightly sour tasting cream with 28–40% fat depending on the brand. The higher the fat content the better it tastes. Should contain no binding agent.

Crème fraîche is excellent for thickening hot sauces, for salads and also for desserts. Like cream, crème fraîche separates at high temperatures (see also Reducing).

Crudités A variety of raw vegetables, trimmed and cut into pieces to serve with a dip or sometimes with a dressing. They can be served alone, as an alternative to commercially prepared snacks and nibbles with drinks. Makes an excellent starter as it stimulates the digestive juices. Crudités also contain a lot of fibre and, as they have to be chewed well, are also good for teeth and gums. Especially rich in vitamins and minerals. Nutritionists recommend that uncooked vegetables should make up 30–50% of our daily food intake.

D

Defat The easiest way to remove the fat from soups or sauces is to carefully soak up the layer of fat floating on the top with absorbent kitchen paper. See also Strain.

Deglaze When cooking meat in a little fat on the hob, a brown coating of sediment forms on the bottom of the pan or frying pan – this can be used as a basis for the gravy. Adding liquid (water, stock or wine) softens it so that it will stir off the pan. Stir vigorously and cook over a high heat until all the juices and sediment are combined. This liquid can be poured over the meat or it can be extended to make a sauce.

Drain Foods that need a lot of cooking water, such as pasta, should be tipped into a sieve or a colander. If there is only a little water in the pan you can place the lid on the pan almost to cover and pour off the water.

Dried fruit No longer dried in the air or sun, but in special drying rooms heated with propane gas. When buying dried fruit always go for quality. It should be free from grit and dirt and preferably unsulphurised – free from sulphur dioxide. This is a preservative which absorbs oxygen and prevents discoloration. Also the lack of oxygen prevents micro-organisms increas-

ing. Sulphur dioxide can destroy vitamin B_1 and in wine can cause headaches. Besides dried fruit, sulphur is also used in dried or frozen potato dishes such as chips or dumplings, in jams and marmalades. Food will be labelled 'sulphurised' or 'highly sulphurised'. Highly sulphurised products should not be bought, whereas sulphurised products need to be washed thoroughly, as recommended in all the recipes that include dried fruit. Dried fruit contains a lot of sugar since all the water has been removed and is high in calories. Avoid eating too much of it and where possible substitute fresh fruit. Dried fruits available include apples, apricots, bananas, pears, dates, figs, prunes and raisins.

E

Eggs Sorted and sold by size and quality.
Sizes by weight:
Size 1: 70 to 75 g
Size 2: 65 to 70 g
Size 3: 60 to 65 g
Size 4: 55 to 60 g
Size 5: 50 to 55 g
Size 6: 45 to 50 g
The quality grade and packing date should be printed on the box. You will usually find only grade A eggs in the shops. This means 'fresh', but not 'fresh-laid' and indicates only that no special treatment has been used to make the eggs keep. Since 1 July 1985 it has been a legal requirement for the packaging date to be given on the box, but even this is no indication of when the eggs were laid and how fresh they really are. There are, however, two methods for testing the freshness of eggs – but not until you have already bought them:
1. Place the egg in a bowl of cold water. An egg about two days old sinks to the bottom since the air pocket inside is still very small. An egg about one week old stands diagonally, while a two to three-week-old egg stands on end; an even older one begins to float. Eggs that rise to the top should not be used.
2. Break the egg into a saucer. In fresh-laid eggs the yolk is

dome-shaped while the gelatinous white surrounds it in a circle. The older the egg the looser it gets, with the white becoming watery and the yolk flat. Eggs about 10 days old taste best of all.

There is no doubt that the usual method of battery farming used today is cruel. In addition it also affects the quality of the eggs for the birds have to be given drugs to prevent disease. In addition they are often fed on low quality foodstuffs which contribute to the flavour of your breakfast egg. With their food hens are fed (harmless) colourings to improve the colour of the yolks, for a deep yellow yolk is seen by most customers as a mark of quality. In fact the colour of the yolk is no more a sign of quality than the colour of the shell.

Wherever eggs are mass produced, free-range eggs from properly reared, 'happy' hens are an impossibility and the birds are treated merely as laying machines. More and more shops and supermarkets are selling free-range eggs, but if you cannot obtain them, the only thing you can do is to drastically reduce your egg consumption, so that with demand falling the producer is able to concentrate on quality and humane treatment of his birds.

F

Fat The most concentrated source of calories. Helps the absorption of and also provides the body with fat-soluble vitamins (in corn, sunflower, soya and wheatgerm oil as well as butter) and essential fatty acids (mainly in thistle oil but also in sunflower, wheatgerm and linseed oil). Edible fats are divided into animal fats, like butter and lard and vegetable fats and oils, obtained from olives, coconuts or cereal germ for instance. Whether a fat is liquid (oil) or solid at room temperature depends on the type of fatty acids it contains. Vegetable oils contain a lot of unsaturated fatty acids. In animal fats the fatty acids are mainly saturated.

Margarine is not always made entirely from vegetable fats. While vegetable oils and

Glossary

The Way to Healthy Eating

fats are mainly used in its manufacture, there are margarines that contain up to 80% animal fat. The manufacture of margarine also involves chemical processes. Margarine is therefore a processed food and as such has not been used in the recipes in this book. Any fats in more or less their natural state can be recommended. Butter is best for spreading; for salads cold-pressed oils are best; for frying and roasting use unhardened fats. For deep frying you need a fat that can be heated to 220c/425f (groundnut or corn oil). Fats which contain protein, like butter, begin to burn at 140 to 160c/275 to 325f. They should not be used for frying but be kept for baking, braising and adding to dishes. Foods fried over a low to moderate heat, such as eggs, can be fried in butter with no danger to health. The basic rule is: if fat or oil smokes it is too hot, and should not be used. See also the fat section in the Introduction to nutrition (page 8) and the heading Oil.

Fillet To separate fish into fillets.

Fish Contains biologically valuable protein, little fat but plenty of essential fatty acids (linoleic acids). Fish is extremely digestible. It is also rich in minerals (calcium, iron, phosphorous, iodine) and vitamins (A and D). Seafish, in particular, are rich in iodine; 200 g/7 oz cod will supply 2 days' requirement, while the same weight of haddock gives 5 days' supply. Unfortunately fish also take in pollution from the water. Fish from farms will be less affected by pollution. Deep-sea fish (cod, herring, mackerel, plaice, sardines and haddock) are also recommended for the quantity of water dilutes the pollution. Fish from coastal waters and polluted river estuaries are best avoided. With a varied diet, however, there is little risk of taking in too much of any particular harmful substance.

Flageolet beans Longish and pale green in colour. Make excellent salads or side dishes.

Flour For thousands of years cereal has been ground into flour to make gruel, soups or bread. Different cultures have

preferred different types of cereal. The Romans used mainly wheat, sifting out some of the bran to give a white flour. In the Middle Ages, mainly rye was grown, which was baked into wholemeal bread. Then at the start of the Baroque and Rococo periods eating habits became more refined and there was increasing use of very white wheat flour. But it was not until the middle of the last century with the invention of the steam engine that milling techniques were 'improved' to such an extent that white flour could be milled in large quantities. It was not long before this refined flour (see separate heading) had replaced the darker flours. With the trend towards natural, healthy foods wholemeal flour has come back into favour. This contains all the goodness of the whole grain; the germ, the outer layers with the indigestible bran and the main body of the grain with its gluten and starches. It is the gluten which gives cakes their fine-grained, crumbly texture. The more gluten the cereal contains the better it is for baking. Wheat flour is best of all for baking, whereas barley is not very good at all. Besides wholemeal or wholewheat flour, which contains 100% of the grain, there are other flours graded according to the amount of bran and wheatgerm they contain. Wheatmeal or brown flour contains 85 to 90% of the grain. White flour contains only 72 – 74%. Granary flour has malted wheat and rye added to it. The less refined the flour, the better it is for you, for it contains more of the goodness of whole grain. Fresh-milled wholemeal flour contains around seven times as many vitamins, six times as much iron, four times as much copper and calcium as white refined flour. The vitamin E found in the germ is not present at all in refined flour. Wholemeal flour should be used quickly after buying, for in the air it loses much of its goodness. In addition, the fact that the germ is milled with the grain makes it quite fatty and it can become rancid in time. Whether you use wholemeal

flour or a more highly refined flour depends what you are using the flour for. When thickening soups or sauces the bran content does not matter so you can use wholemeal flour. To make smooth pastry, for strudel for instance, fine ground wheatmeal is best. The high bran content of wholemeal flour would make the dough tear when you tried to stretch it. There would be no difference in flavour, but your strudel would look less attractive.

Fry To cook in fat with no additional liquid so that food browns and becomes crisp. Use the frying pan for slices and small pieces of meat, chicken portions, fish fillets and cutlets, eggs, potatoes and batters. A similar method using the oven is roasting. This is used for joints of meat from 1 kg/2¼ lb weight and whole poultry.

G

Ginger Tuberous root of a plant from South-East Asia, available fresh, dried, bottled, crystallised or ground. Naturally fresh ginger has the best flavour. This is peeled like a potato and then cooked in the dish to be flavoured, either whole or sliced, and can be removed before serving. Ginger is highly flavoured and should be used sparingly.

Gomasio Mixture of sesame seeds and sea salt. Can be used instead of salt for seasoning. It has a pleasant nutty taste and is excellent in vegetable and cereal dishes. Gomasio has a short shelflife: it loses its flavour and with the high fat content soon becomes rancid. Available from health food shops, or you can make your own. Stir sesame seeds in a dry pan until they begin to give up their oil. Then crush in a mortar with sea salt.

Gratin A dish topped with melted cheese and sometimes breadcrumbs as well. The best known is Potato gratin: thin slices of potato cooked in cream and then sprinkled with cheese and browned.

Grill To cook by direct radiated heat with no contact between the heat source and the food. The rays hit the surface of the food where the protein is

broken down immediately to seal in the flavour. Grilling is an excellent cooking method since it requires little or no fat. If you like grilling on charcoal you can use a barbecue with a vertical coal container so that no fat can drip on to the charcoal.

Groats Coarse to fine-crushed cereal such as oats, wheat or barley as well as buckwheat. Groats cook quicker than whole grain.

H

Hazelnuts Nuts high in protein and fat, delicious chopped and scattered over muesli or salad. Because of the high fat content hazelnuts have a limited shelflife. At their best from autumn to Christmas. It is difficult to be sure that you are getting fresh nuts for often the Christmas rush is seen as a time to get rid of old stocks. Check the sell-by date carefully.

Herb salt see Salt.

Honey Natural product produced by bees from nectar gathered from flowering plants. Honey contains minute amounts of vitamins, minerals and aromatic substances as well as organic acids and enzymes said to have healing capacities. In cooking honey should always be heated gently. Types of honey are differentiated:
1. By flower type, for example, acacia honey.
2. By geographical area, for example, Californian honey.
3. By method of production: comb honey, for instance, is still in the comb, extracted honey is produced by a centrifuge, while strained honey is warmed and squeezed.

Extreme heat destroys the active agents in honey, yet honey is heated to high temperatures to make it easier to filter and pack. In addition, most consumers want clear, runny honey which spreads well. After a time all honey becomes solid. This is not a sign of inferior quality but depends on the types of sugars contained in each type of honey. Honey that has become solid can be warmed in a basin in hand-hot water. Honey can be used to sweeten all foods which do not have to be heated.

Remember that in large quantities honey is just as bad for you as sugar.

I

Infuse This is a method of imparting the flavour of a particular ingredient to a liquid. For example, a vanilla pod is allowed to stand in hot milk for a length of time until it gives up its flavour to the liquid. Fruit rind, spices and other ingredients can be infused in liquid in this way, then strained out before the liquid is used.

K

Kidney beans Large, curved long beans with reddish-brown skins. Essential ingredient in Chilli con carne.

Kiln-drying To dry with hot air, especially cereals. This improves the cooking qualities and flavour and reduces the cooking times. You can buy kiln-dried cereal such as rye or make your own. To do this, soak cereal overnight until most of the water has been absorbed. Pour off the remaining water and spread the grain on a baking tray. Dry the cereal completely in a very low oven.

L

Lactic acid Found in all sour milk products, formed from lactic sugar by bacteria.

Lactic fermentation Method of preserving uncooked vegetables which goes back thousands of years. Best known example is sauerkraut. All vegetables in lactic acid contain plenty of vitamins, especially vitamin C, and few calories. Good for the digestion.

Lentils One of the earliest cultivated plants and the best known of the pulses. Seeds are greenish-brown, red or black. Lentils are rich in vegetable protein which is especially good for you combined with cereal (brown rice, wholemeal pasta). They are also rich in B-group vitamins, iron, calcium and phosphorous. Lentils do not need to be soaked before cooking. The greenish-brown lentils should be boiled for about 1 hour, black (Puy) lentils for 30

to 45 minutes and red lentils for a maximum of 30 minutes. Lentils are delicious in soups, casseroles, side dishes and salads.

Linseed The small, brown seeds of the flax (linseed) plant from which linseed oil is made. They aid digestion and prevent inflammation. Crushed linseeds are available in health food shops. Linseeds contain around 25% protein, 25% fibre and 40% oil. Crushed linseeds have a limited shelflife. They are delicious in muesli, salads, soups and baking.

Lovage A full-flavoured herb, celery-like in appearance. Used sparingly, fresh or dried lovage leaves make an ideal contribution to meat stocks, soups and sauces.

M

Maize Better known as the sweetcorn we eat as a vegetable or starter. Maize was the staple food of the Indians of North and South America. In more recent times it has come to be used worldwide as an animal foodstuff. Contains less protein than other types of cereal (except for rice which contains even less than maize). But if maize is eaten with pulses – particularly beans – the combination provides more valuable protein than a meat or fish meal. Sweetcorn is harvested before it is ripe and is in season from August into late autumn. Corn on the cob is best simply boiled and served with butter. Frozen or canned sweetcorn can be heated and served with butter like other vegetables.

Malt extract Made from barley, wheat, corn or rice. Useful as a sugar substitute although less sweet than sugar. Malt extract is delicious spread on bread, on muesli, in Quark or yogurt and can also be used in baking.

Mange-tout A special variety of pea eaten not for the peas but for the tender pods. This slightly sweet-tasting vegetable is a delicacy (and therefore quite expensive) which is easy to cook. All you need to do is to wash the pods, pull off any tough threads and cook in a little salted water or butter for about 5 minutes. Mange-tout make an excellent vegetable for

a special menu or, served cold in a herby vinaigrette, a delicious salad or starter.

Maple syrup Has been used as a sweetener in the USA and Canada for a long time. Obtained by tapping wild maple trees and boiling the sap to a syrup. Use to sweeten muesli, desserts, waffles and drinks. Contains up to 90% sugar so go easy with it. Also contains small quantities of vitamins, minerals and trace elements. The syrup is quite expensive and has a limited shelflife. Once opened keep it in the refrigerator. You can also buy maple syrup in a more solid, spreadable form.

Margarine see Fat

Marinade Liquid (for example wine, oil, vinegar or lemon juice) with herbs and seasoning, in which meat, poultry, game or fish is soaked for a short time to flavour and tenderise it.

Meat Basically you can eat any meat provided you know where your butcher gets it from, but it is advisable to limit your meat intake and to supply the body with some of the proteins it needs in the forms of cereals and pulses. The quality of almost every type of meat has deteriorated in recent years since more and more meat has to be produced to meet the demand. Pork, in particular, is of much lower quality with modern fattening methods. But there are still farmers and butchers offering meat from naturally fed and raised livestock. Of course such meat is not entirely free from harmful substances for even alternative agriculture can do nothing about air, soil and water pollution, but animals are not artificially fattened nor injected with drugs, antibiotics and hormones.

Microwave This moist cooking method gives results which are similar to steaming.

The microwave oven cooks vegetables very well and quickly, using a small amount of liquid or a knob of butter, instead of the large quantity of water in which they are often cooked. Microwaving vegetables cooperates with attempts to cut down on salt in the diet, as salt is not added to the vegetables

before cooking. Salt tends to produce little dehydrated patches on the surface, so add any seasoning once the vegetables are cooked.

Fish and shellfish cook exceptionally well in the microwave oven. Make a fish dish one of your first experiments if you are new to this cooking method. Small fish steaks and rolled fillets cook particularly evenly. The moist, delicious results will make you a permanent convert to cooking fish by this method.

Milk Not only a drink, but a valuable food which provides many essential nutrients. You can buy milk in various forms:
1. Untreated milk (green top), is natural full-cream milk, bought either direct from the farm or as grade-A milk from health food shops. Production is restricted to certain specially licensed farms under strict hygiene regulations.
2. Pasteurised full-cream milk (silver top), heated briefly to kill germs. Keeps longer, and better for cooking purposes. Pasteurisation is a legal requirement because milk is one of the most perishable foodstuffs, but heating not only kills the germs; it also affects the vitamin content, the composition of the lactic protein and the flavour. Full-cream milk is often homogenised too (red top), which means that the fat is broken up into small particles to prevent it turning to cream. So you now get no cream on the top but have to buy it separately – hygienically packed in plastic cartons.

Channel Island and South Devon milk (gold top) contains more fat than full-cream milk, and so tastes richer.
3. Semi-skimmed (red and silver-striped top) and skimmed milk (blue and silver-striped top) have some of the cream removed, but the vitamin and mineral content is also less.
4. Sterilised milk (blue cap) is homogenised milk heated for several seconds at around 150 C/300 F. This kills all germs so that the milk will keep for several weeks, but the vitamin loss is higher than in pasteurised milk.

Modern methods of production and cold storage prevent the acid-forming bacteria from increasing, while the bacteria which turn the milk bad reproduce unhindered. This changes the normal bacterial relationship so that while milk still smells sour and separates, it tastes bitter and mouldy. For further information on milk see recipe for Home-made Curd Cheese with Herbs, page 29.

Millet Type of cereal recently rediscovered by wholefood cooks.

Molluscs Oysters, mussels and other molluscs are fished off the coast and in river estuaries, where the highest levels of pollution are found. They feed by filtering relatively large volumes of water with which they take in harmful substances – particularly heavy metals. That is the reason why this book includes no mollusc recipes.

Morels Mushrooms with honey-combed caps, usually sold dried. Considered a delicacy and quite expensive.

Mozzarella Slightly sour tasting Italian cheese made from cow's or buffalo's milk. Always make sure it is fresh. Use in hot and cold dishes. See Cook's tip, page 16.

Mung beans Usually used after germination as bean sprouts. Mung beans are small, deep green beans. The white germ is at the side as in Aduki beans. Sprouted mung beans (see Bean sprouts) are delicious in salads, soups, Chinese dishes or as a vegetable.

Mushrooms Contain valuable protein, vitamins and minerals. Low in calories. Wild mushrooms may contain poisonous deposits of heavy metal. So it is not only for conservation reasons that it is better not to pick mushrooms, but on health grounds too. You can buy excellent cultivated mushrooms which contain no harmful substances.

Mustard Usually made from crushed mustard seeds, salt, pepper, sugar, vinegar and other flavourings which vary from type to type. Yellow mustard seeds give mild mustard while brown ones produce a hotter mustard. Mixing the two provides various degrees of hotness. Mustards can also be made from whole or finely or coarsely crushed seeds. Dijon mustard is one of the most expensive and is made with wine or wine vinegar. It is hot to medium-hot and is good in salad dressings or in sauces with fish or eggs. Mustards flavoured with chives, horseradish, green peppercorns and other seasonings are widely available. Keep mustard in the refrigerator in its original jar. The tightly fitting lids keep in all the flavour and hotness. Mustard that has gone dry can be rescued by mixing in a little vinegar, oil and sugar, but it should be used immediately.

O

Oats Cereal with pretty heads. Formed an important part of the diet until the 18th century. As breakfast porridge gave way to bread and the potato became a staple foodstuff, oats began to disappear from the diet. Because of the low gluten content oat flour is no good for baking. Oats contain more valuable protein than any other cereal, plenty of fat with essential fatty acids (linoleic acids), vitamins and minerals. Oats are said to be good for the digestive tract and feature in many invalid diets. Properly cooked oats are by no means bland, but pleasantly nutty. Slow frying in oil or butter brings out the flavour. Whole grain can be cooked in the same way as other cereals. Oat flakes and crushed oats go into muesli, while porridge is really delicious (see recipe page 30).

Offal With the exception of heart, offal should be eaten only rarely if at all. Harmful substances taken in with fodder, even by organically reared livestock, become concentrated in the liver and kidneys.

Oil Liquid vegetable fat in which the terms 'vegetable', 'cooking' or 'table' indicate a mixture of different sources and/or industrial processes. In addition there are pure oils from specific plants, for example, olive, sunflower, sesame seed, wheat or corn. To make oil two different processes can be used, pressing or extracting. Olive oil is the only oil which can be obtained simply by pressing without heating. The best olive oils are cold-pressed and are known as *Olio vergine* or *Huile vièrge*. All other types of oily seeds have to be heated to up to 60 c/140 f, depending on type, to bring out the oil, so the term cold-pressed can only be properly applied to olive oil. However, almost all pressed oils contain valuable nutrients. In their natural state, they are cloudy, usually dark in colour, unrefined and rich in essential fatty acids. In addition, oils of this type can be specially treated to remove unwanted flavourings.

In extraction the oil is extracted chemically to give a greater yield. This produces an oil which is inedible at first so that it has to be refined, skimmed and bleached. This makes the oil neutral in flavour and gives it a long shelflife. But – as with refined sugar or flour – it loses some of its natural goodness.

Natural oils are mainly used cold in salad dressings. They are also suitable for frying or grilling provided they are not allowed to overheat. Their high content of polyunsaturated fats means that harmful substances are produced at high temperatures. Oil that smokes is too hot and should be thrown away. For really tasty salad dressings use walnut, grapeseed or pumpkin oil. Each of these oils has such a distinctive taste that you will not need more than a teaspoonful. Since they soon go bad, buy in small bottles. All oils should be protected from light and heat but not refrigerated, for many oils separate at this temperature, although they return to normal if brought back to room temperature. Even if it does not go bad, any oil will lose its flavour in time. So buy the smallest bottles you can for even the air in the half-empty bottle will affect the smell and flavour.

Olives The difference between green and black olives is that the black ones are ripe. Green olives are picked young and soaked in brine to develop their colour and remove the bitter flavour. Black olives have had time to ripen on the tree and develop more oil before going to the presses. Black olives for eating are preserved in oil or brine and vary from plump and succulent to small and wrinkled specimens. Buy olives loose from good delicatessens, or bottled from supermarkets. Store those you do not eat in a jar of olive oil in the refrigerator.

Oyster mushroom Cultivated on bales of straw. More strongly flavoured than button mushrooms and can be used in any mushroom dish. Delicious grilled with garlic, fresh herbs and oil.

P

Parmesan cheese A very hard, grainy cheese, which when young can be eaten at the end of meals, but which is more usually grated and sprinkled liberally over numerous pasta dishes and soups, or incorporated into sauces. It is most often found ready grated, in packets or cartons. You can buy it fresh instead of grated, and grate it just before use so that the flavour will be superior. A coarse rotary grater is the best one to use.

Peas Leguminous vegetable, sold fresh, frozen, canned or dried. Fresh peas have a short season. Dried green or yellow peas are sold peeled (split peas) or unpeeled. Peeled peas need no soaking and have a short cooking time. Unpeeled peas need soaking and then boiling for about 2 hours. Dried peas are best in soups, casseroles or puréed.

Peanuts Since they are prone to mildew neither peanuts nor peanut products have been used in the recipes.

Pepper Together with salt, the most frequently used seasoning. Unripe, fresh pepper berries are still green and are sold freeze-dried or bottled in brine. Freeze-dried green peppercorns keep for a long time and should be soaked or crushed before use. Black peppercorns are also unripe, but in this case dried. White pepper is ripe, mild and aromatic. Don't buy ground pepper but always grind your own to preserve the hotness and aroma.

Pine nuts: Seeds of the South-European pine. Good in salads or cold sauces. Rich in oil so soon go rancid. Buy in very small quantities.

Pinto beans Beans which are brown speckled like quails' eggs. They need soaking and then boiling for about 2 hours.

Pistachios Extremely aromatic seed of the pistachio tree which grows mainly in the south-east Mediterranean area. Sold shelled and salted or unshelled. Can be used in both savoury and sweet dishes.

Poach To cook in shallow or deep water below simmering point, at 75 to 90c/167 to 194f. The liquid should not boil but just ripple gently on the surface.

When cooking in stock no bubbles should rise. Fish should be poached at the lower temperature; dumplings and meat stocks will tolerate higher temperatures.

Polenta see Cornmeal.

Potatoes Staple food which is also excellent as part of a slimming diet or to clear out the system. Potatoes contain a small amount of extremely valuable vegetable protein as well as vitamins B_6 and C, minerals and fibre. Since they contain about 100 calories per 100 g/4 oz they are not fattening when boiled or steamed, without any butter.

Potato types are differentiated by their cooking qualities. Waxy early potatoes like Arran Pilot, Home Guard, Red Craig's Royal or Maris Peer are best for plain-boiling or jacket-boiling. They are also excellent salad potatoes as they can be thinly sliced without falling apart or going dry. New potatoes, boiled in the skins, are delicious with asparagus, fresh herrings, caviar and other delicacies. For softer boiled or baked jacket potatoes, gratins and bakes, use a floury maincrop variety such as Desirée, Kerr's Pink, King Edward, Red King, Golden Wonder, Majestic, Maris Piper, Pentland Crown and Redskin. Most are also excellent for mashing since they fall as they boil.

In wholefood cooking the idea is to retain the original form of the potato as far as possible. Jacket-boiled potatoes are better for you than peeled boiled potatoes: minerals and fat are found just under the skin of the potato and will be lost in part if you peel cooked potatoes, or lost completely if you peel them before cooking. The skin prevents the protein and vital nutrients being leached into the water to a large extent. Also any harmful substances which pass from the skin into the water cannot find their way back into the potato. Store potatoes in a dark, cool, dry place. Light makes them go green and forms the dangerous substance solanin. Solanin is also found in sprouts, or eyes, which should be completely removed.

Poultry Nowadays most chickens are mass-produced using methods that have no connection with the natural lifestyle of the bird. The only criterion is to produce the most meat in the quickest way possible. This means that the birds have to live in a confined space, never seeing daylight, fed on special foods and injected with drugs until they are a suitable size for killing. It is a good idea to try and find a farmer who raises poultry by natural methods, or shops and supermarkets that sell free-range birds. You will have to pay more and will probably eat less poultry as a result, but you will be able to enjoy your chicken without feeling guilty.

Processed food In this book the term covers all products which are processed industrially and which contain artificial preservatives, flavourings and colourings. For instance, canned soups, bottled sauces, sausages, canned fruit or vegetables.

Pulses Collective name for the seeds of leguminous plants such as peas, beans or lentils. Pulses are rich in carbohydrate, fibre and vegetable protein. If you combine pulses with cereals (pasta, rice, bread or, especially, corn), the two types of protein complement each other so well that the biological value is higher than for a meat meal. For a short season pulses are available fresh but can be bought dried throughout the year. You can find the individual types under the corresponding headings.

Pumpkin Vegetable which often grows to a considerable size. In season from September. Can be used to make soup, in savoury bakes or can be served as a vegetable dish. Can also be made into sweet main courses, desserts or pies.

Pumpkin seeds Seeds of the pumpkin plant. An oil-producing seed rich in protein and unsaturated fatty acids, B-group vitamins, vitamin E and trace elements. Pumpkin seeds are sold shelled or unshelled, salted or unsalted. Peeled pumpkin seeds can be served in sweet and savoury salads, cakes, bread and muesli. The fatty seeds produce an oil which can be used in small amounts in salads.

Q

Quinces Stone-fruit with large fleshy fruit. Varieties divide into apple and the more aromatic pear quinces. Quinces have a velvety yellow peel and cannot be eaten raw. Can be made into jelly, jams or boiled to a pulp. Delicious preserved in vinegar or stewed. Can be made into a liqueur. In addition their bitter-sweet flavour makes an ideal accompaniment to meat dishes.

R

Reduce Instead of thickening a sauce or to concentrate the flavour of a soup, it can be boiled over a high heat until it has reduced to the required concentration. This is the usual way of thickening a sauce in modern cuisine since it has no effect on flavour. Sauces with a cream or crème fraîche base should be reduced by simmering gently because at too high a temperature they can curdle.

Refined flour Any fine-ground white flour. Unlike wholemeal flours, refined flours contain practically no nutrients or fibre since the germ which is rich in vitamins and the outer layer are removed before grinding. Flour of this type keeps well and gives better results in some recipes than the more nutritious wholemeal flours. White bread and fine cakes are made with refined flour.

Refresh To douse boiling hot food with cold water to halt the cooking process immediately and – in the case of vegetables – to preserve the colour. See also Blanch.

Rice With wheat and corn, one of the main cereal crops, on which about half the world's population lives. The same is true of rice as of cereal, in that industrial processing destroys the goodness of a valuable foodstuff. First rice has to be husked. This gives rice with a brown skin and germ which can be eaten. In the last century it was discovered that the brownish-grey rice grain could be turned into an attractive white seed by rubbing off the skin and the germ. Yet it is the skin and the germ that contain the valuable nutrients as well as the aleuron layer which is rich in protein and fat. Parboiled rice is slightly better since a special process is used to put back some of the vitamins, but even parboiled rice contains no fibre worth mentioning. In the recipes in this book you will find only natural brown rice which comes as either long or round-grain. Long-grain rice stays fluffy when cooked and is suitable to serve as a side-dish or for rice dishes like pilau rice or paella. Round-grain rice is more glutinous and is used mainly in risottos and desserts. Even brown rice is peeled, ie removed from the husk, but it contains all the goodness of whole grain including the important fibre. Because of its higher fat content, brown rice does not keep as well as white rice and so should not be bought in large quantities.

Ricotta Italian cheese similar to curd cheese, made from cow's, sheep's or goat's milk. Salted ricotta is used in savoury dishes, while the mild, unsalted type is used in cakes and desserts.

Roast see Fry.

Roasting juices During roasting or frying, small amounts of meat juice escape and form a brown crust on the bottom of the pan. This residue or sediment forms the basis of the gravy or sauce when loosened with a little liquid. See also Deglaze.

Roughage Also known as fibre. The indigestible part of vegetable matter which is essential in a healthy diet.

Roux A paste obtained by cooking flour in butter. This forms the base for a sauce or a thickening for soups and stews.

Rye After wheat the main cereal used for bread. Contains more protein than wheat. Rye flour is dark with a distinctive flavour. Rye bread stays fresh longer than wheat bread. Rye is used in cooking in the same way as other cereals.

S

Saffron Slightly bitter, slightly hot spice that turns food an attractive yellow. Saffron is grown in Southern France, Spain and Iran. It is harvested by picking the orange-red stamens of a type of crocus by hand. These are dried to form saffron threads or may be sold ground to a powder. Because of the labour-intensive harvesting method and the huge number of flowers required to produce a few grams of saffron, this is the most expensive of all spices. It is best to buy saffron threads which hold their flavour longer. Store them in the dark in an airtight container. The threads can be rubbed in a mortar or between your fingers, dissolved in hot butter or water and then stirred into the food. Saffron is excellent for rice dishes, pasta, fish, chicken dishes and baking.

Salt The seasoning we use more than any other and often in too large a quantity. We differentiate between different types of salt by the way it is produced:
1. Rock salt which is mined from either above or below ground.
2. Industrial salt is heated in a smelting furnace to destroy germs and is then cast into blocks for grinding.
3. Salt-pit salt is obtained from the waters of salt springs by vaporisation or from salt-containing rocks after soaking them in water.
4. Sea salt from sea water pumped into shallow artificial basins, salt pans, and left to

crystallise as it dries.

The mineral content of salt is so low that it has no nutritional value. Even sea salt contains only a tiny amount more iodine than other salts. If you want to take in extra iodine you should use iodised salt or eat foods with a high iodine content (sea fish, milk). Apart from ordinary table salt which is extremely fine and sprinkles freely, there are special mixtures, such as herb salt with dried herbs added, which are excellent for salads, sauces and butters.

Sambal oelek Very hot Indonesian paste for seasoning made from crushed chillies.

Scorzonera Winter vegetable with a flavour similar to asparagus and which is cooked in the same way. When peeled scorzonera produce a sap which makes black marks on the skin so it is a good idea to wear rubber gloves. Once peeled, scorzonera should be boiled in water with added vinegar or lemon juice to prevent them discolouring.

Sea salt see Salt.

Seal To brown quickly all over in hot fat. This gives meat a crust which keeps in all the juice. Larger quantities of meat should always be sealed in batches so that the diced meat almost covers the bottom of the pan, leaving just enough room for turning. Otherwise the fat cools too quickly, the juices from the meat prevent it frying properly and it becomes tough.

Semolina Made from hard or soft wheat. If possible buy wholemeal semolina which contains the germ.

Sesame seeds Extremely oily seeds of the sesame plant. Frying in a dry pan brings out the flavour. Delicious in salads, baking and sweets. Do not keep well because of the high fat content. Main products from sesame are sesame oil, Tahini and Gomasio (see separate headings).

Sheep's milk cheese Cheese made from sheep's or a mixture of sheep's and cow's milk. There are soft cheeses like the Greek feta which can be crumbled and scattered over salads, pickled or used like Quark; semi-firm cheeses like the

French Roquefort which can be used for dressings, sauces and gratins; and hard cheeses like the Italian pecorino which is used like Parmesan and which becomes harder and harder the longer you keep it.

Shoyu Naturally fermented soy sauce made from soya beans, wheat and sea salt.

Soy sauce Asiatic seasoning sauce made from soya beans. Japanese and Chinese versions taste salty, while the Indonesian sauce is sweeter. See also Shoyu and Tamari.

Soya beans As well as Aduki, Mung and many other types of bean, there is the yellow soya bean which is mainly used to make Tofu (soya curds or cheese), Tempeh (a soya product of slicing consistency rarely available in Europe) and Tamari. The beans are high in protein which in its cooked form can be only partially broken down in the body, so that they are not particularly nourishing. It is best to eat the products made from the bean rather than the beans themselves for they will provide more nourishment.

Soya curds see Tofu.

Soya flour Available with or without fat. The full-fat flour is suitable for baking. The defatted flour, produced by a chemical process, is added to breakfast cereal, children's foods, bread and sweets.

Soya meat Also known as TVP, short for Textured Vegetable Protein. Contains between 50 and 70% vegetable protein, depending on the brand and has long been used as a tasty and healthy meat substitute. With increased demand for the basic product, the soya bean, pesticides and artificial fertilisers came into use which made TVP less beneficial. In addition, the production of soya meat is highly mechanised so that it can no longer be described as a wholefood. The addition of artificial colourings and flavourings has also turned soya meat into a processed food. It has not been used in this book.

Soya milk Prepared from soya beans, this can be substituted for dairy milk. See Aubergines in Soya Milk, page 96.

Spinach beet For a long time considered to be a poor substitute for spinach which was not popular and therefore rarely sold. Recently spinach beet has reappeared in markets and greengrocers' shops. There are two types of spinach beet, leaf and stalk. Anyone with a tendency to kidney stones should avoid spinach beet for, like spinach, sorrel and rhubarb, it contains oxalic acid which, in combination with animal protein, in milk, eggs or cheese for instance, can cause stones.

Steam Nutritious method of cooking in water vapour at around 100c/212f. Suitable for vegetables, potatoes, rice or fish. You can buy special steamers (see Useful equipment at a glance, page 144).

Stew Cooking method used mainly for meat, which is usually first sealed in hot fat, then cooked gently in liquid in a covered pan either in the oven or on the stove.

Stir-fry For crisp, flavourful results, quickly stir-fry finely chopped ingredients in a little oil over a high heat. A wok is a popular pan for this cooking method as the rounded shape distributes the heat evenly, ensuring that the contents are thoroughly cooked.

Stock Seasoned liquid in which fish, meat or vegetables are cooked. A concentrated stock made from meat or poultry bones or fish heads and bones is called a Fond. These form the basis for many sauces (see also Roasting juices).

Strain To pour soups or sauces through a sieve, possibly lined with absorbent kitchen paper, to remove solid ingredients such as herbs or vegetables. The process also removes most of the fat so stock will not need defatting when cold.

Sunflower oil Made from sunflower seeds. Rich in essential fatty acids (linoleic acids).

Sunflower seeds Oily seeds that you can harvest yourself if you grow sunflowers. The seeds are rich in protein and vitamins and the minerals phosphorous and fluoride. They can be added to mueslis and salads or used in baking or sweets. Like all oily seeds they do not keep well.

Glossary

T

Tabasco sauce Hot sauce made from chillies; use a few drops only.

Tahini Sesame paste, high in calories, which can be used as a spread or added to salad dressings or dips such as Hummus.

Tamari Thick, naturally fermented soy sauce made from soya beans and sea salt.

Thyme Fragrant and piquant, with parsley and bay leaves, thyme is one of the famous three herbs that compose a bouquet garni, flavour-enhancer of soups and stews. Thyme also complements the flavour of tomatoes, aubergines, courgettes and salad dressings, and a small quantity will pep up scrambled eggs or omelettes. Thyme can be grown in a pot indoors, or in the garden if you have one. Use it fresh, or hang bunches in a warm place until dried, then rub the leaves off and store in a tight-lidded jar to preserve the aroma.

Tofu Soya bean curds or cheese. A staple Asiatic food for centuries which is becoming better known in Europe with the move towards healthy eating. Tofu is rich in valuable vegetable protein, easy to digest, low in calories, contains little carbohydrate and is the most versatile of foods.

Tofu is made from soya milk from yellow soya beans, to which is added an acid such as vinegar or lemon juice or a salt known as Nigari. As in curd cheese, the solid ingredients form lumps and are pressed together to remove all the liquid and form a solid mass of cutting consistency. Depending on how long the tofu is squeezed it will contain varying amounts of water so that one can differentiate between soft, normal and firm tofu. The soft type is suitable for dressings, soups, sauces, a filling for cannelloni or for spreading, while the normal or firm tofus are fried or braised. Firm tofu can be cooked in the same way as meat. It can be coated in breadcrumbs and fried like a cutlet, made into meatballs or burgers, deep-fried, grilled or cut into cubes and stewed. In addition you can buy smoked tofu in health food shops which has a stronger taste than the ordinary tofu. Tofu freezes well with no effect on its structure. Leftovers can be refrigerated in water in an airtight container for up to a week.

Since tofu has very little flavour of its own, always soak it in soy sauce, seasoned oil or some other marinade before cooking.

Turmeric Made from the root of a type of ginger plant. Colours food yellow. Used in curry powder. You can buy ground turmeric in most supermarkets, health-food shops or chemists.

V

Vegetables Foods low in calories, but providing lots of vitamins and minerals. We need to eat plenty of vegetables, not only cooked, but also raw in salads. It is best to combine plants that grow under the soil with those that grow above it to get a full range of nutrients. Good combinations include: beetroot and apple (recipe page 25), cucumber, radish, carrot and peppers (recipe, Uncooked vegetable salad, page 21), broccoli, cauliflower and carrots (recipe, Sweet and sour vegetables, page 97) or kohlrabi with fresh herbs (recipe page 102).

Vegetable stock Base for soups and sauces. Like meat stock, it can be made in advance and frozen (see recipe page 38) or you can buy instant stock granules from health food shops. Instant stocks contain herbs, yeast and sometimes salt. Freshly made stock should be refrigerated in a covered container, where it will keep for up to three days.

Vinaigrette Cold dressing made from vinegar, seasonings and oil, sometimes with herbs too. Use with green or vegetable salads.

Vine leaves Sold fresh or in brine like cucumbers. Any filling can be used for stuffing vine leaves. Fresh vine leaves should first be softened in boiling water to make them roll more easily. Preserved leaves should be rinsed in cold water to remove excess salt.

Vinegar Produced either from the fermentation of alcohol by acetic acid bacteria or by the thinning of artificially manufactured vinegar essences with water. As with oil, one tends to pay for what one gets. Cheap vinegar has a sour taste and has no aroma. Real or pure wine vinegar has a host of uses. The strongest flavoured of these is made from red wine, the milder one from white wine. Wine vinegar, without the word 'real' or 'pure', will consist of only 20% wine, the remainder being spirit vinegar. Wine or spirit vinegars are also made flavoured with herbs such as dill or tarragon. Fruit vinegar is made from various fruits, the precise fruits often not indicated. Vinegar should be bought in small quantities and stored in dark-coloured bottles.

W

Walnuts Buy only from health of wholefood shops otherwise your nuts will have undergone various chemical processes before reaching the shops. Naturally-grown nuts are rare and therefore expensive. They are usually smaller than normal nuts and have a hard, dark shell for they are not artificially bleached.

Wheat The main bread cereal. Its high gluten content makes it ideal for baking. Whole wheat grain (wheat berries) can also be braised or boiled like any other cereal.

Wheat bran The outer, indigestible covering of the wheat grain, removed for refined flour, and then sold back at quite a high price by health food shops and chemists to add fibre to muesli. If you eat wholemeal products regularly you won't need extra bran. If you eat 'pure' bran you will have to drink a lot of water with it to make the bran swell and carry out its digestive function properly.

Wheatgerm The germ which is separated before milling. Rich in vitamins (especially vitamin E) and fat, with a limited shelflife. Usually sold in the form of flakes. You can also get all the goodness of wheatgerm from wholemeal products. Wheatgerm should not be confused with germinated or sprouted wheat, that is, the whole grain. Sprinkle wheatgerm on muesli and salads. Can also be added to bread and baking. Wheatgerm pasta is softer than wholemeal pasta and you probably won't like it unless you are used to 'healthfood' pasta.

Wholefood Refers in this book to foods high in vital nutrients and low in harmful substances. These are usually foods which have not been industrially processed, but left in their natural state, which means fresh fruit instead of canned, fresh meat, whole grain or wholemeal products instead of those made with white flour, home-mixed muesli instead of packet mueslis.

Wholemeal products Foods with all the goodness of the whole cereal grain, but not necessarily containing whole grains.

Y

Yeast extract Made from brewer's yeast and at one time simply a by-product in beer-making. Contains B-group vitamins and vegetable protein. Delicious as a spread and an excellent substitute for salt.

Yogurt Skimmed milk soured with a special beneficial bacterial culture to make it ferment and turn acid. It is better to add fresh fruit and, if necessary, honey to natural, unflavoured yogurt than to buy fruit-flavoured yogurts that usually contain a lot of sugar.

Useful Food Values

	Quantity	Fat (g)	Sodium (mg)	Calories
All Bran	50 g/2 oz	3	830	135
Apple	125 g/4½ oz	0	3	50
Avocado pear	100 g/4 oz	22	5	220
Bacon	25g/1 oz	9	400	90
Baked beans	150 g/5 oz	1	720	110
Banana	125 g/4½ oz	0	1	90
Beef, roast lean	50 g/2 oz	2	30	90
Beer	300 ml/½ pint	0	40	90
Biscuits:				
digestive (1 biscuit)	15 g/½/oz	3	65	70
shortbread (1 biscuit)	25 g/1 oz	7	65	70
Bread:				
white (1 medium slice)	40 g/1½ oz	1	180	95
wholemeal (1 medium slice)	40 g/1½ oz	1	220	85
Butter	15 g/½ oz	12	110	110
Cabbage, boiled	50 g/2 oz	0	4	10
Carrots, boiled	50 g/2 oz	0	20	10
Cauliflower, boiled	50 g/2 oz	0	4	10
Cheese:				
Cheddar	50 g/2 oz	16	300	200
Cottage	50 g/2 oz	2½	250	55
Cream	50 g/2 oz	23	180	130
Edam	50 g/2 oz	11	490	150
Stilton	50 g/2 oz	20	575	230
Chicken, roast	50 g/2 oz	7	40	90
Chocolate, milk	50 g/2 oz	15	60	270
Cod	100 g/4 oz	0	80	95
Corned beef	50 g/2 oz	6	480	110
Cornflakes	25 g/1 oz	0	230	75
Cream:				
double	2 tablespoons	14	8	130
single	2 tablespoons	6	12	60
Egg, boiled	60 g/2¼ oz	6	80	100
Gammon, lean, boiled	50 g/2 oz	3	550	80
Gin	1 measure	0	0	55
Grapefruit	100 g/4 oz	0	1	20
Herring, grilled	100 g/4 oz	13	170	200
Honey	1 tablespoon	0	2	45

Useful Food Values

	Quantity	Fat (g)	Sodium (mg)	Calories
Ice cream	100 g/4 oz	8	80	160
Jam	1 tablespoon	0	3	40
Kidney, lamb's	50 g/2 oz	1	110	45
Kipper	50 g/2 oz	5	500	100
Lamb, roast lean	50 g/2 oz	5	30	80
Liver, grilled	50 g/2 oz	6	80	130
Liver pâté	50 g/2 oz	13	430	160
Macaroni, boiled	100 g/4 oz	0	8	110
Margarine	15 g/½ oz	12	100	100
Milk: whole skimmed	 300 ml/½ pint 300 ml/½ pint	 11 1	 140 140	 190 100
Oatmeal, raw	4 tablespoons	2	4	80
Olives	25 g/1 oz	3	560	25
Orange	100 g/4 oz	0	3	35
Orange juice	150 ml/¼ pint	0	4	50
Parsnip, boiled	100 g/4 oz	0	5	60
Peach	100 g/4 oz	0	5	35
Peanuts, salted	25 g/1 oz	12	110	140
Peas, boiled	50 g/2 oz	0	3	25
Pork, roast lean	50 g/2 oz	4	40	95
Potato, boiled	175 g/6 oz	0	10	150
Prawns, cooked	75 g/3 oz	1	1,200	90
Prunes, soaked	40 g/1½ oz	0	5	30
Rice, boiled	50 g/2 oz	0	1	60
Sausage, grilled	40 g/1½ oz	10	430	120
Sugar, refined white	15 g/½ oz	0	0	60
Sardines, canned in tomato sauce	50 g/2 oz	6	350	90
Yogurt: low-fat natural low-fat fruit	 150 ml/¼ pint 150 ml/¼ pint	 1 1	 110 90	 70 140

Note: This chart offers a guide to the fat, sodium (salt) and calorie contents of certain foods. This information will give you some guidance if you are trying to adapt your diet to include a lower intake of fat or salt, or if you are trying to cut down on the calories.

Index

A

Almond milk shake 138
Apple:
  Apple milk shake 138
  Apple pancakes 133
  Apple yogurt 34
  Beetroot with apple vinaigrette 25
  Grapefruit juice with apple 139
  Red beans with apple 127
Apricot:
  Chicken with apricots 90
Artichokes with tofu sauce 16
Asparagus with two sauces 103
Aubergines in soya milk 96
Avocado cream 19

B

Baked courgettes and tomatoes 52
Banana milk shake 138
Banana and sesame purée 30
Barley casserole 53
Barley soup with herbs 44
Bean:
  Bean salad with tomato vinaigrette 23
  Black beans and sweetcorn 125
  Black beans with tomatoes 126
  Red beans with apple 127
  White beans provençal 127
Bean sprout pie 56
Bean sprout salad with prawns 27
Beetroot with apple vinaigrette 25
Bilberry pudding 136
Black beans and sweetcorn 125
Black beans with tomatoes 126
Boiled potatoes with mushroom sauce 108
Braised chicken with vegetables 89
Braised wheat 116
Bread:
  Flat bread cakes 19
Broccoli and potatoes with cheese sauce 105
Broccoli soup 45
Buckwheat:
  Buckwheat dumplings in Gorgonzola cream 115
  Buckwheat gratin 116
  Buckwheat pancakes with scorzonera 118
  Buckwheat soup 44
  Cabbage rolls and buckwheat 94
Bulgur with vegetables 121

C

Cabbage:
  Cabbage rolls and buckwheat 94
  Chickpeas with Savoy cabbage 120
Cannelloni with tofu and spinach 58
Carbohydrates 9–10
Carrot:
  Carrot and courgette soup 41
  Carrots with nut vinaigrette 25
  Leek and carrot curry 104
  Orange and carrot juice 139
Cauliflower curry with potatoes 104
Cauliflower soup 45
Celery gratin 17
Cheese. *See also* Quark
  Broccoli and potatoes with cheese sauce 105
  Buckwheat dumplings in Gorgonzola cream 115
  Cheese dumplings 134
  Cheese and semolina bake 54
  Cream cheese dip 28
  Fried mozzarella 16
  Home-made curd cheese with herbs and pumpkin seeds 29
  Mooli salad with cheese dressing 21
  Olive cheese 19
  Wholemeal spaghetti with cheese and cream sauce 110
Cherry:
  Cherry quark 31
  Quark and cherry strudel 132
Chicken:
  Braised chicken with vegetables 89
  Chicken with apricots 90
  Chicken breasts in Savoy cabbage 85
  Chicken rissoles 85
  Chicken with sage 87
  Chinese-style chicken 91
  Exotic chicken 91
  Leek salad with chicken and almonds 27
  Rice salad with chicken and bean sprouts 24
  Stuffed chicken 86
Chickpea:
  Chickpea soup with lamb 48
  Chickpeas with Savoy cabbage 120
  Vegetable stew with chickpea balls 51
Chicory:
  Leek and chicory soup 41

Chilled tomato soup with herbs 39
Chilli with lamb 50
Chinese-style chicken 91
Cod:
  Steamed cod on vegetables 67
Corn fritters, mushrooms with 114
Cornmeal pancakes 40
Country-style casseroles 53
Courgette:
  Baked courgettes and tomatoes 52
  Carrot and courgette soup 41
  Courgette gratin 59
  Courgette pasties 57
  Courgette soup 45
  Courgette vegetable dish 102
Couscous salad 23
Cream cheese dip 28
Crispy gratins with potatoes and vegetables 61
Cucumber:
  Cold cucumber soup 38
  Fish and cucumber stew 71
  Stuffed cucumber 59
Curd cheese with herbs and pumpkin seeds 29
Curry:
  Cauliflower curry with potatoes 104
  Lamb curry 82
  Leek and carrot curry 104
  Nut curry 125

D

Desserts. *See* Puddings and desserts
Dips with vegetables 28
Dried winter vegetables 98
Drinks 138–9
Duck with spring onions 88
Dumplings:
  Buckwheat dumplings in Gorgonzola cream 115
  Cheese dumplings 134

E

Elderflowers in batter 137
Exotic chicken 91

F

Fat 9
Fennel salad with sesame dressing 22
Fibre 10
Fish. *See also* Cod etc.
  Fish and cucumber stew 71
  Fish in foil 66
  Fish paella 73

Fish soup with vegetables and cress 47
Fish with vegetables 70
Herby fish in lemon butter 66
Steamed fish with ginger 69
Whole fish with tomatoes 68
Flat bread cakes 19
Fried lamb with tomatoes 75
Fried mozzarella 16
Fried rice 122
Fried tofu with vegetables 124

G

Garlic bread 61
Ginger, steamed fish with 69
Gnocchi:
  Potato gnocchi in herb sauce 109
Gorgonzola cream, buckwheat dumplings in 115
Grape:
  Vanilla quark with grapes 31
Grapefruit juice with apple 139
Griddle cakes 133

H

Herb drink 139
Herb soup 46
Herb spätzle 112
Herby fish in lemon butter 66
Herby lamb steaks 77
Herring fillets with potatoes and quark sauce 71
Honey ice with orange salad 135

J

Jacket potatoes with quark 106

K

Kohlrabi pasties 57
Kohlrabi with walnuts 102

L

Lamb:
  Chickpea soup with lamb 48
  Chilli with lamb 50
  Fried lamb with tomatoes 75
  Herby lamb steaks 77
  Lamb curry 82
  Lamb cutlets in thyme sauce 76
  Lamb noisettes with rosemary potatoes 76
  Lamb ragoût with yogurt 74
  Lamb stew with oranges 82
  Lamb stew with quinces 74
  Lamb with tarragon 83
  Mexican-style breast of lamb 80

Potato soup with lamb meatballs 49
Roast leg of lamb with garlic 81
Sesame lamb balls 83
Simmered leg of lamb with vegetables 79
Stuffed cucumber 59
Stuffed peppers 84
Stuffed shoulder of lamb 78
Leek:
Leek and carrot curry 104
Leek and chicory soup 41
Leek salad with chicken and almonds 27
Wholemeal pancakes with leeks 118
Lemon butter 66
Lentil:
Russian-style lentils 126

M

Macaroni:
Wholemeal macaroni with garlic oil 110
Menu suggestions 142–3
Mexican-style breast of lamb 80
Milk shakes 138
Millet pudding 54
Millet and rice griddle cakes 133
Millet soup with vegetables 43
Minerals 10
Mooli salad with cheese dressing 21
Mozzarella, fried 16
Muesli:
Crushed muesli 33
Muesli with flakes and fruit 32
Muesli with wheatgerm 32
Roasted malted muesli 33
Three-grain muesli with fruit 33
Mushroom:
Boiled potatoes with mushroom sauce 108
Mushroom gratin 17
Mushroom pasties 57
Mushroom with corn fritters 114
Onion and mushroom salad with smoked salmon 26
Tofu schnitzel with green rye and mushrooms 123

N

Noodles:
Wholemeal noodles with sesame 112
Nut. See also Almond, Pinenut etc.

Carrots with nut vinaigrette 25
Nut curry 125
Peaches with nut meringues 134
Pudding with nuts and sprouts 131
Yogurt with nuts 34

O

Oat flake waffles with soft fruit 35
Olive cheese 19
Omelette:
Vegetable omelette 99
Onion. See also Spring onion
Onion and mushroom salad with smoked salmon 26
Onion pasties 57
Stuffed onions 101
Orange:
Honey ice with orange salad 135
Lamb stew with oranges 82
Orange and carrot juice 139
Yogurt with oranges 34

P

Paella 73
Pancakes:
Apple pancakes 133
Buckwheat pancake with scorzonera 118
Cornmeal pancakes 40
Wholemeal pancakes with leeks 118
Wholemeal pancakes with vegetables 113
Pasta. See also Cannelloni etc.
Vegetable soup with pasta 42
Wholemeal pasta with uncooked tomato sauce 110
Pasties:
Vegetable pasties 57
Peach milk shake 138
Peaches with nut meringues 134
Pepper:
Stuffed peppers 84
Pickled fillets of trout 14
Pine nuts, spinach salad with 22
Pistachio milk shake 138
Pizza:
Wholemeal pizza with tomato and mushrooms 60
Plaice:
Clear vegetable soup with plaice 46
Plaice fillets in herb sauce 64
Plums with custard 135

Polenta bake 55
Polenta slices with tomato sauce 119
Porridge with dried fruit 30
Potato:
Boiled potatoes with mushroom sauce 108
Broccoli and potatoes with cheese sauce 105
Cauliflower curry with potatoes 104
Herring fillets with potatoes and quark sauce 71
Jacket potatoes with quark 106
Lamb noisettes with rosemary potatoes 76
Potato fingers with sage butter 107
Potato gnocchi in herb sauce 109
Potato soup with herbs 45
Potato soup with lamb meatballs 49
Potato and tomato gratin 61
Potato tortilla 107
Potatoes in herb sauce 106
Prawn:
Bean sprout salad with prawns 27
Grilled prawns 72
Prawns in herb sauce 72
Protein 8–9
Provençal-style tofu ragoût 52
Puddings and desserts:
Apple pancakes 133
Bilberry pudding 136
Cheese dumplings 134
Elderflowers in batter 137
Honey ice with orange salad 135
Millet and rice griddle cakes 133
Peaches with nut meringue 134
Plums with custard 135
Pudding with nuts and sprouts 131
Quark and cherry strudel 132
Strawberries with dates 136
Wholemeal savarin with stewed fruit 130
Pumpkin soup 45

Q

Quark:
Cherry quark 31
Herring fillets with potatoes and quark sauce 71
Jacket potatoes with quark 106
Quark and cherry strudel 132

Quark pasties 57
Strawberry quark 31
Vanilla quark with grapes 31
Quince:
Lamb stew with quinces 74

R

Ravioli with herbs and ricotta 111
Red beans with apple 127
Rice:
Fried rice 122
Millet and rice griddle cakes 133
Rice salad with chicken and bean sprouts 24
Risotto with peas and saffron 117
Vegetable pilau 117
Rissoles:
Rye rissoles 115
Vegetables rissoles with tofu 99
Roast leg of lamb with garlic 81
Romanian-style marinated vegetables 20
Russian-style lentils 126
Rye dumplings 44
Rye rissoles 115

S

Sage butter 107
Salads:
Bean salad with tomato vinaigrette 23
Bean spout salad with prawns 27
Beetroot with apple vinaigrette 25
Carrots with nut vinaigrette 25
Couscous salad 23
Fennel salad with sesame dressing 22
Leek salad with chicken and almonds 27
Mooli salad with cheese dressing 21
Onion and mushroom salad with smoked salmon 26
Rice salad with chicken and bean sprouts 24
Romanian-style marinated vegetables 20
Spinach salad with pine nuts 22
Sprouted salad 26
Uncooked vegetable salad 21
Salmon carpaccio with chervil 15
Salt 10–11
Savarin with stewed fruit 130

Index

Scorzonera, buckwheat pancake with 118
Semolina:
  Cheese and semolina bake 54
Semolina soup 44
Sesame:
  Banana and sesame purée 30
  Sesame dressing 22
  Sesame lamb balls 83
  Vegetables with soy sauce and sesame 97
  Wholemeal noodles with sesame 112
Simmered leg of lamb with vegetables 79
Smoked salmon:
  Onion and mushroom salad with smoked salmon 26
Soup:
  Barley soup with herbs 44
  Broccoli soup 45
  Buckwheat soup 44
  Carrot and courgette soup 41
  Cauliflower soup 45
  Chickpea soup with lamb 48
  Chilled tomato soup with herbs 39
  Clear vegetable soup with plaice 46
  Cold cucumber soup 38
  Courgette soup 45
  Fish soup with vegetables and cress 47
  Herb soup 46
  Leek and chicory soup 41
  Millet soup with vegetables 43
  Potato soup with herbs 45
  Potato soup with lamb meatballs 49
  Pumpkin soup 45
  Semolina soup 44
  Vegetable soup with cornmeal pancakes 40
  Vegetable soup with pasta 42
  Vegetable soup with tofu 40
Soy sauce and sesame, vegetables with 97
Soya milk, aubergines in 96
Spaghetti:
  Wholemeal spaghetti with cheese and cream sauce 110
Spätzle 112
Spinach:
  Cannelloni with tofu and spinach 58
  Spinach beet gratin with garlic bread 61
  Spinach salad with pine nuts 22
Spring onion:
  Duck with spring onions 88
Sprouted salad 26

Starters. *See also* Soup
  Artichokes with tofu sauce 16
  Celery gratin 17
  Fried mozzarella 16
  Mushroom gratin 17
  Pickled fillets of trout 14
  Salmon carpaccio with chervil 15
Steamed cod on vegetables 67
Steamed fish with ginger 69
Stock:
  Vegetable stock 38
Strawberries with dates 136
Strawberry quark 31
Stuffed chicken 86
Stuffed cucumber 59
Stuffed onions 101
Stuffed peppers 84
Stuffed shoulder of lamb 78
Stuffed vine leaves 95
Sweet and sour vegetables 97
Sweetcorn:
  Black beans and sweetcorn 125
  Mushrooms with corn fritters 114
  Sweetcorn with tomatoes 120

T
Three-grain muesli with fruit 33
Tofu:
  Artichokes with tofu sauce 16
  Cannelloni with tofu and spinach 58
  Fried tofu with vegetables 124
  Provençal-style tofu ragoût 52
  Tofu balls in caper sauce 124
  Tofu dip 28
  Tofu schnitzel with green rye and mushrooms 123
  Vegetable rissoles with tofu 99
  Vegetable soup with tofu 40
Tomato:
  Baked courgettes and tomatoes 52
  Black beans with tomatoes 126
  Chilled tomato soup with herbs 39
  Fried lamb with tomatoes 75
  Polenta slices with tomato sauce 119
  Potato and tomato gratin 61
  Sweetcorn with tomatoes 120
  Tomato dip 28
  Tomato juice 139
  Tomato pasties 57
  Tomato quiche 18

  Tomato vinaigrette 23
  Tomatoes stuffed with wheat 100
  Whole fish with tomatoes 68
  Wholemeal pasta with uncooked tomato sauce 110
Trout:
  Fish in foil 66
  Pickled fillets of trout 14
  Steamed fish with ginger 69
  Trout with cream and herbs 6

V
Vanilla quark with grapes 31
Vanilla sugar, to make 31
Vegetables. *See also* Artichoke, Bean etc.
  Braised chicken with vegetables 89
  Bulgur with vegetables 121
  Clear vegetable soup with plaice 46
  Dips with vegetables 28
  Dried winter vegetables 98
  Fried tofu with vegetables 124
  Millet soup with vegetables 43
  Romanian-style marinated vegetables 20
  Simmered leg of lamb with vegetables 79
  Sweet and sour vegetables 97
  Uncooked vegetable salad 21
  Vegetable omelette 99
  Vegetable pasties 57
  Vegetable pilau 117
  Vegetable rissoles with tofu 99
  Vegetable soup with cornmeal pancakes 40
  Vegetable soup with pasta 42
  Vegetable soup with tofu 40
  Vegetable stew with chickpea balls 51
  Vegetable stock 38
  Vegetables with soy sauce and sesame 97
  Wholemeal pancakes with vegetables 113
Vine leaves, stuffed 95
Vitamins 10

W
Waffles:
  Oat flake waffles with soft fruit 35
  Wholemeal waffles 35
Walnut:
  Kohlrabi with walnuts 102
Wheat:
  Braised wheat 116

  Tomatoes stuffed with wheat 100
Wheatmeal pastry 56
White beans provençal 127
Wholemeal macaroni with garlic oil 110
Wholemeal noodles with sesame 112
Wholemeal pancakes with leeks 118
Wholemeal pancakes with vegetables 113
Wholemeal pasta with uncooked tomato sauce 110
Wholemeal pizza with tomato and mushrooms 60
Wholemeal savarin with stewed fruit 130
Wholemeal spaghetti with cheese and cream sauce 110
Wholemeal waffles 35

Y
Yogurt:
  Apple yogurt 34
  Lamb ragoût with yogurt 74
  Yogurt with nuts 34
  Yogurt with oranges 34